Memories of
My Father

Memories of My Father
Copyright © 2023 by Ray Burk

All rights reserved. No part of this book may be reproduced or transmitted in any form or by any means without written permission from the publisher and author.

Additional copies may be ordered from the publisher for educational, business, promotional or premium use.
For information, contact ALIVE Book Publishing at:
alivebookpublishing.com, or call (925) 837-7303.

Book and cover design by Alex P. Johnson

ISBN 13
978-1-63132-202-0

Library of Congress Control Number: 2023908513

Library of Congress Cataloging-in-Publication Data
is available upon request.

First Edition

Published in the United States of America by ALIVE Book Publishing and ALIVE Publishing Group, imprints of Advanced Publishing LLC
3200 A Danville Blvd., Suite 204, Alamo, California 94507
alivebookpublishing.com

PRINTED IN THE UNITED STATES OF AMERICA

10 9 8 7 6 5 4 3 2 1

Memories of My Father

Ray Burk

Alive Book Publishing

*Special thanks to my editors,
Eliza McKenna,
Jennifer Holmes,
and Mimi C.*

Memories of my Father,
I hope you enjoy reading about my father.

This book is a compilation of my memories, about 80 years worth, experiences, and teachings from my father. Because my father was a very honorable man, and I am writing this book to honor him. I feel highly honored to be his son. I want to express to my readers the type and kind of person he was. My father, over the years, taught me so very many, many things. He showed me how to work together. This book will mention other people because we may have been working on many different projects. But I have many memories, some in detail, and some just briefly. My father was a very good person and well-respected by everyone who knew him. At his funeral, there were a couple hundred visitors. A lot because he always lived in a rural community. He was a very hard worker and knew how to make money with the farming industry. The biggest thing he taught me is, "Everyone has a Heart." His explanation for these words was that everyone has feelings. Everyone has Love if they want to show it.

Everyone deserves respect because we are all persons in this universe. My father never said anything unfair about anyone. Yes, he did not like everyone, but mainly because they had not treated him fairly at some point in his life. Most of the time, he would explain his reasons for not liking them. But my father was not a judgemental person. He gave everyone the benefit of the doubt. And now I know, for sure, that he was trying to pound that theory into my hard head. When I think back about him and how much I now remember, I genuinely appreciate every one of his teachings. To me, he was a remarkable person.

My father's legacy to me was "Everyone has a Heart." Sadly, dad died in 1973 at age 55 years old. Years after his death, I also acquired some of his property, souvenirs, and mementos. But I would - give it up to have had him live a few years longer. This book is all from my memory, except for what I learned from Ancestry.com. Everyone mentioned in it is deceased except for my sister and brother. My sister and brother probably have lots of memories also. I wonder how my father knew the saying "Everyone has a Heart," maybe from the Price family. The Price family was my great-grandmother's family. I think the Price family was more religious than the Burk family. I have mentioned Uncle Johnny Price, he was my great-grandmother's brother. And he lived across the road from Ollie and Anise's house. I never heard anyone else in the Burk family saying anything like "Everyone has a heart". I wonder where dad learned this saying?

Dad

Elvin L. Burk, my dad, was born June 29, 1917. Dad was about 5 feet 9in tall. And he weighed around 175-180 pounds. He had brown eyes. He was predominately right-handed. He had very strong hands and a muscular body. Dad's hair was very thick and black all his life until he became ill in May 1972. His hair turned from solid black to almost white in the last 3 to 4 months of his life. It seems that the color change was almost overnight. He never fought with anyone and usually had something good to say about everyone. Dad never disciplined me physically, but he would tell me if I had done something wrong. I know when I disappointed him, but he never held anything against me. Dad was a great man.

Dad was the youngest of three boys. His father was a blacksmith and had a small 19-acre farm with two milk cows and a few chickens. They lived in a rural community, close to Union City, Indiana. They were not a wealthy family, and times were tough. Dad was born around the beginning of the depression.

My grandfather drove the school bus for the neighboring school community when my father was born. Two horses pulled the bus because motorized buses were not around rural communities then. Grandad delivered the children to Wayne school. I imagine he also took his sons with him to this school. My sister and I went to this same school for two years, many years later. Granddad shoed the horses used by this school to pull these buses, and he also repaired the buses. These buses were just a wagon enclosed with wood, canvas, and windows. Most schoolhouses were the red, one-room brick type. Wayne School built a larger building some years later. My grandmother cleaned houses for some of the neighbors to help out financially. And about this time in society, around the '20s and '30s, the depression was hitting every family. My father went to school, but I think he only went through the eighth and maybe part of the ninth grade.

 Dad did everything he could to try to make money for his family. He did a lot of hunting, especially rabbits, for food when he was young. Dad learned to play the guitar and violin. As he got older, he played music with a couple of cousins for anyone who would hire them to entertain at their get-togethers. There was not a whole lot of demand for their music around the area, but he did meet our mother at one of these events. But this group of musicians became well recognized in their immediate area. I do recall one of our relatives who were part of the group, telling me how much they all enjoyed playing their music together.

 Because dad was the youngest child, his older brothers received the largest share of food at the dining table. Dad often told me he only had bread and water to eat and drink for days. These must have been very rough times. This is one of the stories dad told me about when dad was a child. Their house had an enclosed back porch. But it was separate from the heated part of the house. But one night, dad needed to go to the bathroom, which was outside. And when he returned to come back into the house, he wanted to get a drink of water. A pail of water was kept on this back porch for a drink of water when needed, especially after a long day's work and many times after using the bathroom. There was a dipper hanging on the side of the pail. But one night, dad stopped for a drink of water and realized something was in the water dipper. Whatever it was, it brushed his lips. It was a dead rat and ended up in the dipper where dad was about to drink. I suppose they threw out the water and rat the next day. But water during the depression played a large part in everyone's survival. And according to dad, that was about all he had to survive on, along with a few bread scraps. Dad explained to me how hungry he had gotten sometimes.

My father told me many things, this is another one. My dad always said my sister came along soon after he and my mother married. Now our father was a farmer and had one child. Our dad was at the draft age, early '20s. Men at that age could be drafted to go to WWII. But he told me that if a man was a farmer with two children and still at draft age, they were exempt from the draft. But if they only had one child, the farmer could still be drafted. According to dad, this is why I came into this world in 1943. Being born must have worked because I do not think dad wanted to get into war. His one brother and many of his cousins were drafted into the Army during WWII. Our mother's brothers and one sister were in the military during WWII. I have no idea how our father knew about these guidelines. Several of these relatives told many stories about their war experiences serving in the military during WWII. I do not know if any of them were out on the front lines of the war. But our mother said she knew nothing about what dad had told me about farmers being exempt from the draft. But this is what dad told me. I never questioned my father about this subject.

Another thing my father always told me was, that a person needs to work for a reason, whether monetary, animal, or machine, and of course, family. And he usually thought using a person's hands was the best way of earning anything. Dad also told me, "You cannot count your labor as worth anything." I never agreed with that because his hands and labors brought him everything he had accumulated and gained. His mind was essential too. All his labors represented dollars and investments. That is why he always invested each dollar back into his business. "It takes money to make money," he told me. He purchased more cows, pigs, chickens, and other animals. Dad took outstanding care of all his animals. He also purchased better and newer farming equipment, over time, which could do a better and more efficient way of producing crops.

    Dad was always in debt to the equipment company because he was always looking at things that could help make him more inventory. Dad never had any cash in his wallet. If a cow was not a very good milk cow, he would sell it and look for a better one. And similar was his thinking about farm equipment. Dad would instead invest in equipment that would do a better job pulled by an old tractor than a new tractor pulling old inefficient equipment. My father was a brilliant man. And just like he used to tell me that everyone has a heart, he also kept telling me that it takes money to make money! Now that I am older, I realize how smart he was. We would not have what we have today if it wasn't for his teachings.

    My father may have been excessive in his ways of thinking sometimes. Maybe because he was born during the depression. Dad always told me he wanted something to show for all his efforts. That meant he wanted to own land, farm equipment, farm animals, etc., which would help him make more income and allow him to acquire more land, and inventory to help provide for his family. And he wanted something he could physically touch. Dad's thinking was about some of our relatives, who did not have much to show for all their efforts. He felt they needed to change some of their priorities. Some drank quite large amounts of alcohol. Dad never drank any alcohol. Our dad always wanted more attached to his name.

For this reason, dad always worked hard to acquire more of everything. Dad was not greedy but just worked hard with his hands and back. Dad always told me that his reason for working so hard was that some people only had a little to show for all their efforts. No property, money, a pot to pee in, or a window to throw it out. I can't tell you how many times dad told me this. And I know my dad wanted to be more profitable and successful than his brothers. Dad had a different personality than either of his brothers. Dad always had so much more to show for all his hard work and efforts. I have always tried hard to follow my father's teachings.

Another thing my dad always showed me, not physically but by his doing, was when it came time to harvest products from the rental properties. Dad always split everything evenly down the middle. In those years, there was very little cash rent for farmland. The land rental worked because the landowner paid for ½ the seed and ½ the fertilizer costs. Then dad paid for the other half of these costs. Dad was responsible for tilling the soil, planting and caring for the crops during the summer, and maintaining weed control. Dad was responsible for mowing the grass around the fields and lanes too. Then when harvest time came, it was the same. Dad received ½ of the crop, and the landowner received the other half. Sometimes I think he cheated himself by giving more of the harvest to the landowner than to himself. He always told me that if two shovels were full, one went to the landowner and one to him. And if there was a half shovel total left over, that went to the land owner.

My father has been away from this earth for many years. There is not anything I would not do, to be able to see and talk with him again. I loved my dad. I also know he loved his family and me. He died much too early in his life. He is undoubtedly a big part of my life and my makeup today. Dad really liked my wife too. I genuinely Hope dad respected me and understood everything I was trying to do with my life and relationships. I remember dad telling me to purchase a farm. I probably would have, but I could not ask for his help. I wanted to acquire things my own way. Owning farm property did not turn out for me until many years later, a long time after his death. Now that I have one of his farms, he is probably looking down on me and saying, "I told you so." Golly, I miss him, so I am writing a book about him to honor him.

After graduating high school, I knew I would have to join the military. The Military Draft was still going on in 1961. For sure, I would qualify as IA. Being graded as 1A meant that you were physically and mentally strong, and would be a good candidate for the US military. And because I had a younger brother at home, who could help with the farming, this would make me more qualified to serve in the military. Plus, my brother needed to learn some of the things I had already learned. And my long-range plan was to get the military behind me, find a wonderful wife, settle down, and at that time, look at purchasing farmland and begin a farming career. I needed to be more realistic, but I thought I knew what I was doing. I probably should have told my dad of my intentions, but I never did tell him. Dad and I talked a little when he was in the Muncie hospital. By then, I had settled on other goals and challenges. I wonder if dad ever understood me.

The Three Sons'

Dad never said too much to me, but the three Burk sons did not get along with each other very well when they were young. Dad and Uncle Roy tolerated each other and worked together most of the time without problems. Uncle Roy was a farmer too, but only cultivated the original Burk property acreage. Uncle Roy never had the updated equipment dad had, but dad did help him harvest his crops. And because Uncle Roy and dad purchased a hay baler together, Uncle Roy helped us bale hay, and we helped him bale his hay. Grandfather also usually helped us. Dad helped Uncle Roy with some other farm issues too, and Uncle Roy also helped dad some too. Dad always combined Uncle Roy's wheat and oat crops. Uncle Ira worked in the factory all his working career, and we never saw any of Uncle Ira's family after they moved away from the green shingled house in the early '50s. They purchased and moved to a place in Winchester, Indiana. Uncle Ira's wife, Aunt Grace, was a cook at Wayne and Winchester schools. The sad thing, as I remember, we (all the 3 Burk families) always got together for Christmas celebrations. And we exchanged gifts by drawing names. It was always fun, and each family brought good food to eat. But that all ended after our grandmother had a stroke.

Our Burk Ancestry

I have learned much about my dad's Burk/Mullen ancestry. What I have may not be exact, but I think it is pretty accurate. Ancestry.com has some dates labeled as considered, meaning close to the date they have listed.

Our Burk Grandparents were Ollie Burk and Anise (Mullen) Burk. They were married in June 1910. Ollie was born in 1889 and died in October 1973, in Union City, Indiana. Anise (Mullen) Burk was born in May 1892 and died in May 1957, at Aunt Edith's home in Greenville, Ohio.

Our- Great Grandparents on the Burk side were William and Barbara (Price) Burk. They were married in May of 1874. William was born in 1855 and died in 1941. Barbara (Price) Burk was born in 1858 and died in 1945. William Burk must have dropped the "E" on Burk.

Our- Great Grandparents on the Mullen side were Curtis Mullen and Manda (Hiatt) Burk. They were married in November 1882. Curtis Mullen was born in 1863 and died in 1942. Manda (Hiatt) was born in 1864 and died in 1893.

Our- Great Great Grandparents on the Burk side were William Burke and Mariah (Cole) Burke. They were married in 1839. William Burke was born in 1812 and died in 1881. Mariah (Cole) Burke was born in 1820 and died in 1902. They had an "E" on the name Burke.

Our- Great Great Grandparents on the Price side were John Price and Sarah (Davis) Price. They were married in 1852. John Price was born in 1826 and died in 1898. Sarah (Davis) Price was born in 1834 and died in 1897.

Our- Great Great Grandparents on the Mullen side were Calvin Mullen and Leah (Bales) Mullen. They were married in 1855. Calvin Mullen was born in 1833 and died in 1897. Leah (Bales) Mullen was born in 1835 and died in 1905.

Our- Great Great Grandparents on the Hiatt side were Wilson Hiatt and Maria (Blackman) Hiatt. They were married in 1859. Wilson Hiatt was born in 1834 and died in 1880. Maria (Blackman) Hiatt was born in 1837 and died in 1875.

Granddad and Grandmother Burk's Place

My Burk Grandparents' house is where dad and his brothers were born. This house sits at the intersection of County Rd 650E and Indiana State Highway 32, with a Union City, Indiana 47390 Zip Code. It was on the RR4 mail carrier's route. It had no indoor plumbing and only cistern water to drink until our grandfather drilled a well in about 1948. I remember the man who drilled the well, and then my father and grandfather built a building around the new well and the well pump. If I remember correctly, the well is about 130 feet deep. Then dad and granddad dug trenches for the underground pipes to carry the water into the barn and the house. My grandparents were happy to have clean running water from the new well. Of course, there was no hot water in the house. Hot water needed to be heated on the kitchen stove. But a few years later, dad gave granddad a hot water tank to heat water, and it sat on the counter next to the kitchen sink. Dad had used it in his milkhouse until he installed a regular 30-gallon water heater. Hot water was needed to clean some of the milking equipment. But this small tank that dad gave granddad used electricity to heat the water, but you had to pour the water in the top first. Getting warm water in the kitchen was several years after my grandmother moved away, to Aunt Edith's house.

However, before running water and hot water came into our grandparent's house, they washed their bodies and clothes with only cold water plus a small amount of hot water. The kettle on the wood cookstove provided the heated water. A wood stove provided heat to the house in the living room and the wood cookstove in the kitchen. On cold winter nights, sometimes the stoves needed more wood to burn to furnish heat. Extra wood was stacked on the back porch. They had an ice box out on the back porch, with block ice in it to keep things cold. Later electricity was installed in the house, and then a refrigerator was installed in the kitchen. The back porch was never heated. Our grandmother wasn't too good at cooking. But she always had Ritz crackers and Pepsi to give us kids. This always impressed me. In the late '30s or early '40s, electricity was installed along highway #32. I think our Uncle Ira did a lot of the electrical wiring inside granddad's house.

The Greyhound Bus ran weekly down the State Highway in front of their house. Every week, grandmother would get dressed up, always looked very pretty, and she would ride that bus to town to do her ladies' shopping and then ride the bus back home. Then on Saturday nights, my grandparents would take my sister and me to town, and my grandmother would do her grocery shopping at the A&P (Atlantic and Pacific) grocery store. On these Saturday nights, my sister would go with my grandmother to the grocery store, and I had to go with my grandfather. Granddad and I would go to the corner, where there was a bus bench. There were a couple of older men there too, and they would talk, and talk, about nothing interesting to me. They chewed a lot of tobacco and spat in their can, not on the street.

Golly, I was bored! I was about 3 to 5 years of age at that time. But I was happy to be with my grandparents. Sometimes, my sister and grandmother would come to the corner where we sat and the men conversed. The store on this corner was an FW Woolworth's store. Grandmother and my sister usually went inside this store to look and buy things grandmother wanted. I would have been happy to go with my sister and grandmother inside the Woolworth's store. I did not want to buy anything; I just wanted to look at all the exciting and different things. I just wanted to do something besides listening to the older men talk about their neighbors, Agriculture prices, Politics; and spit tobacco. FW Woolworth stores was a chain all across the country. Everyone in this area of the farming community called them the "Dime Store"; I never knew exactly why.

Our grandfather, Ollie Burk, constantly chewed Mail Pouch tobacco. He always had a chew in his mouth. Granddad had an overstuffed rocking chair in their living room, which sat beside the entrance door from the porch outside. Before TV, they sat in their living room and listened to the radio. But after TV came into existence, the TV sat in the corner, and granddad had a direct view of it. Beside granddad's rocking chair, he had a beautiful blue ceramic spittoon. And on the wall beside his chair, he had newspapers taped to the wall, several pages too. At night while he was watching TV, granddad would chew his tobacco and spit in the spittoon. And as you can imagine, he did not always hit the spittoon, and the spit ended up on the wall, floor, chair, or wherever. And it smelled!! And if granddad were out someplace and could not spit out, he would swallow it. Yuk!!

As I first remember, my granddad drove a car. I believe it was a 1939 Chevrolet sedan automobile. Green in color. He carried a spit can inside the vehicle, but the driver's side door had spit streaming down the outside, and much of it on an angle, because he spit out the window while driving. I can see in my mind, that car. Today some people paint their cars with stripes, but grand-dad had his car striped with tobacco spit. Granddad also smoked cigars, but only outside the house. But he did not smoke many cigars. He chewed most of them.

On the northeast corner of granddad's house was an open porch. Around 1948, I remember my granddad tearing out the old porch. It had been made of wood. Then granddad and dad poured a cement floor and built an enclosed porch. It had a lovely roof and brick walls on two sides, about 42 inches high. The upper part of the porch walls was enclosed with screen wire and a door for entrance from the yard. The walls of the house made up the other two sides. It was a lovely porch when granddad finished. The exit door from their bedroom led out onto this porch from inside the house. And on this porch, granddad had a glider for himself and a wooden rocking chair for our grandmother. I remember a small table with some magazines on it. And granddad was a big Cincinnati Reds baseball fan. Almost every day, when they were playing, he would sit on this porch glider, with a radio playing, and listen to those ballgames. And as you can imagine, my sister and I would visit them, and my sister and grandmother would do things inside the house. And I would be sitting on the glider, slightly gliding with granddad, spit can beside him, listening to the ballgames. Yes, I was very bored!! We usually tried not to bother granddad on ballgame days.

A couple of other things about our grandparent Burk's house: the upstairs had only one room covering the whole top of the house. Dad told me this is where dad and his brothers lived when they were young. Our grandparents had a beautiful Library table up there, and granddad gave it to my wife and me. We use it today. On the wall In their living room was this New Haven wind-up clock. Every night we were visiting, granddad would wind this clock. It ticked pretty loudly, and it kept accurate time. Many years later, I acquired this clock after my grandfather passed away. It now sits on our fireplace mantle and has for many years. I rarely wind it, but it used to run when it was wound. My granddad told me he purchased this clock when his first son was born in May 1911. Our middle uncle was born in 1913, and our father was born in 1917. My grandparents never said they celebrated these two later sons' births with the purchase of anything. They may have celebrated all birthdays, but no one ever said anything about celebrating anyone's birthday. I am not sure our grandparents had the finances. Grandmother never purchased much of anything, only groceries.

Grandmother Burk had some jewelry, nothing special that I remember. Primarily things that had been given to her by her Aunt Sally. Aunt Sally was Curtis Mullen's sister. She had enough wealth to afford some jewelry, which she handed to Anise. Anise gave my sister two sets of glass beads when my sister was seven years old. Then after our grandmother had passed, granddad gave my sister a ring and brooch, which grandma had—only sentimental value. Many years later, my sister had the glass beads restrung. Dad's parents did not have much money for extravagant things. I do have granddad's old cane. I guess granddad had his tobacco and cigars, those kept him happy.

One of my favorite memories about our Burk grandparents was some of the Christmas decorations grandmother had. At a couple of Christmas's, which we celebrated with them, grandmother had this beautiful Christmas decoration. She had it sitting in the window. It had colored electric light bulbs, maybe ten on it. It was manufactured using a heavy wire and made in a circle. It had a base of about 20 inches in diameter. And attached to the heavy circular wire were the colored Christmas lights, connected with an electrical wire. I do not know how the lights were attached. But around each bulb were small mirrors cut in triangular shapes, maybe six mirror pieces around each bulb. And I have no idea how these were attached, either. Then the whole wire parts were covered by some type of garland or something which looked like garland. And when it was lit after dark, it was the most beautiful, unusual decoration I had ever seen. The colored light bulbs, when lit, reflected off the mirrored pieces. I had never seen anything like it before, nor since. It was so beautiful. I wonder where grandmother found that decoration and what happened to it.

Another of the things we did with my Burk grandparents was going to free shows. The shows were always shown on Friday evenings in Bartonia, Indiana. Bartonia was about 2 miles from our home. We went to these shows for several years, both before our grandmother's stroke and a few years later. Both grandpa and grandma just sat in their car and watched. Even after grandmother had had her stroke. Our grandfather would get his milking finished early; he only milked 2 Jersey cows. Then he would put our grandmother and his chewing tobacco in his car. He also had a spit can in his car. Then he and our grandmother would drive to the area and park his car close to the projector man's automobile. The projector/operator man placed the projector on top of his car. Other automobiles parked around, but my grandfather got the best space by getting there early. We would take small individual benches or chairs to sit on, and we usually could sit in front of our grandparents' car and lean back on it. Sometimes, our mother would sit in their car with them, but rarely. The shows were projected onto a large white canvas screen. The canvas screen was fastened to a vertical metal frame. It was a distance away, close to the property fence.

The shows were accessible to everyone. These shows were a neighboring thing, and some other small areas also sponsored free shows. Usually, a local grocery store supported the movies and evenings. During the show, people would go into the store to purchase ice cream, candy, snacks, popcorn, sodas, etc. And usually, many people attended. It was an excellent way to have good entertainment for the community. About 75 people were there, and lots of children. The projector man showed a cartoon first, some recent newsreel after the cartoon, and then the main feature. Over time, the projector man showed several westerns and other kinds of movies. He would announce the following week's free movie title when the projector man had finished that evening's film. Sadly, sometimes it would rain and cancel the show until the following week. I liked the rain, but not on free movie nights.

Some of the time, our father went with us to these shows. Dad's going depended on the time of year; he'd miss the show at harvest time. When dad was there, sometimes I would lean over against dad's leg. My sister, brother, dad, and I usually sat on our little benches, which we had brought from home. Mom also sat with us, but I do not remember what she sat on. My brother sat in front of us on a small bench or blanket. We usually brought something to eat from home. Sometimes we crossed the street to purchase ice cream and popcorn, but rarely. Pat Byrum always had the popcorn concession. We always were cautioned to watch out for automobile traffic.

Our Burk grandparents had six grandchildren. Uncle Roy had a daughter, Uncle Ira had two sons, and dad had three children. Yes, I spent a lot of time with our Burk grandparents. I worked with granddad quite a lot on many different projects. And I watched him work as a blacksmith. Granddad liked me and told me I was his favorite grandson. After I went into the military, I felt terrible about having to leave all my family. But I was drafted. And then, when I was discharged from the military, my wife, Dee, and I lived in Indiana for a little over a year. I loved all four of my grandparents. However, my grandfather Gibson died in 1945. I do not remember much about him, only the things my mother told me about him.

Granddad Burk's farm was 19 acres, I believe. It had one big field, which granddad planted part of in corn one year, along with oats in another region. There was also an area of clover in this field too, for the cutting and baling of hay for his cattle feed during winter. His property had a fair size wooded area, maybe about 3 acres. His cows grazed in this area during summer, and the chickens scratched and looked for worms and insects. The barn was not very big, but large enough for a couple of cows and a milking area. On the outside southeast corner of the barn was a wooden silo for storing chopped corn for his cows. Grandad had a manure spreader and his tractor stored inside the barn, along with a corn shocking machine and a silo-filling machine. This corn shocking machine was used to cut the stalks of corn, then it would hold about a dozen stalks in a bundle and drop them on the ground in a pile. Corn shocking and silo filling happened around September each year. These bundles of corn shocks would then be loaded on a wagon by hand and pulled into the silo area beside the silo-filling machine. Dad's Farmall "H" tractor would be connected to the silo-filling device using a big flat belt. A large pipe was tied to the outside of the silo and connected to the machine. It ran over the top into the silo to put the corn material inside for the cattle's food during the winter months. When using the silo-filling machine, the tractor would run at full engine speed to run the chopper, which had a big fan, and cutting knives. It would cut the corn, make it into small pieces of corn silage and blow it up into the silo. Someone had to feed the shocks of corn onto the conveyor belt feeding the chopping machine. I stayed far away from that area because it was hazardous. Silo filling for grandad was sort of a family get-together thing. Dad and I usually hand-cut the shocks of corn at the corners of the field. I was about 8 to 12 years old when I was helping fill granddad's silo. We also opened some corn ears to see how ripe the corn was. Then granddad and the corn shocking machine could cut the corn from the straight rows. Then Uncle Roy would show up, and we would load the wagon with the corn shocks and proceed with the filling process. Uncle Roy placed the shocks of corn from the wagon onto the silo-filling machine. After we filled the silo, during the following winter, granddad shoveled the silage daily to feed his cows. Granddad, Dad, Uncle Roy, and I were the crew for filling this silo. It took a couple of days to do this project.

On the west side of grandad's barn was a corn crib to store ears of corn for grandpa's animal food after the corn had dried out. One year, it had become infested with rats because the corn crib had a wooden floor with space underneath the stored corn. The rats lived underneath the corn in this void area. On one Saturday, dad and I and our rat terrier dog, Andy, went to grandpa's to empty that corn crib. I was about 10 years old then.There was not much corn in it at the time, as harvest time was still several days away. But there were many, many rats. When we finished clearing out all the corn, we killed over 60 rats. Andy caught most of them, and we killed some with clubs and shovels. But many escaped and probably went inside the barn where the hay was stored. Emptying the corn took us several hours. When we finished, poor little Andy was exhausted. I was tired, too, from chasing the rats. But we emptied the corn crib. Then later, dad, grandpa, and I filled the void with cement under the crib to prevent the rats from being able to live there again.

The memorable thing about this corn-clearing episode was that a rat had gotten into granddad's bib overalls at some point during that day. It climbed up his leg, inside his pants, and jumped out beside his face. Standing beside him, I saw granddad jumping around just before the rat jumped out. Granddad exclaimed, "Oh, Jesus Christ." That was one of granddad's favorite sayings. We laughed about this, and we told dad about what had happened. I must say, I always enjoyed working with dad and granddad on any projects they were working on. I liked both of them quite a lot.

In front of the west side of granddad's barn was a round wooden bin used to hold oats for the cattle and chickens. Next to it was grandpa's blacksmith shop. Inside the blacksmith shop was a giant forge to heat metal, a large wall drill press, and a wall grinder; grandpa had the most enormous anvil I have ever seen. Many hammers, tongs, and other blacksmithing tools too. Grandpa also parked his car his building at night. Then on the outside corner of this building was the outhouse. It was part of the blacksmith/garage building. During those years, no one locked any of their facilities—only their house.

Sadly, sometime late one night, someone went into the blacksmith shop and stole that anvil. Dad used it for working on his combine and mower sickles. It must have taken at least two men to carry that anvil. Dad often used that grinder to sharpen those sickles used for the hay mower and combine. The sickle is a knife-like piece of steel, which operates back and forth, to make the cutting motion. The hay mower is the machine used to cut the clover plants, where they have come up through the soil. A combine is a machine, used to remove the grain from the dried up plants. It knocks the grain off the straw, which is the dried up plant, after that plant's growing season is complete. Most common is wheat, that is ground into flour, which people make bread from now days. Chefs use wheat flour every day for their preparation of many different baking needs.

Our Burk Grandparents House

I was told that our Grandmother Anise (Mullen) Burk inherited this property. Somehow she inherited some money from someone. It was never clear how or where she inherited any money. I asked dad, but I cannot remember his explanation. It probably came from her Aunt Sally. Aunt Sally seemed to be the only person with any wealth of any kind. I understand Aunt Sally was fond of Anise. Grandmother was the only child of Curtis Mullen, and I believe Aunt Sally was Curtis's sister.

The interesting layout of this house was that it was built as a simple, solidly built house. I imagine it was built in the early 1800's. Most houses in the area, which were built around that time were much larger. I wonder if it housed slaves at some time, as the underground railroad is not far away. This house was small, but very well setup for a family, even a large family. And with the large single room upstairs, there could have been many beds installed up there. The roof sloped, which made the ceiling of the upstairs roof slope too. And under some of the sloped area were closet-like areas, which were very small, but could easily hold folded clothing. The house on the 39-acre property had similar areas, and it was fun to hide in them from my sister. I guess I liked wandering around this house and property mostly because our father lived here, and it belonged to my grandparents who lived in it.

The house where dad lived as a little boy was between the blacksmith shop and the State Highway. This house was a two-story building. It had one bedroom downstairs and one large room across the entire upstairs. It also had a medium-sized kitchen, no dining room, and a medium-sized living room. The house had a large back porch. It also had a cistern and a hand pump to supply water to the sink. The sink sat on the floor above the cistern and connected to a drain pipe outside. There was an area for the men to remove their dirty clothing and shoes before entering the house. Their clothes washing machine, and later a freezer, was in this area too. Granddad did not heat this area during the winter. Inside the house was the kitchen with a wood cookstove, but later, a natural gas line was installed along the highway, and then the kitchen had a natural gas cookstove. What happened to the old wood cookstove? I do not know.

The design of this house has the living room on the eastern side of the wall behind the kitchen cookstove. This specific wall enclosed a brick chimney. The kitchen cookstove and the living room stove had flue pipes connected to this chimney. The living room had a large wood and coal-fueled stove in the middle of the room to provide heat for the house. It was centrally located to best heat the entire house.

On the wall behind this living room stove was a shelf. And on this shelf sat the family clock, which grandad would wind every evening. The clock chimes on the hour and dings on the half-hour. This shelf also held some of grandma's collectibles. Grandmother's rocking chair used to sit under this clock. Now, grandmother's rocking chair sits in our living room. I recently refinished my granddad and grandmother's library table and rocking chair. Now they both sit in our living room in Oakland, California and are beautiful. They always bring back memories of the times we used them at granddad's and grandmother's homes. Then in the front part of their house was grandpa's and grandma's bedroom.

A door to the south side of the living room opened to a small wooden porch. I only saw my grandmother's rocking chair on this porch. I remember her rocking in her chair on this porch before her stroke. After grandmother had her first stroke, she sat in it. I do not think she could rock in it then. This was the chair given to her for house cleaning during the depression. Next to this porch was the enclosed back porch. There were two cement walkways when you went out of the back door or the side porch. One ran straight towards the barn area, and the other went to the outhouse door. Both porches, the enclosed one and the open one, at the rear of this house, were connected by one concrete walkway.

The barn and all the outbuildings were painted red. The house was covered with brown/tannish asphalt siding. It was designed to appear and look like bricks, but it wasn't real bricks. Many homes built in this time era had this type of siding. This was a medium size house compared to other homes. Our house on the 39 acres was about the same size, but the 80-acre house was much more prominent.

West of granddad's house was a fair-sized vegetable garden and a couple of acres with some big trees growing there. I believe they were Oak and Elm trees. Dad and granddad cut some of them down at some point, and they cut the small limbs into firewood. But I know dad put the logs on the '41 truck, took them to Miller's sawmill, and had them cut into the different sizes which dad wanted for later use, for building dad's new hog barn.

More of our grandfather Burk will be mentioned later in this book, but I wanted to insert this one thought. When I was home from the military on leave for a few days, dad suggested that he and I visit granddad for an hour or two. This was the second time I had been home on leave after I had entered the Navy. While I was in the military, we did not get much time off to go home to visit. But I know it had been more than a year since I had been home. So this one evening, after milking and our evening meal was over, dad and I drove to granddad's house. Inside granddad's house, granddad's chair always sat next to the living room door. This visit was after the darkness had settled. Dad knocked on the door, I waited until dad had gone inside. Dad asked granddad if he wanted to see someone. I do not know if granddad answered or not. But then I stepped through the door and gave granddad a big hug. It surprised granddad a lot, and he sort of lost his breath. Granddad had to stay seated because it kind of gave him a shock. But everything was perfect after a couple of minutes. I truly loved my grandfather. I wish I could have spent more time with him. Talking with granddad was always interesting. He had tons of information. I have always enjoyed listening, especially to older people, because they have a lot of knowledge and experience. I have always felt a little honored because my birthday is one day before my grandfather's birthday. Granddad's was December 10th, and mine is December 9th. Very close!

Our Grandmother Burk

I do not recall too many things in detail about my grandmother Burk. Probably because she had her first stroke when I was about 6 years old. I liked her, I thought she was an interesting woman. She was very pretty when she dressed up. I never heard anyone say anything about her cooking and baking. I remember her at their Christmas celebrations, and some of the times we visited them. I do recall her rocking in her rocking chair, while sitting in her living room next to the stove. I remembered her giving my sister and I Pesi Cola. No one else had any Pepsi Cola, mom said it was too expensive. And grandmother always had Ritz crackers to give us. I remember her rocking on granddad's front porch after he had remodeled the porch. I suppose I did not feel very close to her because I never spent much time with her, I was always with grandpa. I never knew why she did not do many of the chores outside their house. I remember her sitting in the barn, and watching granddad milk his cows. My sister spent a lot of time with grandmother, went shopping with her, etc., but I do not remember her buying anything for us. I spent most of my time around my grandparents, with my grandfather. Our Burk grandparents did not socialize together with anyone, except family. I do not think grandmother ever visited us inside dad's 80-acre house. She had had her stroke by then.

I do recall grandmother sitting in her rocking chair, which we have now. I described this chair later in this book. Dad had moved it out to their backyard, and close to the cement walkway. Granddad had carried grandmother out to this chair, and she sat there and watched us. I do not remember if we were baling hay, or filling the silo. I mainly remember her complaining about her physical condition. And she was pitiful. She did do a little better after she had moved to Aunt Edith's house. I remember trying to show her pictures in the magazines when she was at Aunt Edith's house. She paid little attention, only complained to dad. Grandmother's complaining to dad all the time must have been hard for dad.

As I recall, our grandmother Burk had her first stroke sometime in the late summer of 1949. It left her paralyzed on one side. My sister and I were at our school, Wayne school. I remember our Uncle Ira came to our school that afternoon to pick up my sister and me. He took us to our grandparent's house. When we arrived at their house, my mother and father were there, along with Uncle Roy, Aunt Grace, and Uncle Ira. I remember all three Burk sons were there. The family doctor had been there and gave grandmother some medications but did not send her to any hospital. Concerns and disagreements arose among family members about how to best care for grandmother in the future. She was pretty much bedfast unless my grandfather picked her up and put her in a chair. Working with my grandmother was hard, as my grandmother was a sizable lady. There was no hydraulic medical equipment available in those days. But granddad did the best he could to move her from the bed to a chair or the portable toilet, but she frequently used a bedpan. The bathroom was the main issue, as there was no toilet inside the house, only the outhouse outside.

Some of the women did help for a while to wash grandmother and keep her clean, but no one could pick her up completely, only our grandfather. That meant grandfather had to be there just about all the time to help pick grandmother up. But granddad did not want to be there all the time, he had farm chores to attend to. Plus granddad liked to get together with other farmers at a local store in Harrisville. They would sit and talk (gossip) about things happening locally and chew and spit a lot of chewing tobacco. I had to go there with my granddad a few times. I did not want to go for sure, but I did, and of course, I was bored. I was around 6 years old at that time.

Not long after my grandmother had her stroke, Uncle Ira hired a lady to come and live upstairs at our grandparent's house and to take care of our grandmother. This lady was a sizeable strong lady. She could handle grandmother. But granddad did not like her because she was demanding and challenging! Granddad and this lady argued and fought about things. I do not remember precisely what the issues were. Then granddad fired her, she was gone. Granddad should have accepted her help and followed her suggestions. Dismissing the lady started the whole problem of caring for grandmother again. Our grandfather did his best but had no money to hire extra help. His only income was the little grain he sold from the farm each year. He did not have enough milk from his cows to sell to a creamery. He did have his Social Security check each month. He even needed help to pay the farm real estate tax. Dad helped him. All his sons and their families were too busy to stay with their grandmother all the time. Plus, grandmother was large, and most ladies could not pick her up to put her in her wheelchair. All the adult family members tried to decide what was best for our grandmother.

Greenville, Ohio

Somehow, someone got in touch with a lady in Greenville, Ohio. Then, for my grandmother's proper care, she was moved into an assisted living facility in Greenville, Ohio. The lady who owned the home was a distant relative. Aunt Edith Armstrong was her name; she somehow was connected to our Great Grandparents. Aunt Edith had a substantial two-story house. Aunt Edith cared for a couple of other older individuals, and she said she had room and could take grandmother into her home and feed and care for her too. Aunt Edith's husband (Carl) was a large man who would help move the patients around. Aunt Edith and her husband were very friendly, and kind, and cared very well for our grandmother.

Luckily grandmother did lose some of her weight. When grandmother moved to Aunt Edith's place, this is when my mother and father and my two Uncles came into the picture. Our middle Uncle said he had hired that lady to stay with grandfather and grandmother, but then she was fired, and he refused any further help. I wonder if Uncle Ira visited his mother after she moved to Greenville, Ohio. So our father and Uncle Roy paid each month for our grandmother's care while living with Aunt Edith. Grandfather had very little income to offer any financial help. But grandfather visited his wife at least once or more a week. Edith's husband usually had grandmother sitting in a chair in their living room when we visited grandmother.

My father, mother, and us children visited our grandmother on Sundays. Grandmother was a pitiful person. Yes, I felt so sorry for my grandmother. Dad and Uncle Roy agreed this was the best way to care for grandmother. And Aunt Edith's home was very nice. Sometimes grandmother lay in bed or sat in a chair when we visited, but she always complained about everything. It was sad she had to live this way. Plus, she would not do anything to help herself or enable the people caring for her. She was in a physically sad existence. And the stroke affected her mind, causing her to complain much of the time. After about 6 years at Aunt Edith's assisted living facility, grandmother passed away on her 65th birthday. I believe the year was 1955. To this day, I do not know why she would not try to improve herself. We, children, tried to talk with her, but it was difficult. Aunt Edith had a wonderful Assisted Living /Nursing facility.

We took grandmother magazines. Grandmother would not exercise the muscles that were not affected. She just complained. Most people try to fight their declining health and be optimistic about their future. I sat beside my father at my grandmother's funeral. That was the first time I ever saw my father physically cry and have tears in his eyes. I think I was about 13 years old then. Now I know why people shed tears at funerals. Dad loved his mother, even though the last few years of her life brought stress for our parents. I never knew how my grandmother's will finally worked out, but our grandfather gave us children souvenirs from our grandmother's belongings. He gave me my grandmother's rocking chair and their library table that I mentioned earlier.. The rocking chair was made around 1850 and was assigned to our grandmother because the homeowners she cleaned the house for during the Depression did not have enough money to pay her wages, so they gave her the rocking chair. She had to carry that chair home on her head, as she told me, about a ½ mile. This chair is made of Mahogany wood and is heavy. As I mentioned before, it's in use in our living room.

I mentioned we visited grandmother and Aunt Edith almost every Sunday. Uncle Ira and his wife never saw his mother, and their two sons never visited her either. I think Uncle Ira was always angry. But I know Uncle Roy told me he visited his mother at Aunt Edith's house but did not say how often. But even though the weather may not have been too great, we, dad, mom, and us children, always visited grandmother. I think we three children of dads, were the only grandchildren who visited grandmother at Aunt Edith's house.

Grandfather Burk

Our grandfather died in 1973 after our father had died earlier that same year. He was brokenhearted because he had lost his wife and two sons. Uncle Roy had died in 1966, granddad's oldest son. Grandfather did not get along very well with his remaining son, Uncle Ira. I do not know why people cannot work out their differences. I think there must have been hard feelings between my father and his brother Ira too, from way back. Because in our earlier years, we all visited quite often. Then after my grandmother was in the assisted living facility, I can not remember getting together with Uncle Ira's family after that time. All three of the Burk sons did not appear to have much love for each other. I hope all three Loved their parents. I Loved all my grandparents, both my father's and mother's side.

Granddad had a Farmall "F-12" tractor. It had three gears forward and one reverse. It was not the kind of tractor large farmers would want to use, but ok for grandad and the 19 acres. Granddad built a wooden blade on the front to push dirt and snow to level out surfaces. The homemade pushing device had a large piece of metal across the bottom. A couple of times, dad put me on this tractor to drive it down the road to the Shaw farm, about 3 miles from Granddad's farm. I am trying to remember what dad used it for there. It traveled very slowly, but I drove it down the highway with no problems. Granddad's tractor had knobby tires on the rear, and the engine had a small amount of horsepower. We used it to pull the wagon around the field to haul the shocked corn when we were filling grandad's silo. Granddad used this tractor to pull his manure spreader when he needed to clean his barn. I have no idea what ever happened with granddad's tractor.

At our Grandfather Burk's house was this vast mulberry tree. It was a big tree; I do not think it is there anymore. The mulberries then were big, sweet, and great to eat straight from the tree. This tree produced a tremendous amount of berries. Picking these required a step ladder and dad's truck. Dad would take his 1941 Dodge truck and park it under the tree, and then we would stand on the step ladders placed on the truck bed, just like we did for picking sugar pears from the sugar pear tree on the 39-acre farm. Then mom and all us kids, and maybe other adults, would harvest the mulberries, buckets full of them. Then dad would move the truck around to a different location under the tree. Granddad's mulberries were shared with everyone. Mom would make the best mulberry pies. They were delicious. Mom gave granddad a pie too. We picked mulberries two or three times each summer. After gathering these berries, our fingers would have turned purple, but the stain washed off. I cannot remember eating mulberry pies baked by anyone except our mother.

Another thing I remember about granddad Burk. Granddad had a green 1939 Chevrolet automobile. The car with the tobacco stains on the driver's side door. The thing I remember about this car was the time dad and Uncle Roy repaired the engine. I was about seven years old, and this was after we had moved to the 80-acre farm. But there was something wrong with the automobile. I wonder if the engine needed a new head gasket, if they needed to grind the valves, or what it needed. But I remember dad meeting Uncle Roy there at grandad's blacksmith shop; this is where granddad kept this car. They opened the door and proceeded to take the top of the engine apart. It took all day, and they stopped for a short lunch, then it became time for dad to do his milking. Dad and I left granddad's place, and

Uncle Roy said he would finish the project. Somehow dad and Uncle Roy knew how to repair automobiles and their engines. Dad rarely talked about his early years, I do not know if dad had his own vehicle to care for, but he said he was driving an old Ford when he met my mother. I do not know if dad owned it, and I never heard Uncle Roy or Uncle Ira mention having their own cars.

While Dee and I lived in Indiana for that 14 months, we had to go to the grocery once in a while. At the grocery, we would purchase our groceries and add a couple extra bags for my grandfather. Then on our way home, we would stop by granddad's house and drop off the groceries we had purchased for him. We did not want him to go hungry. Sometimes Dee baked a cake for him. But after Dee and I moved back to California, we felt terrible that we could not buy groceries for him, so we sent him a few dollars each month to help him with his grocery bill. His $46 Social Security check did not cover much of his expenses. That seemed to be the best Dee, and I could do to help granddad. I do not think my mother brought grandpa any food of any kind, even though she did bake several things. When Dee and I decided to move back to California, we thought about how to help granddad. Sending him a few dollars seemed the only way to help him. But we had to make the move.

My Earliest Recollections of the 39 Acres

When I was born in 1943, we lived on a 39-acre farm west of Union City, Indiana. Dad and mom purchased this property in March of 1946. Dad said they had rented it before they bought it. Dad told me they purchased it from Mrs. Clark, who lived on the corner just down the road. Dad and mom were married in May 1939, and I do not know when they moved to this property. We lived on the 39-acre farm until February 1951. Then my parents sold the 39-acre farm and purchased an 80-acre farm south of Union City, about five miles away. I had just turned seven years old when we moved. At the 39 acres, dad raised corn, oats, hay, tomatoes, and possibly other crops. Dad had two workhorses to do the cultivating, Pete, and Daisy. I recall riding on the blind horse (Pete) when dad was working with the team of horses. I recall my sister riding Daisy, and I remember dad using the horses to pull the tomato planter and tomato cultivator. I always rode old Pete. Old Pete had a broad back. I think dad must have had a neighbor with a tractor do the plowing of the ground. I cannot remember dad plowing any of the 39 acres.

The 39-acre farm had several large trees around the house and barnyard area. A border fence around the barnyard encompassed the entire square area to contain all the farm animals. It had a gate in the fence over the drive to allow access to the barn area. A small entrance gate led from the house to the chicken house, the outhouse, and further down was the barn.

At some point earlier, when we were living at this farm, dad purchased a milk route. It must have been about the time I was born. I remember dad and mom talking quite a lot about this truck used for this job. It was a 1937 Chevrolet truck that dad used for this milk route. This truck had an insulated truck body to help keep the milk cool before delivering it to the creamery. Dad would drive around to the farmers who milked cows. Dad had a specific route to farms, where he would pick up cans containing the milk and deliver them to the creamery for processing. The truck also held empty cans to replace the full cans at each stop. Then the farmer would fill the empty cans with milk at the next milking. Then dad would pick them up the next day and leave empty cans for the next milking. A job like this was a seven-day-a-week job. There was a "Red 73 Creamery" in Union City. This creamery provided homogenized milk, butter, and ice cream. The products were processed from the farmers' milk cows. I have no idea of the number of farmers on dad's route. Dad said the 1937 Chevrolet milk truck was constantly breaking down. That truck made dad angry, and he said he would never own another Chevrolet truck again.

When dad came home, dad always had something for me to eat. It could have been leftover from his lunch, something he brought home from a farmer, or possibly the creamery. But he always took it out of his lunchbox and handed it to me. Of course, I could carry his lunch box into the house. I can remember how tired he was when he returned home after he had parked the truck in the driveway. And I clearly remember running out to the driveway to meet him daily. Dad coming home each evening was the highlight of my day!

Dad wanted to start doing other kinds of work, primarily using his truck to haul things. I would like to know the year he made this decision. To do this work, he sold the 1937 Chevrolet truck and milk route and purchased a 1941 Dodge truck for trucking the grains and hay south. Dad would buy grain and hay in Indiana, haul it to Kentucky or Tennessee, and sell it to someone there. On one of these trips, the man purchasing the corn dad had brought to him could not pay dad the entire amount needed, so dad accepted a bicycle as part of the payment. Dad gave me that bicycle after I was older, and I rode that bicycle many miles when I was a teenager. I have that bicycle, stored in our garage in Oakland now. Dad told me it came from Tennessee. He also told me several other stories of loading the truck with sugar beets, which he loaded by hand with a heavy metal fork (picture) from the fields around Indiana and Ohio. That was hard work. Then he hauled the truckload of beets to the sugar mill in Union City. How long did dad do this kind of work? It was seasonal. Dad told me my mother said that dad had to give up trucking and be a farmer. I wonder if this was really what my father wanted to do, but that is what he did.

I think dad would have been successful with anything he wanted to do.

After dad had purchased the "41 Dodge truck, it enabled him to buy grain, hay, etc. for dad to haul south to Kentucky, and Tennessee, and sell those items there. Dad told me this was his best way of making money relatively quickly. Dad told me about several experiences he had while delivering these supplies to the farm owners in Kentucky and Tennessee. Most were not very rewarding stories. He delivered to some plantation owners who enslaved people. Dad was unhappy with the way the enslaved people were treated.

Our father always told me he wanted something to show for all his hard work. I never knew precisely what he meant because when he pulled his wallet out of his pants pocket, it only had a couple of dollar bills. But as time moved along, he accumulated a sizable amount of farming equipment, property, and farm animals. This was his investment and value, a very sizeable amount. When dad told me, "you cannot count your labor," I do not think dad understood that all his energy and hard work, his labor, created enough funding for all the things his struggle rewarded him with. Dad had a reputation. He could buy anything anytime without a contract. Dad always paid his bills, bought lots of equipment on credit, and never missed any payments. Dad's word was his contract. Dad had an open account at the local service station.

My brother was born in 1948 while we lived on this 39-acre farm. Sadly, he was born with club feet, and because of his handicap, mom needed to take him to a doctor in Dayton, Ohio. She had to take him to the doctor often at first and not so often later. My brother had foot surgery at some point. But the thing I remember most was the tall buildings there and the drive there and back. Usually, my sister and I went with mom, and sometimes one other family member would also go along. But I remember dad meeting us when we returned to the 39-acre farm. Dad usually wanted me to do something as soon as I changed my clothes.

I remember pushing corn down in the corn crib. Steering the tractor out in the field when dad and others were baling hay. I also helped with the tomato planting. Tomatoes are planted as plants and not from seed. I needed to help ensure the plants were placed on the planter straight so that the person putting them into the ground could pick them up more quickly. The tomato planter carried water to put at the roots of each plant as the two men placed the plants into the ground. However, I am trying to remember what job dad wanted me to do. The horses pulled the planter while I was riding old Pete. I remember dad seemed to like having tomatoes on his farm. The profits may have been sizeable. And I remember the Latino people coming to pick them. I think they were from Mexico. They were only there for about two or three days, then the tomato picking would be finished, and then they moved on and picked tomatoes for other farmers in the area. They must have had someone representing them and arranging the places they would be picking the tomatoes. It may have been arranged by the tomato canning factory in Union City. I believe they were in the area for several weeks. They had a specific area where they made their living quarters during that time. They had some trailers and tents, and plenty of water was available. They had an outhouse too. I also remember some children getting on the school bus and going to school. They were hard-working people.

More 39-Acre Recollections

When I was 3 to 6 years old, I remember my chores included feeding the chickens and gathering the eggs. The chicken house had about 20 chickens. The eggs were for our use and our aunt, who lived just down the road. I remember I had a bucket with oats to scatter on the floor for the chickens. Then I would reach into the nests, take out the eggs, and put them into the empty bucket. But the big problem for me was a rooster in there too. And when I would go into that chicken house, he would flop me (attack me). This rooster was about the same height as me. He would jump on me with his feet aimed at my face. His claws would scratch my face and arms. I hated this creature! But I learned how to defend myself by getting the bucket between him and myself. Then I would gather the eggs and get out of the chicken house as quickly as possible. I am sure I broke some of the eggs. I don't know what happened to that rooster. And I don't care! I do not know if mom and dad realized my problem with that creature.

One of my other chores on this farm was feeding ear corn to the pigs. I had a little red wagon. I would put a wooden bushel basket in the wagon, go to the corn crib, and put the corn in the basket. I always put more corn in the basket than needed, but I needed about half a basket full. But the problem was, at the entrance to the corn crib was about a 3-inch hump of cement placed there to hold the barn doors from pushing in during wind and rain storms. Dad would open the doors for me because I could not open them. At first, I could not get the wagon and the filled basket over that hump. So I learned to leave the wagon and basket outside the hump and carry the corn to the basket, about six feet. Then I could go and feed the corn to the pigs. After feeding the pigs, I needed to go up to the top of the barn to push hay down for the milk cows and straw for their bedding. Dad had told me the amount he wanted down for each stall. There was a large hole area in the upper floor. This hole in the floor is where I would push and pull the hay and straw close to it and let it fall to the lower part, where the cattle were. At first, most of the hay was loose, and later some baled hay. I had to slide everything across the floor to get the materials to the opening on the floor. It took a lot of work; the hay bales were heavy, but I always made it without falling through the space.

When I was three years old, my father and an uncle built a new chicken house. Because my mother wanted more chickens. She planned to sell more eggs. Anyway, I was in the garden beside the new chicken house one afternoon. I found a Kro-Kay mallet. And I don't know why, but I took that mallet and broke all the windows in the new chicken house. Our mother was supposed to keep an eye on my sister and me. Mom was probably inside the house preparing food and trusted I would be ok out in the garden beside the new chicken house. I did not get hurt by any of the broken glass. I probably was reprimanded for doing this, but I do not remember any spanking. I remember my father telling me never to break any glass again because I could get hurt. I listened and never did anything like that again. To this day, I still do not know why I did this. Afterward, dad had to take all the broken windows to Montana's hardware store to re-install the new glass.

Dad had built us a new outhouse north of this unique chicken house. It was deluxe. A nice two-holer, painted red, had a new door and was windproof. It sat beside the fence, which enclosed the barnyard and kept the chickens, pigs, and cows from running wild.

The north and south sides of this outhouse had firewood stacked as tall as the fence. I don't know where the wood came from, but there was much of it. We would carry this stacked wood inside the house for heat and cooking. Taking wood into the house for the stoves was quite a task. Also, I liked to play outside on top of this wood when it was sunny. I probably should not have, but I did anyway. I often got thorns and splinters in my feet and body. I was barefoot most of the summertime. And I do not remember wearing short pants. There were ants, bugs, and snakes on top of the wood, sunning themselves. The snakes scared me. But I specifically remember getting thorns in my feet. Then I would run to our mom, and she would take a pair of pliers and remove these painful objects. I was always into something.

More wood was neatly stacked between the new outhouse and the new chicken house. The area for trash, empty cans, bottles from home, and other debris was close to the new chicken house. Anyway, a drinking glass in the house somehow broke. And if you know about broken glasses, they usually break in a sort of "V" shape. Mom had told me to put that glass outside in the trash. I did, but instead of placing it in the garbage, I threw it. And somehow, my right index finger was in that "V" shaped area, consequently cutting the tip off my finger. I remember standing there watching the blood spurt out. I supposed I was crying because mom came running from the barn. Mom got a clean white pillowcase and wrapped my hand in it. Dad had also run out of the barn to see what the commotion was. Dad wrapped his handkerchief around my arm and told mom to take me to the doctor. Mom drove me to Dr. Wills, who lived above his office there in Union City. He looked at my hand and said he could sew the end back on if he had it. Mom went home, and they all looked for it, but because of the darkness, they could not find it. So Dr. Wills pulled the skin over the bone and bandaged it. And that took care of my finger. But it did not affect the bone because I could still pull the trigger on a gun. That was all the military cared about when I got older. The next day after I had cut the tip off my finger, we found the severed end. Too late to sew it back on then. And I never threw any broken glass again. I have always remembered that, and I learned my lesson! I was five years old at that time. Since then, I have always been conscientious around broken glass.

The 39-acre house had no running water, but it had a brick-lined cistern on the north side of the house. Most cisterns were hand-dug and lined with brick and mortar. Cisterns were used to hold rainwater, with drain pipes connected to the house roofs. Cisterns were used to hold the collected rainwater inside them for storing the water for later use. A hand pump was on the top covering to draw the water out of the cistern. It was good drinking water and pure and clean. I never saw any creatures in it. But I remember my father telling me to get down in there to clean it. I did. It was circular and about 6 feet deep. It was about 2 feet in diameter. It had some moss growing on the sides, which my father wanted me to remove. He had a rope tied around me to pull me out if I fell too deep. But there was not much water in the bottom when I cleaned it. I am sure this cistern was filled in when the new owner took over the property.

My father learned I could and would do this as I cleaned Russel Shaw's every year. But Russel's was made of concrete and was square inside. His was only about 2 feet deep and was 4 feet square inside, and covered with concrete. It usually had sediment all over the bottom. I suppose the sediment of dirt is what they wanted to be removed. Our mother bought Russel Shaw's house years later and told me she filled the cistern with dirt. The house on the 80 acres also had a cistern. It was made of brick and large enough to stand in. It had a square concrete pad over the top and a large piece of metal covering the opening. It did not have very much water in it or not much dirt. We stored apples in it for a few years. I had put boards on the bottom to sit the baskets on to enable air to circulate these baskets. The one at the 80-acre house is still there, as far as I know. Cisterns stored water, and fruit cellars were placed under the ground to keep fruits and vegetables cool during summer. Fruit cellars were frequented on the hot, humid summer evenings, as they were consistently calm, cool, and inviting. We would use a kerosine lamp inside because there was no light inside the fruit cellar.

A sugar pear tree was west of the barn on the 39-acre farm, in the middle of the field. That is what people called it. Golly, the pears were good. It was not a big tree and did not produce many pears, but many people wanted them. I remember dad parking the 1941 Dodge truck underneath to enable people to put step ladders on the truck bed to stand on to pick these pears. I specifically remember Aunt Mary coming to help pick the pears. Did mom make pies with them? I only remember eating apples. I tried to reach as many as possible and climbed the side of the truck to gain some, but I was not tall enough! I specifically remember Aunt Mary trying to get up on the truck bed. Aunt Mary was a sizable lady at that time.

At the very back of the 39-acre property ran the Pennsylvania Railroad tracks. As I recall, they all were steam trains in the late '40s. There was a large water tank along the tracks for the engines to stop to fill their water container for the engines. We would always wave at the men working on the train. Along these tracks were many wild berry vines and strawberry patches. When the strawberry and raspberry season was right, our mother would tell my sister and me to pick enough for a pie and some to eat. We picked these fruits each year while we lived on the 39-acres. I was young when going back there, 3 to 6 years old. I also remember Aunt Mary's daughters going back there with us too. All of these plants were organic and had no cultivation at all. I suppose we took some back to mom, but I know we ate a lot of them while picking. They were delicious!

Baby Chickens @ 39 Acres

My mother and father had a brooder house used for raising baby chickens. It was about 10 X 16 feet, and built on wooden logs. I do not know if my father or someone else made it. But because it had been constructed on logs/skids, you could move it around with a tractor. At the 39-acre property, most of the time, the brooder house was placed west of the house, but at the specific time I am referring to, the brooder house was east of the house and barn, about 50 yards out in the field.

My mother and I were in it one afternoon. I think I was 5 years old. Mom wanted to do something with the young chickens inside. It sat out in the pasture where the cattle ran, and the cattle could eat the grass around it. Our father had borrowed Virgil's bull a few days earlier to breed the cows. Many farmers loaned out their bulls to eliminate the cost of keeping an extra animal around. Bulls do not produce milk or any income. Most breeding of cows nowadays is done through artificial insemination. This bull was known to be mean. But this afternoon, mom and I started walking from the brooder house back to the barn area. At this time, this bull came around the corner. It was snorting and was showing great danger to both of us. We went back into the brooder house. We tried to get out again, but the bull would not leave. Somehow, my mother started yelling for my father to alert him of the problem. We were stranded in this building for many minutes before our father heard my mother. So dad and another man started walking to the brooder house, then the bull started running towards them. No one was hurt. Because my father got on his tractor and drove it out to the brooder house, and my mother and I climbed up on it. The other man stayed by the gate in the fence. That crazy bull tried to attack the tractor, but dad steered away from him. Finally, dad drove the tractor through the gate area, and the man closed the gate behind us.

My father went to see Virgil that evening, as we had no telephones. Virgil came and took the bull away the next day. I was pretty young then, but as I understand animals today, this bull was similar to the rodeo bulls used today for rodeo events. I do not know how long my mother and I would have been caught in that situation if my dad did not show up when he did. I do not know how mom and I would have gotten out without that tractor. I remember the field area where the brooder house was sitting. The soil surface was pretty muddy from the recent rains. That bull scared both mom and me.

The 39-Acre House

This house was a two-story, solidly built house with a metal roof. It was a beautiful house. It had one bedroom downstairs, two bedrooms upstairs, and an area for storing supplies. There also was a storage room on the first floor too. The west room of the downstairs part of the house was not heated and was just a storage space. This house had a large living room with a Base Burner stove in the middle of the room to heat the home in the wintertime. Dad purchased coal to burn in it at night because coal kept the fire and heat much longer than a wood fire. But during the day, in winter, they burned only wood in it. I wonder where dad got the firewood. At night the metal sides would turn red from the fire inside. Close to this stove was the sofa, where I slept many times when I was sick. Especially when I had measles, and chicken pox, with only one day between those two illnesses. The house house had something like an enclosed back porch. The back porch of this home had a smaller wood stove used to heat this part of the house. The stove always burnt wood in it too.

Our mother had a large copper tub to pour hot water into for us to sit in to bathe. When I took my bath, our mother put that copper tub beside the stove on the floor. The stove would also help heat the air around the copper tub, so the air would not be so cold. But wintertime in Indiana gets pretty complicated. There was lots of snow, and it was cold all winter long. There was also a wood cookstove in the kitchen to prepare food and heat the water for our baths. It primarily used wood for fuel in this cook stove too. I bet the water was pretty dirty after my bath. Mom heated water in pans and then poured it into the copper tub. I also remember mom using lye soap, which she had made for us. Baths were an experience, but we all survived!

There was no electricity in this house for the first years of my life. Hurricane lamps were used inside the house at night, and lanterns were used for the back porch and outside after darkness had set in. Kerosine was the fuel used in them. Lanterns were suspended on nails overhead in the barn and other outbuildings. I remember dad lighting them and hanging them up. The outhouse did not have any lights, that I remember. I do not remember using it at night. I used a pot. The outhouse was far from the house, at least 75 feet from the back door. The kitchen had an ice box. The iceman delivered ice and put the blocks in it on a schedule. It was about every other day. Inside this house was a landing space at the bottom of the stairs. Our mother had a library table sitting there. I remember leaning on this table for quite some time, at different times of the day, but always at night. I would be looking through coloring books and picture magazines. Mother had a hurricane lamp sitting on this table, and that is how I was able to look at pictures and books in the evenings after dark. I know there was a tablecloth on this table. There was also a radio sitting on this table. It was connected by wires, with the batteries sitting on the floor. Dad always liked to listen to the Fibber Mcgee and Molly radio programs.

Back then, almost everyone kept magazines, newspapers, books, etc., to share with friends, family, and neighbors. Our mother shared with family and neighbors. The same with the garden's rewards, such as tomatoes, sweet corn, watermelons, green beans, and other vegetables. We had a big garden. Mother harvested Concord grapes from grandmother's house, which she shared with neighbors too. I do not think mom shared the sugar pears, only with Aunt Mary. I do not think there were very many to share. Also, farmers helped each other, especially at hay-making time and harvest time. And when cutting firewood, sometimes there would be other people helping. I remember dad and granddad cutting some of the trees from our grandfather's wooded area. I do not remember helping much on that project. But I remember stacking the firewood next to granddad's garage for him to carry into his house for heating. I know some people helped other neighbors construct needed buildings. Uncle Roy had neighbors help him build an addition to his barn in about 1947. That was the custom then.

The bedroom downstairs was dad and mom's bedroom. The upstairs had two bedrooms. The one to the south was for my sister, and the one to the west was mine. The ceiling in my room sloped, similar to many other houses, because of the roof's exterior slope. My room had a walnut bed and dresser. The walnut bed is stored in our Oakland garage, and I have the dresser in our Oakland home now. This dresser has a large beveled mirror. That door to my bedroom was always closed, and it was always frigid and was not heated as best as I can remember.

I specifically remember to this day, the nightmares I experienced in that room. A big dark creature thing was coming to get me. The demon was something like a big cloud. These were terrible nightmares; if I cried, my mother or father would come to the room and tell me to go back to sleep. That is the reason the door was closed. Of course, I was afraid to go back to sleep. But I finally outgrew the nightmares. The worst were when I was 3 years old.

In the center part of the upstairs area was an old double bed given to my parents by my grandfather. The thing I specifically remember about this bed was after my brother was born and needed to have surgery, we both had to sleep in it. The bed was tight against the wall, and I had to sleep on the side next to the stairwell. The reason is my brother had braces on his feet and would squirm around and could fall out of bed. So I had to ensure he did not slip out of bed, which he never did. But he used to roll around, and the metal brace would bang against me, wake me up, and then I would push him back next to the wall. The one good thing about this was it was heated some. But the downside was constantly being bumped by my brother and his brace. Of course, my brother was innocent and never knew what was happening. I do not remember getting angry; I did whatever mom and dad told me to do. These are just memories from this house, and I liked this house.

The 39-acre home had no electricity or running water when I was born. Electricity had been installed only a short time before we moved. I do not recall any running water. We always carried in cistern water. After we moved from this house down to the 80-acre house, this 39-acre house was picked up, moved about a half mile away, and remodeled. My sister and I were able to see the inside of it again just a few years ago—lots of memories.

I also remember my father putting me on the tractor seat on this farm to steer it. I was about five years old then. Dad was baling hay with other men, and I steered the tractor around the field. They would put it in gear to get it moving, and I could pull or push the throttle in or out to go faster or slower. I remember doing this same procedure for many years at different locations when they were bailing hay. And I remember doing this when Dad was helping neighbors. I steered other farmers' tractors around. But my dad would always start and change gears. I drove, but I knew how to turn off the ignition switch if I needed to stop. Of course, we were traveling less than one mile per hour.

The 1941 Dodge 1+½ ton truck. was a big truck to me. Dad would start it, put it in gear, and I would stand on the seat and steer it around the fields. And I also knew to pull the throttle out to go faster and push it in to go slower. And I knew where the ignition switch was to stop it. This truck was also the truck dad parked in the field, which allowed us to put step ladders on the truckbed to stand on. Standing on these ladders on the truck bed enabled picking those delicious pears. This procedure was used at the mulberry tree at granddad's house to harvest the mulberries. It was a grand old truck.

Dad said he used the Dodge truck to haul sugar beets (pictures) and other hauling and to transport grain and hay down to Kentucky and Tennessee. He would tell me how long (about an hour) it took for the loaded truck to climb the large grade in Covington, Kentucky. And dad used this truck to haul his fertilizer from Cincinnati, Ohio. I went on this trip with him many times. He would leave early in the morning after milking and be home in the middle of the afternoon. Dad usually stopped at a fruit stand in Hamilton, Ohio, on our way home. Dad purchased a bushel basket full of peaches to bring home for mom to make preserves, and we ate several too. I suppose dad saved money by buying and trucking his supplies. The '41 Dodge was a good solid truck. Dad always kept a wool blanket in the cab of this truck, usually on the seat. Dad kept it there if he wanted to sleep or nap while waiting to load or unload his truck. When dad traded trucks, he kept this same blanket on the seat of the '54 Dodge truck. My wife and I have used this blanket every winter, or it is stored in our closet during summer.

Dad never kept any books for his business. How he remembered everything the way he did, I will never know. The only recorded information I know was a tiny little black book and an Agrico fertilizer book. They showed some figures and names, which dad must have recorded when he was hauling sugar beets. But there was only 1 page in the Agrico book, and 3 in the black book. The only date showing is 1943. Some figures recorded in this book showed the same farmer's names, and some showed other farmers' names too. All figures had been recorded by dad, and mainly on a single page. The other pages only had figures for mathematics.

These figures were the amounts dad transported for each farmer. All statistics were weights; no money amounts were listed. Dad loaded all these beets on his truck by hand, and he never had any help. At least, that is what he told me. There is a picture of dad standing beside his vehicle at the time he was loading the sugar beets. Dad was never afraid of hard work. At tax preparation time, I remember dad and mom sitting at the dining room table, with dad telling mom the figures to write down on the tax forms. I marvel at how dad could retain so many statistics. To my knowledge, they never had any problems. Years later, they hired an attorney to file their tax forms. Dad must have sat beside him, and given him the figures.

The 39-Acre Barn and Farm

The barn on the 39-acre farm was a big old red barn. Inside, it had a corncrib on the west side. Which seems to me was added sometime after the original barn was constructed. There was space between it and the west side of the barn to store equipment, supplies, etc. Dad kept the '41 Dodge truck in this area too. The space was approximately 10 feet wide, with a dirt floor. The horses were in the northern middle section of the big barn, and the cows were housed on the east side. Dad milked his cows by hand. No machines during those years. I remember sitting on the foundation edge on the inside and watching dad milk the cows. I sat about 6 feet behind the cows and was not allowed any closer to the cows or the horses. But the horses (massive) were in the next stall over. I stayed far away from them too. This barn had a full hayloft, with an area in the middle to drop down hay and straw for the animals. The site's opening for pushing down hay and straw from the upper part of the barn was toward the middle and more toward the southern region to allow dropping the hay and straw down into an area in front of all the animals. The space was called a feed way. There the hay and straw would fall, and then dad would place it in the feeding troughs and place the bedding on the floor for the animals. Outside the barn, toward the east, was the watering trough.

Dad kept the milk cans in this trough to keep the milk cool. There was a big tree beside the watering trough. Southeast of the tree and barn was the old chicken house. I mentioned the chicken house because that is where the rooster would get me. But my chores were to feed the chicken oats, gather the eggs, get corn to feed the pigs, throw down hay and straw for the animals, and carry wood into the house for the stoves. I did not have any problems with the oats, but getting corn for the pigs was much different. I had to take our little red wagon, put a wooden bushel basket inside, put corn in the basket, and give the corn to the pigs. Dad kept the pigs behind the barn in 2 or 3 hog houses. Getting the wagon out of the corn crib required getting it over the cement ledge which held the doors. This ledge was only 3 inches high, but I needed to be stronger to get the wagon wheels over it. So I would take the corn out of the basket, move the wagon over the ledge, and then put the corn back inside the basket in the wagon.

I remember that the top of the basket in the wagon was about the same height as I was. I was about 3 or 4 years old. I remember how difficult this chore was. And after I had finished feeding the chickens, gathering the eggs, and feeding the pigs, I was to slide hay and straw over to the hole in the hayloft and drop the hay and straw down for the cattle and horses below. This chore was easy for me to do. I had to ensure I did not fall through with the hay and straw. After the hay and straw were in the bottom of the barn, dad took care of placing them where he wanted them. And the carrying of wood into the house was an endless chore. I carried two or three pieces at a time if they were manageable. The stoves used many chunks of wood in the winter but a much smaller amount in summer. I think mom or dad carried in the coal for the Base Burner stove, which we used during the wintertime's cold winter nights.

This big red barn had a hay track mounted to the inside upper roof area. Farmers used this track at hay baling time to move both bales of hay and loose hay into the barn for the wintertime food storage for the animals. On the wagon parked beside the barn, dad would take the hayfork mechanism's forks and put them into the bales, about four at a time, as I remember. The metal track ran from one side of the barn to the other. The automobile connected to the large rope would pull the mechanism holding the hay bales into the barn. The rope ran through a series of rollers. The rope was attached to the car's front bumper, which our mother was operating. The process required mom to back the car up, which pulled the bales of hay up into the barn. Dad would pull the trip rope, and the bales would fall inside. At dad's signal, Mom would drive the car forward again. Dad would pull the mechanism and large cord back down to the top of the wagon. Dad would repeat this process over and over again. Our uncle Roy stacked the bales inside the barn in the hayloft. My job was to pull the rope attached to the car forward so the car wheels would not roll over it. This rope was pretty heavy, but I always managed, I was 5 to 6 years old. Dad pulled some from the other side, which helped, but he could not see how close the car's tires were to the rope. My job was to drag the rope to keep the vehicle from running over it. And one-time, dad accidentally scraped his leg badly with the hay fork, but it healed.

 Someone invented this process at some point, and it worked well. Moving in of the hay bales was replaced with metal grain elevators in my later years. Before hay balers were invented, farmers put all hay and straw into the barns as loose. A horse-drawn mower cut the grass, hay, and oats. Sometimes they loaded the wagons by hand, using long-handled pitchforks. Mostly the loose hay would be picked up and placed on a wagon by another machine, called a hay loader. Then the wagon loaded with the hay would be placed next to the barn. The loose hay would then be brought into the barn for winter feed for the animals by using the same overhead track system similar to what I mentioned before, except horses were used to pull the rope instead of an automobile.

The earliest I remember being out in the fields with dad was when he used the horses to prepare the soil for planting. For a couple of years, dad planted and grew tomatoes in the area by railroad tracks. There was a tomato canning facility close by in Union City, and it was straightforward to haul tomatoes to that canning factory. Someone had a tomato planter, and they came to plant this field for dad. It was some kind of planter, where two people rode seated, side by side, and they placed the tomatoes in the ground, in a furrow, along with a small portion of water for each plant. I do not remember dad having a tractor when we were out in the tomato field, and I know Pete and Daisy pulled the planter. Before the tractor, dad used the two workhorses, Pete and Daisy for soil preparation. They both were pretty old. Pete was blind, and I don't remember much about Daisy. But when dad worked in the field with the horses, I would sit on old Pete and ride him around while pulling the tomato cultivator and other farming equipment.

I never knew if tomato raising was a profitable way of making money. When tomato harvest time came, the Latino people would come from the Texas area to pick the tomatoes and then place the full hamper baskets filled with tomatoes on the Dodge truck. Then dad would stack the full baskets neatly on the truck. Several other farmers raised tomatoes in the area around Union City. Harvesting the tomatoes would make it profitable for Latino families to come and work for the summer. Their whole families would come, children and all. I helped pick some tomatoes, but only a few because I was too small. But several years after we moved to the 80-acre property, dad and I helped another farmer (Stanley) pick his tomatoes. We worked at that for a few days, and dad was paid ten cents per hamper basket full. Dad and I picked almost 50 hampers full each time we worked, usually only half a day at a time. This 39-acre farm tomato field is my last recollection of riding and using dad's horses, Pete and Daisy. I know that before we moved to the 80-

acre farm, dad sold the horses. Dad told me they made soap from the horses; I could not understand that.

Dad also raised corn for the cows and pigs. I remember dad going out to the fence posts to cut the ears of corn to feed the cows. Cutting up the corn took place when the corn was still in its growing form. Corn, at this age, was suitable for the production of milk. Dad used a corn cutter blade to cut the ears of corn. Dad would cut up about 8 or 10 ears at a time. One time dad cut his fingers with the corn cutter. Dad cut his finger but never went to the doctor. Dad was tough and did not care to go to any doctor. In between the fields was a lane. An extended narrow area that enabled the cattle to go into one field but kept the cattle out of the other fields. Using this route also allowed farm equipment passage from one field or barnyard to a different area. I remember this lane had the most beautiful Jim-son weeds. There were several big ones, probably six feet tall when mature. Jim-son weeds have beautiful blooms. Blooms may have been 6 inches in diameter. However, the pods on these weeds are poisonous. The blooms on these plants were beautiful, purple, and white when they opened up. The farm animals never bothered these weeds. The farm animals instinctively knew they were dangerous. The pigs liked to wallow in the mud puddles next to these weeds. The pigs wanted to lay in the shade under them.

This 39-acre house and farm were about ½ mile from Union City. To the north of this farm was the Pennsylvania Railroad, with only one set of tracks going each way. We, kids, used to pick wild strawberries and blackberries along these train tracks. Harter Park and the Union City Cemetery were on the other side of the railroad tracks. Several of our relatives are buried there. There was a water tower along the tracks for the steam engines to fill their water tanks. I watched the train employees do this many times.

Our cousin's husband was a painter for the railroad, and he

painted this water tower periodically and the train bridges in that area. He said he liked painting them. And he had to paint using a brush, no spraying. I do not know how many years he did this work. He was a lovely person. He, dad, and I, along with others, played a lot of baseball in the field across from their house. We all had lots of fun. That is the only time dad would play ball with us for any length of time. And some Sundays, on the 80 acres, some of them visited our house, and we would all go out to our large barnyard and play baseball, croquet, and sometimes we just wrestled each other. Croquet is a game played with wooden balls, wooden mallets, and metal arches to hit the balls through. I think it was a common European game.

I remember walking down the gravel road to our Aunt Mary and Uncle Bill's house. Behind Uncle Bill's house was another set of railroad tracks. Dad said they were the Big Four. Their daughters were a year or two older than my sister. Our Aunt Mary always received her milk from dad and his cows. Our mother supplied Aunt Mary with eggs from mom's chickens too. I remember my sister carrying our Aunt Mary's milk can.

We would go to our Aunt and Uncle's house on many Saturday nights. The adults liked to watch wrestling on TV. And several Sunday mornings, I would wake up on our Aunt's couch. I had fallen asleep, and mom, dad, and my sister, had gone home and left me there. It never seemed to upset anyone. Then I would go home the next morning.

I remember my first day of school. My cousins and sister always rode the school bus, and I just got on the bus too. I don't know much about school, except the teachers and their names. I recall getting sick one time and vomiting on the school floor. I liked looking out the school windows across the field where a hand-dug well was in the corner of the area. A few farm animals were out there too. Also, dad had some business dealing with our first-grade teacher's father, Mr. Platt. I remember going to her and her father's house in Union City for this. Miss Platt was our first-grade teacher's name. Mrs. Butcher was the second-grade teacher's name.

And a couple of other things I remember while living in this house. One was the wonderful sugar pear tree out in the field west of the house, which I had mentioned earlier. Another thing I remember was my sister's piano teacher coming to give her lessons. He drove a model "T" Ford automobile. And this Model "T" had to be cranked by hand to start it. This teacher always wore a white shirt, tie, and suit, very neatly dressed. But one time, the old Ford would not start. I remember him taking off his coat and necktie, rolling up his sleeves, and working on the engine for a bit, then cranking it, it started, and then he put his coat back on and drove away. I don't remember how long he gave my sister piano lessons, but I think it was until we moved in 1951.

Another thing I remember, one winter, it snowed a lot. The snow was about fence high, probably around 4 feet deep. No one could go anywhere, but my sister and I went to our Aunt's house just down the road. But that was after Mr. Mote drove his giant caterpillar down the road to open it for some travel. Dad waited for the sun to melt the snow away after that particular snowfall. But I remember walking through the snow to get to the school bus.

The 39-acre house sat many, many feet back from this road. There were several giant trees in the front yard. I think they were Maple trees. There were many trees all over this property—lots of leaves for raking in the fall of the year. I remember rolling in the piles of leaves—many fond memories of that whole property while we lived there.

Going to Church

My sister and I walked to the Methodist Church in Union City on Sundays if the weather was good while we lived on the 39-acre farm. It was not too far to walk, maybe one mile each way. I was about 3 to 6 years old then. I know I had to go upstairs in the church for Sunday School and then downstairs for the Church Service. The ladies upstairs could not understand me when I told them my name. They finally asked my sister what my name was. I did not speak too well at that age. After Sunday School was over, my sister and I would go downstairs to the main seating area of the church. I only remember a little about what was said. It did not interest me at that young age. But my sister and I would sit on the church pew, and I would lay on the bench with my head on my sister's lap and sleep. I had no idea why I was there. Then after the service was over, we would walk back home. Sometimes our grandfather would come in his Chevrolet to pick us up. And sometimes, dad would ride in the car with granddad. But I remember enjoying the walk and looking at the stones on the street and roads. Many years later, my sister played the organ in this church for their Sunday Services.

After we moved to the 80-acre farm, my sister and I went to the South Salem Methodist Church for a while. I think mom took us to this church on Sunday. It was about 3 miles from our house. I also remember going to Vacation Bible School at this church during some summers. For some unknown reason, we stopped going to church anywhere. Mom and dad never went to church on Sundays. Dad explained that he did not have a good enough suit to wear. I accepted his response then, but I would not buy that response today. But after I was a little older, I started riding my bicycle to the Bartonia Methodist Church. Mrs. Harder, who lived up the road, was my teacher at first.

About 40 people attended this church on Sundays, and about 20 children. However, I remember precisely that I rode my bike each Sunday for two years and three weeks and never missed a Sunday service. The last time I went to this church, I became sick, and one of the young men drove me home. Mom had taken me to church that day. I had tonsillitis frequently during those years, which was my problem that day. I was very sick. The sad thing about this was that I was so embarrassed that I never returned to that church again. Mrs. Harter called occasionally and asked me to return, but I could not get there. Part of my fear was I was timid and shy.

Mrs. Harter's granddaughter attended this church. She was very outgoing and talked a lot. And for sure, I knew nothing about the teachings of the Bible. The granddaughter made me feel small and dumb. And sometime later, Mrs. Harter had a birthday party for this granddaughter. Mrs. Harter insisted that I also attend her granddaughter's party. I did, but I was the only boy there, and there were 4 or 5 other girls there too. Being shy, I was so embarrassed. That is why I never went back to that church. And for sure, dad never went to church, so I just decided I would not go to church and stay home and work on the farm catching up on cleaning up and organizing different ideas I had. Sundays became another typical work day. I usually cleaned the feed way area of the barn on Sundays. However, after Dee and I were married, we started going to church every Sunday. We enjoyed going to church.

Uncle Ira's Electrical

At about this same time, in the late 40s, our Uncle Ira built the house across the road from the 39-acre home. I wanted to know who wanted to have a home built there. It was a beautiful house, but not very big. And I don't know who moved into it when Uncle Ira finished the building. Uncle Ira's family did not, but our cousin did live there many years later. I remember my father and grandfather digging out the basement area with grandfather's big scoop. It was a tough job. It was designed as a horse-drawn scoop, but they pulled it with a tractor. And I remember them making the foundation forms. I do not recall who framed the house, but I know our Uncle and father did some of it. But the part I remember primarily about this house was my Uncle wanted me to help him do the wiring. I remember my job was keeping the wiring straight, with no kinks or twists, while Uncle Ira pulled the wire up and through the walls. I don't know if the wiring was color-coded or not. I think the year would have been 1947 or 1948. I also remember trying to shovel dirt around the foundation. And I remember my dad, and Uncle Roy, and I were walking out on the east side of this new building. And somewhere as we were walking in the tall grass, we came upon a pile of dirt, with a bunch of garter snakes laying there sunning themselves. Uncle Roy immediately picked me up and carried me for a distance. Maybe they scared me. But Uncle Roy carried me to safety. That is all I remember about this house, but I do remember how pretty this house turned out after completion. And it still is. I suppose our Uncle purchased the small plot of land, which initially belonged to the larger farm across the road, and he paid for all the material costs and construction. I would have no idea if dad and Uncle Ira had any kind of agreement about this house. I only remember it looking pretty, and it was light green outside.

    I mentioned that a cousin of my dad's lived in this house across from the 39-acre farm. He did, but maybe 35 years later, after it was sold to the first buyers. This cousin (Charlie) and his wife worked at the same factory as our Uncle Ira. Charlie and his wife lived north of Winchester, Indiana., out in the country. Charlie was a great musician and loved to play the guitar. He would play his guitar and he and his wife would sing at some of the taverns around Winchester. People said they were a good duo. But sometime later, the two of them decided to get a divorce.

I think the wife remarried, but Charlie did not, but he had a girlfriend. As near as I remember, Charlie and his girlfriend rented this house that our uncle had built, probably 35 years after our uncle completed building this house. Charlie must have been unhappy, he committed suicide while living there. The whole situation seemed very sad! I do not know why Charlie would do that. He and I spent quite a lot of time together when we were out hunting, and he always seemed pretty happy to me, although I think he was afraid of the dark. It is so sad that the house our father helped build would be the same house where Charlie would lose his life. Our father would have been distraught if he knew about this, but our dad had already died several years earlier. Dad liked Charlie, and we visited him and his family several times each year. Charlie owned a Harley Davidson motorcycle at one time. It was light green and white, a deluxe one at that time. He was so proud of it but was afraid to ride it. As I remember, he only had it for a short while.

Across the road from the 39-acre farm was another great family; Patterson was their name. Mom said they originally came to that area from Kentucky. The father was a farmer, the mother was a lovely mother who baked things, and there were several children, about 4. We shared apples, pears, raspberries, strawberries, and garden vegetables. I only remember picking these fruits and vegetables. I liked the father. He was a very slow-talking, skinny man. He helped my dad bale hay, and in turn, dad helped him bale his hay. The Pattersons also had farm animals. My sister probably knew some of the daughters who lived in that area after we moved. And our mother corresponded with them for a while after we moved to the 80-acre farm. Their farm was a little small. Behind it was a small creek, and over it was a set of railroad tracks. The creek flowed west to east, and some Union City factories used water from that little creek. That set of railroad tracks was what my dad called the Big Four. I never knew who the Big Four Railroad was. I assume they belonged to all the trains that were not Pennsylvania trains.

Grandmother Gibson's Farm

Dad cared for our grandmother Gibson's farm in my early years. Grandmother Gibson was my mother's mother. Grandmother Gibson was married two times. With her first marriage, she had three children. Then her first husband died, Mr. Moore. Then she married John Gibson, who was 20 years her senior, and they had seven children. John Gibson had three children from his previous marriage.

Grandmother (Maude) Gibson's maiden name was Alexander. She had two brothers, whom I met and talked with a few times, Harry and Harley. Grandmother lived on the 59 acre property as a child. When she married Mr Moore, it is unclear where they lived. When Mr Moore died, grandmother married Mr Gibson. They lived in a small house in Drake County Ohio, on 5 acres, about 20 miles from her parents home. Mr Gibson was a lumberjack, this was his work. All 7 of the Gibson children were born while living in this house. Our mother was born in 1921. Our grandmother's father died in 1928, while living on the 59 acres. The 59 acre property was sold, and grandmother inherited $3,300 from that sale. She then purchased back the 59 acre property where her parents lived. That is when John and Maude Gibson moved their family to the 59 acres. John Gibson cared for the farm until his death in 1945. I do not know the year grandmother purchased the 59 acre property. I only know our mother went to school from this home, and most of her siblings too. Then their eldest son cared for the property after Mr Gibson died, but their eldest son did not want to be a farmer.

Grandmother asked our father to take over caring for it. I do not know when that was. But my father purchased the 39-acre property, about 1942. He rented it from Mrs Clark before he purchased it.

While we were living on the 39-acre property, dad was caring for his land and our grandmothers. Grandmother's property was about 4 miles away. That meant that dad had to haul his equipment over the roadways back and forth until he was finished for the year. It was pretty challenging to load tools on trailers, haul them there, unload them, do the work, and then again load them back on trailers and transport them home. Moving equipment requires time. Every day dad needed to care for his livestock plus his property too. Many times spring rains would interfere with the schedule. It could rain on one farm and not the other. I remember hauling the equipment there, unloading plus connecting it, and doing the work dad wanted to get done.

And when I was older and working at my grandmother's farm by myself, about 12 years old, my mother would always tell me to tell my grandmother that I was working her property and that I would be there for dinner/lunch. Grandmother would always fix my food, and plenty of it. Grandmother's cooking was always excellent and tasty. Grandmother Gibson used the old wood cookstove for her cooking and baking. Those stoves are all collector items now. But again, our mother was an excellent cook and baker. Our mother's mother (grandmother Gibson) would make the very best pies, and all different kinds of pies, in this old wood-fired stove. Golly, they were so good. And luckily, she would almost always make a chocolate pie for me when I was at her farm with a tractor, working the ground, planting, mowing, or doing other farming duties. Grandmother would tell me when to come into her house to eat. Mom's brother, Uncle Calvin, was always there to eat too. I liked grandmother Gibson. Sadly grandmother Gibson passed away in 1963.

At grandmother Gibson's farm, I would only be there one or two days at a time. As I was younger, dad would help me unload the equipment and connect it. But after I was a little older, I could unload the equipment and go straight to work. Many times, If I needed to be working at my grandmother's, and the end of the day came, I would ride my bicycle home to the 80-acre farm. It was easy to put my bicycle on top of the loaded farm equipment on the trailer, allowing me a way home. This way, no one needed to come to pick me up, which was so far away, about 11 miles. Sometimes at Grandmother's farm, I needed to ride the seeding drill while dad drove the tractor to top-dress wheat with grass seed and fertilizer in spring. I made sure everything was feeding down correctly.

Grandmother was constantly questioning dad about the days and times to plant and harvest crops on her farm. Grandmother had a neighbor who visited her frequently and told her she should follow the "Almanac." The Almanac was a book that many farm people believed contained the messages to follow, to receive the best turnout of harvests, and everything it mentioned and contained about farming practices. Her neighbor had convinced grandmother to plant at certain times when the Almanac said it was the best time to grow and harvest. Grandmother felt that the Almanacs' words would make more profits for her. Dad did not go by the Almanac. Dad tried to accommodate some but wanted to do the work when he had things ready and was not interested in waiting a day or two or more. Or stopping work at another property to go to work at our grandmother's. Dad hoped the neighbor would stop visiting our grandmother until he had finished his work at our grandmother's farm. But I think she changed her mind because dad always had successful harvests. Dad stored a little corn at her farm, but most of the time, dad would fill wagons with the harvest, and I would take them directly to the elevator in town to unload while dad kept on harvesting. This way, the elevator weighed the loads and amounts, and they would have records of how much the harvest produced. Dad was the most honest man I have ever known. He would never cheat our grandmother or anyone. I also knew dad, if there were a half shovel full of product remaining at harvest time, it would automatically go to the land owner, not dad. I was not old enough to legally drive the truck, so I had to pull the wagons from my grandmother's farm to the elevator with the tractor. I do not know how the haymaking worked out. We never put any hay in grandmother's barn. Dad always hauled all the hay from her property to the 39-acre barn. I am sure dad paid her for her share.

The first I remember steering the big truck was when we were baling hay at our grandmother's farm, across from the wooded area. Dad did not own a hay baler then, so he had contracted Elvin Stump to come and bale this hay field. Mr. Stump had baled hay for dad at the 39-acre farm also. Mr. Stump's son, Ronald Stump, came to do the baling that day. I remember he had a New Holland baler and pulled it with a Jeep. That type of Jeep had a transmission that was geared to go slowly. Plus, it would travel down the road faster than a tractor.

Mr. Stump, using this equipment, took little time to bale all the hay, a little over two hours. The baler did not pull a wagon, and all bales fell to the ground from the baler chute. That is when I came into the picture. Per my dad's instructions, I would steer the truck around the field. Dad would put the truck in gear to get it moving. I just stood on the seat to drive. I could pull the throttle out to make it go faster or push it in to go slower. Dad and Uncle Roy walked beside the truck, one on each side, and picked up the bales and put them on the truck, and gave me signals to go faster or slower or where to steer. Someone else was on the truck bed, probably granddad Burk or Stumpy, stacking the load of bales. I cannot remember exactly, about 5 years old, but I know we still lived on the 39-acre farm. Doing this work involved the truck, but I remember steering the tractors around the fields, too, many times before this specific time. My first recall of driving the tractor was in the field west of the house and barn on the 39-acre farm. Mom, my sister, my brother, and I had just gotten home from a trip to Dayton, Ohio, from my brother's doctor's appointment.

Across the road from grandmother's property was a wooded area. A neighbor owned it. Several times when working there on my grandmother's farm, I needed to go to the bathroom to relieve myself. I had to be very careful to watch out for poison ivy. And I had to clean myself with leaves and grass. Not the most pleasant experience, but it worked. I had to watch out for snakes too. I cannot express how many happy memories I have from the time we were working on this property—planting, harvesting, and arguing with our Uncle Calvin, lots of happy memories. And one time, when we went to check on the crops at grandmother's, it had rained, and there was a puddle of water in the road. The road surfaces were gravel at that time. For some reason, the pool of water was close to where dad wanted to stop. For some reason, I looked into the puddle of water, and there was a snapping turtle. Anyway, dad wanted to take the turtle home to eat. It was of modest size. We took it home. Dad took care of preparing it for cooking. It was tasty, but I could never do that to any animal today.

Another thing about grandmother's farm was that the side ditches were reasonably small, not deep at all. Crossing them with the equipment was pretty easy. We could even drive across them with the pickup truck. But they remained large enough to drain the property after heavy rains.

One time when dad and I were coming home from grandma's farm, dad took a hopper wagon load of his share of ear corn home with us. This specific wagon was dad's. It did not trail too well. Dad was driving the '49 Dodge pickup towing this wagon and only going maybe 10 MPH. The roads were all gravel then, and asphalt was rare on country roads. This road is now called Boundry Road. At that time, there was another vehicle coming to meet us. Well, dad drove just a little too close to the right edge of the road surface, and the earth along the side of the road dropped down several inches.

Dad had been going slowly. The wagon swayed, and the tires on the right side ran off the road surface. Dad stopped the truck, and we got out and looked at the situation. I thought the wagon was going to tip over. Some of the corn slid off into the ditch. But dad got back into the truck; I pushed on the side of the wagon, and the wagon was back on the road surface in just a few feet of travel. We picked up all the ear corn that had fallen off the wagon and proceeded home. We were fortunate the wagon did not tip over. We made it home safely, and I learned not to drive too close to the road's edge. After that experience, I usually pull over to the side of the road and wait for the other vehicle to pass.

At another time, we had been baling hay at grandmother's farm. We used Uncle Roy's F-20 tractor to pull the baler and wagon. I do not know the reason we were using his tractor. However, it did do a good job pulling the hay baler. After we were finished, I was to drive the F-20, pulling the baler with two empty wagons behind it, back to Uncle Roy's home. That was something I had done many times. But as I was driving down Boundry Road, I met a car coming from the other direction. At this part of the road, there is a 90-degree turn to the left, and then after traveling about 100 yards further, there is another 90-degree turn to the right.

A car was coming towards me at the second turn. I had to run the baler pickup table down into the side ditch for the vehicle to have enough space to get by my equipment. It was necessary because the baler and equipment take up much of the roadway. The only problem this time was some metal fence lay under all the grass, down in the side ditch. It was visible to me after I needed to get enough space for the oncoming car to pass.

Of course, I waited for the vehicle to maneuver around the equipment. But after the car was gone, I needed to back everything up a short distance to allow me to get everything back onto the roadway. This was something normal too. Somehow, a piece of the fence was catching on the bottom of the baler table. Therefore the baler was dragging the fence. I needed to move forward, but first, I needed to get the fence uncaught from the baler. Luckily, Uncle Roy and dad were coming along behind me. I had been stuck for a few minutes before they caught up. But when they arrived, Uncle Roy stomped down on the old fence as I was driving forward, and everything was ok. The only criticism I received from this episode was, dad told me to ask the car to back up the next time. It would have allowed enough space to get around the corner safely without needing to get the baler that far over into the side ditch. I learned a lot from this experience.

One other time when dad was driving the tractor pulling the 62 combine down the road from grandmother's farm, I was riding in the grain hopper of the combine. Dad went by a farm with a dog who liked to chase cars and tractors. The dog chased the tractor this particular time but did not see the combine wheels. The combine wheel ran over the dog, ending its life.

I recently drove by my grandmother's farm. I am still wondering who lives there and who cares for the farm. I looked at the side ditches and entrances we used when moving equipment to and from that property. It brought back more memories. I remember how we tilled the earth and the crops planted there, and the many times riding the grain drill, and making of hay, and how we did it. It was a reasonably productive property. We also hunted raccoons many times in the surrounding wooded area there. One other thing I noticed about this area, the roads were covered with gravel on the days when dad farmed it. Now they are all paved with asphalt.

Dad's Expanding

Dad took over farming more land about the same time dad moved us to the 80-acre farm. That was in 1951. I know dad purchased another large tractor, the Farmall "M," about this time. Dad was also renting the Shaw farm of about 132 acres. Mr. Shaw owned it when our father took over the farming of it. Mr. Shaw was a very nice older man. He always took an interest in what we were doing in the fields. But Mr. Shaw was never a nosey person. Mr. Shaw helped us when he could. He never operated any equipment.

Sometime before dad took over farming the Shaw farm, our Uncle Roy had rented and lived on this property when he was first married. I wonder if Mr. Shaw owned it at that time. Our Uncle had horses and cattle. Uncle Roy had milk cows, and he also had a few pigs. Our deceased cousin, Uncle Roy's daughter, was born in that house around 1935. And when she was young, she accidentally caught the back of the house on fire when the window curtain came in contact with a candle. I do not know why the house did not burn, but only the back half burnt. I remember it being a lovely house inside when Mr. Shaw lived there. By then, someone had built on the new back porch area. The whole home was not very large. After dad purchased this property, dad remodeled it some and upgraded the kitchen and bathroom. This property has 3 barns, and dad was able to store bunches of farm machinery in them. Storage for ear corn, wheat, and oats were in the same building where Mr. Shaw parked his Buick automobile. The big barn had plenty of hay and straw storage. The smaller building only had farm machinery stored in it. Mr. Shaw had no farm animals. This property has a large grassed barnyard planted with bluegrass. We used to mow and bale the grass to feed it to the cattle. I am not sure, but I think we stored some of the hay we baled there from that large yard in the barn loft at the Shaw farm.

Then, in 1951, with dad farming the 80-acre farm he had just purchased, and the Shaw farm, and grandmothers, there was always lots of work to do. When dad was loading the farm equipment, it required efficient timing. Hauling large equipment over the highway can be difficult. And, of course, we always had to be concerned about the weather. And in the spring of the year, at planting time, the rains would come at the most inopportune times and create extra stress trying to get crops planted.

Dad also helped our grandfather plant his 19-acre property. Granddad had a tractor, a Farmall F-12. These tractors were popular in the 1930s. Granddad's tractor only had three gear speeds forward. Ground speed could have been faster! But grandpa usually had his fields prepared well for planting before dad had to plant there. Granddad did not have a corn planter. Grandmother Burk had her stroke by then, and granddad had to take care of her too. I think this is why dad helped out grandfather. Our other uncle, who farmed, had farm equipment but had no way of transporting equipment over the highways. At times, for some reason, granddad's tractor needed to go from one farm to another. Dad would put me on it and tell me to drive it to the other location. I think I was about 6 or 7 years old at that time. I remember it took a couple of hours of driving to get his tractor where they wanted it. Dad drove by and checked on me, but that tractor was slow compared to the ones dad had. But I made it to where dad wanted it.

I had just turned seven years old, two months before dad moved us to the 80-acre farm. I had been operating the tractors some before we moved, but after we moved, I was everywhere dad wanted me to be. I tried my best to help do anything dad wanted, including the fieldwork and working with all the animals. I was willing to try to do my best.

Dad's Corner Farm

In 1964, after I had entered the military, dad and mom purchased a property close to the 80-acre property. It was a half-mile from the 80 acres and contained 168 acres. It had a lovely house, an old barn, and some outbuildings. Long after dad purchased the property, dad built a new barn. Dad rented the house to a man at that time. Dad continued renting the home to the same man. I do not know how many years that same man lived in this house. He took good care of it. But dad asked the man to move, to allow Dee and I to live there.

My wife and I were living in dad's corner house for a short time. While we lived there, I purchased a 1949 Chevrolet pickup truck. And on occasion, after work or on the weekend, Dee and I would have Fanny ride in the truck with us. We would stop at the Dairy Queen for ice cream after shopping for groceries. We always purchased three cups of their ice cream. Usually vanilla for Fanny. Then we would sit in the truck, and all three of us would eat our ice cream. Fanny had her own and licked her lips after she was finished. That little dog could almost talk. She was special. Fanny went almost everywhere we went in the trucks. And she would sit on our laps while we were driving the tractors from one farm to another. Other dogs came and went, but no one ever replaced Fanny.

We also had a vegetable garden there. Dad helped us plow, till, and make it ready for planting. Dad planted corn, beans, and some other vegetables there for us. Dad and I and Dee also planted some cantaloupe seeds, maybe watermelon too. But these cantaloupes were the best any of us ever had. They were so good, and with very few seeds inside, the cantaloupe meat filled the entire melon. Of course, we shared the first ones with dad and mom. Dad loved cantaloupes. Dad was so funny when he was happy. You could see his smile and grin from a mile away. To till this garden, dad bought me a pleasing little hoe to cultivate around the plants. I still use this little hoe to till my garden. Dad has been away from this earth for almost 50 years, but I can still see his smile and grin clearly in my mind. We sowed some morning glory seeds once, and dad made us pull all of them up and throw them away. Dad called them weeds. I found that farmers do not like morning glories, because they spread in the planted crops, and choke the plants.

Dad had planted the field north of the barn on this farm with field corn. The year was 1968. Field corn, pole beans, and pumpkin vines were growing near the field entrance. The corn plants themselves had to be close to 8 feet tall. The pole beans would climb these corn stalks, and the pumpkin vines would wander around between the corn plants. There must have been lots of nutrients in the soil in that specific area. However, dad always raised good yields from his corn, sometimes 200+ bushels per acre. We always liked to eat corn on the cob. We took a few ears, cleaned the shucks off them, mom boiled them, and we ate them. Each ear had to have been at least 10 inches long and extensive in circumference, almost a meal itself. Dad and I both ate our share of this beautiful-tasting corn.

And along with the corn were the pole beans. They were enormous and accompanied the corn very well. We ate like Kings! And for sure, the pumpkins grew large. Dee and mom made pumpkin pies. We also gave some corn to other family members. Mom cooked the extra beans and then put them in the freezer. We gave away several pumpkins, and what was leftover, we fed to the pigs. The season for eating this type of corn, and pole beans, only lasts a couple of weeks. Then the corn gets hard and starts to dry out. Mostly, all the beans not eaten were cooked and put in the freezer. Almost every farm had a freezer in its basement or back porch.

Milking

Dad always milked 2 or 3 cows at the 39 acres property. Mom always had her chickens. They earned their steady paycheck by selling the milk and eggs. Of course, we always had all the milk and eggs we needed for use in the house. Then Dad and mom sold the excess to milk and egg companies. I do not remember how many cows dad had when we moved to the 80-acre farm, but as time passed, we milked 38. Dad purchased a mechanical milking machine and a pipeline machine at some point. These machines were run by electricity. Sometimes the electricity was off because of bad weather, and we had to milk those cows by hand. It took well over 3 hours for us, and I must say how tired my hands and fingers became, along with my feet and legs, from squatting for such a long time.

When we first moved to the 80-acre property, dad sold grade "C" milk to the local milk creamery. When dad was selling grade "C" milk, a different truck driver picked up the full milk cans and left the same amount of empty milk cans. I think the milk was going to the Red 73 Creamery in Union City, Ohio. Then dad graduated to selling grade "B" milk. Dad had to make changes because the creamery paid a little higher price for the milk. For selling grade "B" milk, the milking parlor needed the walls to be painted and the entire parlor washed down after each milking. I think dad added some upgrades to his milking equipment. When dad changed to selling grade "B" milk, dad's cousin Dean started picking up dad's grade "B" milk. Earnie Mason picked up dad's milk for a while, when Dean was on vacation. Earnie may have purchased Cousin Dean's milk route and truck, but I do not remember for sure. I only remember talking with Earnie. Some of Earnie's children went to school with us at Spartanburg. This milk was going to the Nestle

Creamery in Greenville, Ohio. A short time later, dad graduated to selling grade "A" milk. Dad's grade "A" milk also went to the Nestle's Creamery in Greenville, Ohio. Then two different drivers picked up dad's milk. First was a man named Bill, and after some time, dad had a man named Richard picking up the grade "A" milk.

Selling grade "A" milk required dad to have a refrigerated bulk milk tank to hold his milk between pickups. And to sell grade "A" milk meant the cows needed to be clean and udders washed before milking. The milking parlor must be washed after each milking period, and bug spray must be applied every time. And dad's milking parlor had to be inspected each year. That is the main reason dad poured all the cement outside the barn. It kept the cows much cleaner. After some time, dad poured more cement around the back lot where the cows stood most of the time. To help keep them more sanitary. Then dad purchased more milk cows. I do not remember the price of milk then, but I know selling milk was dad's primary steady income. Dad and mom milked cows and sold their milk until dad's death. Then the milk cows were sold by mom.

The evolution of dad's milk business on the 80-acre property was impressive. Dad started steadily increasing his herd of milk cows. He purchased some from other farmers, and a company in Fort Recovery dealt with buying and selling milk cows. Dad purchased several from that facility. About all the milk cows dad purchased were only a couple of years of age and pretty good milkers. Dad kept increasing the number of cows he wanted. At first, dad had about 25 milk cows, but dad kept expanding the herd to 38. I have no idea if milk cows recognize their names or not. But all our cows had names. Dad milked 38 cows every morning and night. With the improvement of dad's milking machines, it only took about 1½ hours from start to finish. Dad purchased a glass pipeline milking system. I think dad bought this system about 1957.

Dad also had his plan to milk six cows at a time.

For each morning and each evening's milking, dad and mom usually watched the milkers to ensure everything was working correctly. The milking parlor had 12 stanchions. Dad had installed the six milking systems connected to the glass pipeline mounted on the pipes above the cows, one on every other stanchion. With this design, dad could attach the milking machine from either side of the cow. Fitting the milker to each cow was pretty simple. The milker was connected by two plastic hoses, which ran up to the glass pipeline. One line carried the milk into the channel, and the other brought the vacuum to keep the teat cup connected to the cow's teat. For dad to sell grade "A" milk, all cows udders had to be washed by dad, or someone, before the milkers could be attached to each cow. First, dad would bring in 12 cows, wash their udders, and put the milkers on six cows. When these six cows were finished milking, dad would switch the milkers, and turn those six cows outside. Then dad would bring in six more cows. When dad finished milking the 2nd group of 6, they would go out, and then dad brought six more in. This procedure was used until all the milk cows were milked, both morning and evening. This method cuts down the time needed to complete the milking.

Switching the milkers to the next six cows would allow me a few minutes to go out and put hay in the hayrack or do some other chore needed. I could only put hay in the hayrack for the already milked cows. The closed gate and fence at the end of the barn would keep the milked cows separate from the unmilked cows. After we finished milking all the cows, we would open the gate again, and all the cows could eat together. Out in the milk cows' feedlot was the rack to hold hay for cows to eat during the day.

Of course, we fed all cows the same kind of feed. Dad's fields produced all the corn, oats, and hay for the feed he needed for his animals. Plus, dad's fields made the straw to apply to the beds to help keep the animals clean and warm. Each evening we would check to see if we needed to add more straw to the cows' sleeping area. All cows slept in the same barn room, which would be very warm there during the cold winter nights. Dad acquired more milk cows and other animals that could be raised and sold for profit. Another example of Dad's saying, "It takes money to make money."

It was about 1957 when dad installed a silo to hold more food for the cows. About two years later, dad had a 2nd silo built. Dad also created a very lovely wooden trough to hold this ensilage. The feeding trough connected to both silos. After milking all the cows, one of us would climb into the silo and shovel out enough ensilage into the trough to feed the milk cows. After a short time, the trough would be licked clean. Putting out the ensilage was another part of caring for the farm chores. At first, dad filled the silo with corn. The following year, dad planted cane with corn to fill the silo. Cane has some sugar content in the stalks. Dad had to hire a neighbor to chop the corn mixture and blow it up into the silo. Later, dad purchased his forage chopper and blower to fill the silos. I assume the corn mixture and the hay must have helped the milk cows produce more milk. And that is always what dad was striving for, more production and profits. Dad was the most ingenious farmer that I knew. The feed in the silos helped cut down on the amount of hay needed each year. And in each silo, after dad had the silos full, dad purchased automatic silo unloaders. We did not have to shovel the ensilage after installing the silo unloaders. These unloaders had electric motors to "shovel" the ensilage down.

But silos are dangerous. Shortly after a silo is filled, it creates hazardous gasses in the space at the top. Many farmers have lost their lives because of these dangerous toxins. Usually, farmers cover the top of the ensilage at the top of round silos with plastic to help keep it from drying out. Immediately after the silo is filled is the time to do this. However, one night, after I had come home from working someplace, (I was 18 years old) dad and I decided to go to the top of his silo and put the plastic cover over the ensilage. A week or more passed after dad had filled the silos. These silos were 40 feet tall.

Dad had two silos, but we were only going to cover one. So I told dad to go up the inside ladder, and I would go up the outside ladder, and after we finished, I would close the exterior door at the top. Dad went up the inside ladder, and I went up the outside ladder, and when I reached the top, I jumped down inside the silo, on top of the ensilage. Immediately I could not breathe because of the harmful toxins. The ensilage had settled down about 7 or 8 feet. Not knowing, when I jumped inside, it forced these toxins up and out into the air. These dangerous vapors could kill a person. After I jumped inside, it pushed the vapors up and out of the outside door and down the enclosed ladder.

Dad had climbed up the inside ladder. I yelled at dad, and told dad to get down because the silo was full of dangerous gasses. Luckily, I was just tall enough to jump up and grab the edge of the metal inside the outside door. I pulled myself up and sat for a moment at the opening. Then I yelled for dad, and there was no response. I hurried down the outside ladder and went to the inside ladder, where dad was stuck at the top. Those harmful toxins had overtaken him. I climbed up and fixed myself under dad so he could not fall. Then I proceeded to pry his feet off the ladder rung, and I was trying to get his hands unclasped from the ladder rung above, but dad had a firm grip. I finally got dad loose, and we moved down about 2 feet, about one ladder door inside the silo.

That was enough for dad to regain consciousness sufficiently to understand that I was behind him, trying to get him down. By then, dad could manage the rest of the ladder to the bottom, but of course, I was under him in case he might fall. Then we just sat there on the ensilage trough for about 5 minutes until I was sure dad was okay. I will never forget that situation, and I always worried about dad going into those silos. But we both learned our lessons concerning covering the ensilage inside those silos. If I had not been able to reach that outside opening, I probably would not be writing this book. Each year, individuals lose their lives because of these hazardous vapors.

It was about 1956 when dad started selling grade "A" milk. Dad wanted to put cement around the 80-acre farm backlot to help keep the cows from being too dirty. That improvement helped tremendously. To do this, dad wanted to borrow granddad's tractor to help level out the earth behind the barn. Dad and I went to grandpa's house one day to get his tractor. To start this kind and age of tractor, a person had to hand-crank the engine; it had no electric starter. Granddad and dad cranked, and I also tried, but I was not big enough to turn the engine over. But the tractor refused to start. Nothing like Starting Fluid had been invented at that time. At this time, dad had the 1949 Dodge pickup truck. Dad and grandpa decided to take the truck and pull the tractor to get it started. Even though this was a small tractor, this was a tough job for this little truck. I had to ride on the side of the tractor to choke the engine as dad pulled it along. I stood on the tractor's frame, held on to the top of the tractor with my left hand, and pulled the choke lever with my right hand. Dad had to start and stop several times. Grandpa was on the seat and would engage and disengage the clutch while the tractor was in gear to allow the engine to turn over. The little truck moaned hard but accomplished the task. The tractor finally started, and dad then towed it down to the 80-acre farm. That tractor helped to level the earth somewhat. But we had to do most of the dirt moving with shovels by hand.

Dad had to have Pat Byrum haul in some gravel from his gravel pit a mile down the road to make the land level enough to pour cement on top. I remember the cement was about 6 inches deep. Dad had contracted for the RediMix cement from a company in Greenville, Ohio. After the truck laid down the cement, dad and I leveled it off with 2x4 boards. It was about 10 feet wide and went all along the edge of the barn. Believe me, this was quite a lot of hard work. This cement work paid off very well. The cows were significantly cleaner after dad had contracted to supply grade "A" milk to the local creamery. It was such a success dad put more cement around this section each year after that. Dad finished cementing the whole backlot sometime after I entered the military. I do not remember how dad got grandad's tractor back to his house.

    We had to haul the hay for the cows' feed during the wintertime. We had to haul it down from the upper part of the barn because the hayrack was outside on the cement area of the backlot. We usually carried it to the hay rack with the Ford tractor. To do this required going through the gate at the end of the barn. It was a small job and only took 15 minutes. I would do this when there was a little time gap doing the milking. But one morning, I forgot that I needed to close the gate. I needed to remember this vital part of the job. It only happened one time during all the years. But this one morning, all the cows got out and started walking down the highway. Luckily, this highway had little automobile traffic. But no harm done; when we saw the cows walking down the road, I jumped over the fences, ran through the neighbor's field, got in front of the herd, and turned them around. I think the cows were happy to experience something new! Sadly, one of the cows was injured, and dad had to sell it because of the injury. Dad was not angry at me. It could have happened to anyone. Even dad forgot the gate a couple of times but caught the cows before they went too far.

    During the milking time, I would feed the baby calves and pigs when we had them and when I had time. Also, during the evening milking, I had to put straw in the sleeping area for the milk cows. Sometimes that only required a couple of bales, and sometimes five bales of straw. We had to drop the straw and hay bales down from the upper part of the barn through an opening on the floor. Then we could move the straw through a gate at the end of the lower part of the barn to enter the sleeping area, then scatter it all over the floor. There was also a manger inside the barn to hold the hay for the cows to consume. We would throw down enough hay to fill this manger each night, about three bales.

We did not put hay in the outside feedlot at night. All of these chores required a little time. But they needed to be done to keep the animals fed and healthy. After the milking finished, we had to clean the milking machines, clean up the milking parlor, haul out any manure, and wash down the floor. Doing the entire milking situation, and taking care of the other chores, usually required 1½ to 2 hours each morning and each evening. If mom or dad had something special to do, I could do it by myself. But it would take quite some time to get everything accomplished. We always prepared early if one of us had something special to do. After I was older and wanted to go out with friends on Saturday nights, I would do all the chores I could and then tell dad what tasks I did not finish. But I always tried to allocate time for everything. During the springtime, when there was work out in the fields with the tractors, I would get up early, maybe 4 am, and go out in the area and work, then come in and help with the milking and do my other chores. I tried my best to help dad as much as I could. If I could save him an hour, I would..

I was getting older. I was 16 when I acquired two cows of my own. We weighed their milk production at each milking. Mom paid me weekly for the amount of milk they produced and its value. It was the only way I could earn any money. I had purchased a heifer, which grew into a fair milk cow, but I could have done better. And later, I went to a farm sale and bought an excellent milk cow. The heifer's name was Sandy, and my good milk cow was Bossie. Of course, dad supplied their feed to them simultaneously with all the other cows. This feed was from dad's supply, which was our agreement. I always thanked mom for the cash when she gave this income to me.

Farm Animals

Dad always had other animals too. Most of the time, he had about 30 to 40 pigs. When we first moved to the 80-acre farm, dad had brood sows that gave birth to the baby pigs. That was hard because the barn was not set up very well for raising baby pigs, and many died because of too large of litter, and the brood sows laid on some. He tried several things to be more successful in raising the piglets. But then, one old brood sow once wanted to bite dad! I was standing beside the pen containing the sow and baby pigs. I saw the sow turn towards dad and start to chase him. Then dad leaped over the gates confining this particular sow; dad was in a big hurry! That was the end of dad keeping brood sows. A brood sow weighing 300+ pounds is difficult to handle. And if she had bitten dad, he could have lost his whole leg. Hogs of that size have giant mouths and many big teeth. Our mother wanted dad to get rid of the brood sows because of the danger they presented. If she, or one of us kids, had accidentally gotten into the sow's pen, it could have been a disaster. From then on, dad purchased feeder pigs at five weeks of age, and would keep them until they reached a weight of around 200 pounds, about six months. Then Dad sold them to the slaughterhouse.

The Demise of Animals

When living on a farm, life is complicated. I say this because I have gotten close to many animals. They liked me, and I wanted them, and they became like pets to me. I had a Barred Rock rooster, which I had gotten from Mr. Teeters' Hatchery. I gave him the name Pluto, and he grew into an enormous chicken that mom did not like. One evening, when I came home from school, mom told us at the dinner table that we were eating Pluto. I wasn't pleased, but I had to accept it. Poor Pluto. I also had a pet pig, Hypocrite. He went to the market while I was in school. I would have other (pet friends), and when it was time for them to go to market, that always made a deep void inside of me, which I will never forget. I tried to help many little pigs, kitties, chickens, and calves survive. I would get attached to them and had names for them too. I had a dog (Reddy), other dogs, and many cats around the farm. We all have a life cycle. And even today, when we need to put one of our animals down, it hits my heart hard. I am not vegetarian, but I try to avoid eating meat.

Over the years, I have seen too many dead people and animals. As a freshman in high school, I saw one of our classmates' mothers drive past our house while I was waiting for our school bus. She was going to the school where she was a teacher. Mom and dad said they heard a big bang. Dad had come running from the barn to the house, not knowing what made the noise. I did not hear the noise. Mom told me to get on my bicycle and ride down to the corner, about a half-mile away, where she thought the noise had come. That is where the automobile accident happened. When I arrived, I saw our classmate's mother lying underneath her car. For some reason, a man had neglected to stop at the stop sign. His vehicle struck the teacher's car and spun it around. The teacher fell out of her car as it turned around. She probably died at that moment because the car's right front wheel was sitting on the teacher's chest. The man told me to go home and call the sheriff, which I did. Mom called the sheriff. Our bus driver usually went by that corner, on the way to our school. When the bus came, I tried to tell the driver to turn around and not go past that accident.

But he would not listen and said he would be careful. But I knew what had happened, and I was sure the kids on the bus knew that lady, and would recognize her car, which they did. The sad thing was that the school children on the bus saw this lady under the vehicle. Many girls started crying. Then when we arrived at school, the children on our bus told the teacher's children that their mother had been in an accident. And because I had been right there, seconds after the accident, the teacher at school asked me to explain what I thought had happened. It was sad how this excellent parent/teacher had lost her life and how her children learned about her death. I have always disliked that bus driver for not listening to me.

This specific intersection of roadway, had several accidents. Mostly because people did not stop for the stop sign. The Main highway had the right of way, and the other cross road was supposed to stop. Also, when I worked on highway construction, there were automobile accidents, and sometimes I would be the first on the scene—so much unnecessary destruction and deaths. And when I was in Vietnam, I saw many dead bodies, too many.

When I was young, I trapped animals and hunted animals, not for food, but to sell their fur. I am not proud of that. I never could understand how my father did not seem to have any feelings for any animal that did not represent dollar signs to him. I am sure he must have; he kept his feelings covered. The crazy thing was when we slaughtered hogs; my father would never shoot them to kill them. Dad would make our Uncle shoot them. But when we slaughtered a beef, dad would shoot the animal. Mom always took care of slaughtering the chickens, but I had to help pick off the feathers, after they were dead. It was hard eating one of my pets. Life on a farm has its disadvantages.

Slaughtering

Dad always slaughtered the beef at the 80-acre farm, usually once a year. I could not help much because dad had to skin the carcass alone. And I needed to learn how to cut the meat. And once a year, we always killed 3 or 4 pigs at our grandfather's house, by his blacksmith's shop. At pig slaughtering time, I had my responsibilities. I had to keep the fires going as hot as possible to heat the scalding water and later cook the pig skins. Back inside Granddad's blacksmith shop, next to the forge, was a large metal tub-like container, where I would build a fire underneath to heat the water for the slaughter and, afterward, the cooking of the pigskins. Outside, for the slaughter, were two other heavy metal tubs to heat more scalding water. When I was smaller, about 8 years old, my job was to keep the fires as large and hot as possible. That kept me plenty busy by pushing new wood into the fires. As I got older, I guess I graduated from getting the fires going and hot to help cut up the animals. Slaughtering these pigs was an all-day affair. These pigs were dad's because he had raised them to slaughtering age and size.

The pig's fat and skins would be cooked in this large kettle, inside the blacksmith shop, with a hot fire. Then after it had cooked for a particular time, someone would dip the cooked skins and the lard and put it over into a lard press to squeeze out the excess liquid fat. Depending on how many pigs were slaughtered, usually three pigs, this would determine how much space would be needed to hold the lard. Before this could happen, the pigs would need to die, and the entire animal had to be dipped into scalding water with lye in it to enable the scraping of the hair and dirt off the skin. They used a wooden barrel to hold the hot scalding water. They would dip each pig in and out of the scalding lye water. A series of rope pulleys connected to the shop's roof allowed the raising and lowering of the carcass. This usually took two healthy men to do this, as each pig weighed about 200 pounds. After I was older, I helped scrape the hair and dirt off. After the animal had been cleaned and cut up, the skins were cooked.

Then we put the cooked skins into the lard press, and after the lard was pressed out, the skins were called cracklins. Our Uncle Ozro, who lived in Dayton, Ohio, would come to pick up these cracklins. I do not know what he did with them. We ate a few cracklins ourselves. After the animals were slaughtered, we shared meat with grandpa and our Uncle Roy. Then mom would take our share of the meat to a facility in Union City, which cut up the meat to the requirements that mom wanted. Then they would put the meat into their freezers and keep it frozen until mom had made space for it. By doing this, it would be our family's meat supply for the year, then next year, slaughtering would be done again. Dad was a big meat eater. He wanted to have some kind of meat to eat at every meal.

When dad was going to slaughter the beef, dad had to shoot the animal. After the animal died, dad inserted a chain between the animal's tendons on its legs, then hung it upside down. Dad used the tractor with the manure loader to raise the carcass. I remember slaughtering a beef before purchasing the Ford tractor with the loader. Skinning the meat was much harder to do with the body lying flat on the ground. But the tractor loader made the job much easier. After cutting the animal in quarters, mom would take those sections to the store in Union City, where they would cut the meat and package it as mom wanted. Very similar to the process of slaughtering pigs.

I hunted cottontail rabbits. Luckily, I never shot any, even though I did see several. But sadly, I raised domestic rabbits for a few years for their fur. We ate a couple of them, but I sold most to fur traders. Rabbit meat tastes similar to chicken. I am trying to remember how I decided to make money this way. I am not proud of doing this. I wish I had not done this. But many of the older people around the area talked about eating raccoons, possums, squirrels, etc. Maybe that was part of survival during the depression. I know dad said he was always extremely hungry during the depression.

The 80-Acre Farm

This property had a beautiful house, a large white bank barn, a chicken house, and an old corn crib. The Orchard had many apple trees, about 25, which we sprayed each year. There was a large crab apple tree, but its fruit was bitter. There were several peach trees around both sides of the garden. A large row of black raspberry vines grew along this row of peach trees. We staked these vines up to make it easier to harvest their fruits. We picked many quarts of raspberries and strawberries each summer. And along the other side of the garden was a large strawberry patch. During the summer, raspberries and strawberries ripen for harvesting. We ate many of the peaches. Mom also baked peach, strawberry, and apple pies too. Along the driveway, along the north side of the bank barn, was a productive white peach tree along with some yellow rose bushes. On the south side of the bank barn driveway were different kinds of red and yellow roses. The entire barnyard area needed quite a lot of work and care when we first moved there.

We moved to the 80-acre farm in February of 1951. I had just turned 7. The first thing I remember was that one evening in January, dad and I went to this new farm with the big truck loaded with stuff we put in the barn. It was difficult because the drives around the barn area were mud. Any car or pickup truck would get stuck quickly. These mud gutters were a foot deep in most places, and many had water in them. That evening after we had finished unloading the truck, dad wanted to go to the house, go inside, and look around. We took our shoes off when we went in. It was totally empty. We sat on the bottom two stairway steps, dad on the second, and I sat on the first, and we just looked out over the beautiful hardwood floors. I remember leaning against dad's leg. He said a few things, but I do not remember his words. But this house was beautiful both inside and out.

Early one morning, Dad had taken the tractor and slid the brooder house down the road when there was quite a large amount of snow on the roadways. Dad had borrowed a set of tire chains to fit the tractor's tires to enable them to grip the road surface. A day or two later, dad and a couple of relatives moved all the household furnishings in. The old upright piano was the hardest and the heaviest thing to carry. Because it was moved during the wintertime, and subject to the coldness of being outside, the piano's tuning board cracked, making it untunable and useless. Eventually, dad tore it apart and burned all the wood. But everything was moved in, piano and all, and mom put down some throw rugs. It was only a short time until mom installed carpeting over almost all the hardwood flooring. That was the only way to protect all those beautiful hardwood floors.

I mentioned the beautiful hardwood flooring throughout the main floor, and the stairway to the upstairs was also hardwood. Even the handrail was made of beautiful hardwood and varnished the same as the flooring. The main downstairs floor had a kitchen, dining room, and large living room; mom and dad's bedroom was also downstairs. Upstairs were three bedrooms. The one to the north was our sisters, and my brother and I shared the bedroom to the south, and the bedroom to the west was used as an overflow room. But it did have a nice full-sized bed for guests to use once in a while. Downstairs, the one thing I wanted to mention was the kitchen. There was a built-in breakfast nook next to the dining room entrance.

While sitting at the breakfast nook, people could watch the

TV in the living room through the doorway leading to the living room from the kitchen. There was also an entrance to the living room from the dining room. We ate all our family meals at this breakfast nook. And dad made it clear, though, that we were supposed to eat everything on our plate before getting up from the table. I always did, even if I was overfull. Dad said he reasoned that there were starving children all around the world. It was because dad was pretty hungry when he was a child at home. But we all loved this breakfast nook.

Dad and mom usually sat across from each other next to the outside wall, which had a nice window where you could look out over the garden and fields. I usually sat beside dad, and my sister usually sat beside mom. My brother usually sat in a highchair at the end of the table. His back was facing the TV. This setup was very big-time to us after dad had purchased the Sears TV in Greenville. We were living modern then, or so we thought. If mom had other things she wanted to be served, or if any of us wished to have seconds of food, I usually would get up to get those. Mom was marvelous at preparing the food. I do not know how she did it all the time, and she always had her timing perfect.

I made a lot of homemade ice cream during the winter, and mom never hesitated to prepare it for me to take to the ice cream freezer. I would get the milk and eggs, and she would cook the mixture and put in the sugar. I did not mind cranking the old ice cream freezer, but the metal container where the mixture goes became damaged and was leaking. So I purchased a new electric ice cream freezer from Sears. I could get the ice from the cows drinking water trough at the barn. It usually had ice in it during most of the winter. After I was a little older, I made my sister help me clean the kitchen after we finished the evening meal. I would wash the dishes, and my sister would dry. My sister put the dishes away in the cabinets too. After supper, we all went to the living room to watch TV. Sometimes my sister and I did some of our school work on the dining room table after eating the evening meal. But I always tried to do all my school homework during our study hall time at school. I had too many other chores and work to do at home.

I remember how mom prepared the food and did the laundry. The kitchen had a refrigerator and an electric kitchen range. There was a medium size freezer in the basement. At first, mom also had the washing machine in the basement. She had a clothesline strung through the main floor of the house to hang the clothes on to allow them to dry during the wintertime. The clothes were hung on a line in the backyard during summer. Later, after they built the new garage, mom moved the washing machine to the garage. We had no clothes dryer. Also, the coal/wood burning furnace was in the basement for central heating. The shower was next to the well pump, and the water softener to condition the well water was next to the shower stall. Dad had to put salt in the water softener about once a week. There was also shelving for all the many jars mom had to hold the foods and vegetables she had previously canned. I remember mom canning things on the old wood stove at the 39-acre farm. All of those were moved to the 80-acre farmhouse basement. There were quite a lot of them. Mom canned some things after we moved to the 80-acre house, plus she made many fruit ellies.

Also in this basement was a large 50-gallon electric water heater. Mom used the other unoccupied space for pickling pickles, making lye soap, and probably some other proper farm/household supplies. To the south end of this basement was a large area for storing coal and wood to burn in the furnace to supply the heat in the wintertime. We did not need the furnace heat in the summertime. Every winter, we would haul several loads of wood, and sometimes coal, to the window leading to this basement area. This area was large enough to hold 3+ trailer loads of wood at a time. Dad usually did not buy much coal, only if the weatherman said there would be a long spell of frigid weather. The coal would hold better fire/heat during the night than ordinary firewood. But every winter, we would cut many trees for firewood, pile it up, and then haul it to the basement later. We never threw away wood. We burnt all the wood we could get in the furnace. Dad had purchased a 17" Homelite chainsaw to do most of the cutting. Dad also had a buzzsaw, which fit on the front of the tractor, to help cut the wood into shorter lengths. Dad would operate the buzzsaw to cut the wood. I handed the limbs to dad, then I stacked the cut wood or put it in the trailer to take home for the furnace.

After a few years, dad did some remodeling of the kitchen. We used the outhouse built onto the backside of the garage until dad installed a toilet in the kitchen closet. Then he moved the kitchen stove a little, and mom could purchase a new washing machine to sit beside the stove. After the contractor had built the new garage, mom had the old clothes washing machine put in the garage. It made it much easier to wash clothes. Mom also had the egg washing machine out in the garage as well. And some years later, dad did more remodeling of the kitchen, which allowed mom to have another new washer and dryer sitting beside the stove, all in the kitchen. While I was in the military, dad remodeled more of the kitchen and built in a bathroom behind the stove and washer and dryer. Dad did all this work all by himself!

Another thing I remember was probably around 1954; dad wanted to insulate the crawl space above the kitchen and dining room area to help with the heating loss during the winter. The entrance to this crawl space was through my sister's bedroom. You could enter through a door in the wall about 2 square feet. It was on hinges in the east wall. Dad purchased a bunch of rock wool used for insulation. It came in big bags. Dad and I moved these bags into my sister's bedroom and the crawl space above the kitchen. Then we removed the insulation from the bags and scattered the insulation all around by using our hands. That area is significant, and it took a couple of days to do this. Of course, we could not work on this all at once because there were other farm chores to take care of. But we did it. Unfortunately, that rock wool gets into your clothing, and then it itches. The warmer your body gets, the more it itches, and our pants held that rock wool for quite some time. But it finally went away after several washes. Dad always had lots of good ideas, and dad was never afraid of hard work.

This property had a large fenced-in barnyard. Of course, there was an excellent bluegrass cover over all the lawn areas. But this barnyard had had cattle grazing on it before dad acquired it. Dad did not want cattle feeding on this area, even though a fence enclosed it. Later, the entire fence was removed, and no animals were allowed on this lawn area. There was a driveway to enter the barn area and a separate driveway to enter the house and garage area. We covered both of these driveways with crushed limestone. The driveways were smooth after dad and I were able to get all of them covered. But dad did not want any gates to block either of these driveways. That meant we had to mow all the lawn area with a lawnmower. At first, we only had a push lawnmower. Using a push lawnmower was impossible! I could not push a push lawnmower. I just wasn't big enough at 7+ years of age to push a mower through the tall grass. And dad was too busy doing other things, more important than mowing the lawn. Dad somehow purchased a Huffy Electric Lawnmower. It would easily cut the yard, but it needed several electrical cords to supply power to the motor. We ended up needing about 300 feet of power cords. Pushing the mower, and dragging all the electric lines, was a pretty tough job. And it required some time to mow everything.

After we took down the fences, we mowed the side ditches too. From start to finish, it probably took a couple of hours. But we usually did the mowing in spurts, some now and some later, rather than doing it all at once. After we finished the mowing, it looked beautiful. It made a wonderful place to play baseball, plus all the other games that could be played on lawns. Dad never allowed any automobile parking on any of the lawn areas. Sometimes we needed to drive tractors and wagons across small sections to allow the unloading of hay and grains. As time passed, gas-powered lawnmowers replaced electric lawnmowers. Riding lawnmowers were around, I wonder if dad was ever able to mow the lawn using a riding lawnmower before he passed.

After moving to the 80-Acres

Dad and mom purchased this property in December 1950. They had sold the 39-acre property to the Westinghouse Electric company. A lumber company now owns that property.

I remember coming home from school on the bus several nights shortly after moving to the 80-acre farm. Earlier in the day, dad had been to the limestone quarry and had the 41 Dodge truck loaded with crushed limestone. Then he and I started filling all those gutter/driveways ruts and holes around the barnyard with this material. Surfacing these driveways would allow any vehicle to move about without getting stuck. I was not very big, but I did my best to help shovel the limestone off the truck and down into these gutters and level the material off. I wonder how many loads of limestone; dad purchased and hauled in to make these driveways pleasant, even, and usable. I know it was at least a dozen. Some loads dad helped unload, and some loads I unloaded by myself, but I had a smaller shovel, and it took me a long time. After a few months, most driveways were leveled and surfaced nicely. Dad did most of the raking and leveling of the crushed limestone. He knew better how to do it than I did.

I remember having a few farm chores to take care of at that age. At about 7 years old, I had to feed oats to the chickens, provide the baby calves with their milk supplement mixture, check on the baby pigs, and feed the dogs and cats each evening. Mom gathered the chickens eggs. Helping with the bedding and feeding of all the animals and chickens, caring for the sows, plus checking their feed, were part of my duties. All animals had to have clean bedding to sleep on. My job was to get the hay and straw down from the upper part of the barn for bedding in the cow's sleeping area and the hay to feed to the milk cows while dad and mom were finishing the milking. I also helped clean the milking parlor. After I was a little older, I helped milk the first six cows. Then I would go and do some of my chores and then come back to the milking parlor. Then help change the milkers and do the rest of my duties.

About every four days, dad and I would have to grind feed for the milk cows before milking. We would put the corn and oats in the pickup truck, back it next to the hammer mill, then connect the tractor to the hammer mill via a sizable flat belt. Then have the tractor run at top RPMs, to turn the hammer mill as fast as possible. Dad fed the mixture to the hammer mill, and I usually changed the burlap sacks containing the cows' food. We provided a small amount of this food mixture to each of the cows during their milking time. After we finished grinding the feed, we would put the bags into the truck and then haul them down to the bottom of the barn. Then we put the food in the container which held the food. This procedure allowed us to scoop a certain amount of food for each cow before and during the milking session. Sometimes dad added supplements to the food, and we mixed in cake mix food a couple of times. The cake mix was pretty good, but mom said it made very poor cakes. That is why it was being used as cattle food. But the cattle ate it up. Then after we finished the milking, either dad or I would get into the silo and shovel out enough ensilage for the cows to eat each morning, and we did the same thing after the evening milking. It was not a big job, but it took about 20 minutes. Later, while I was in the military, dad purchased automated/electric silo unloading machines. At some point, dad extended the ensilage feeding trough.

Many times in the fall of the year, dad would have harvested ear corn at one of the other farms while I was in school. He usually had his share of ear corn on the '54 Dodge truck, close to 300 bushels. After dad had driven the truck home, I would back the truck into the corn crib, and after the evening meal that night, I would go down and shovel the load of corn off the truck and up into the corn crib. I had a little transistor radio that I could listen to. Mostly, I listened to the Beatles. Then dad could refill the empty truck again the next day, bring it home, and I would empty it again. I unloaded this truck probably three times each fall of the year. I think I did this for about five years. Later, dad made other more convenient storage for his share of the corn harvest. Shoveling this amount of ear corn off this truck took me over an hour. I usually was not in any hurry.

At the 80-acre farm, dad and mom had about 200 chickens most of the time. Those chickens produced many eggs. Mom had an egg washer. The egg company supplied big boxes to hold the eggs. The egg company truck picked up the big boxes about once a week. Each large box contained 30 dozen eggs; mom usually had four boxes each week. But egg production dwindled as the years moved along. I helped gather the eggs some, and sometimes I washed them. But mom's egg production did not last but maybe ten years. The chickens did not produce as many eggs as they got older. Then mom would buy more chicks, and they would grow up and produce more eggs. Some neighbors purchased eggs once in a while, and Aunt Mary purchased eggs almost every week. Aunt Mary was a fabulous cook and baker. That's probably why Aunt Mary used a lot of eggs. But I think mom became a little tired of caring for the chickens. I do not remember them having any chickens around the time dad passed.

There were also some sheep out in the orchard for some time. I think dad had these sheep to keep the grass down in the orchard. They did a great job. I remember shearing them. I remember dad saying he sold the wool. I also remember dad slaughtering one of the young sheep. Dad nor mom liked the taste of that meat. I tasted it, but I have never been a meat eater. I prefer fruits and vegetables. I think dad acquired the sheep while I was in the military. Dad also had two hound dogs, most of the time. The dog houses were close to the chicken house. There were always kitties of all sizes around the barn. Most had foul distemper in their eyes. Dad refused to treat any of them. He said he would not spend money on any animal, which did not make him any money. Those kitties killed many rats in the winter, which lived and bred in the ear corn cribs. Rats ate some of the corn, and that was a monetary loss. I always wished we could do something for the poor kitties' eyes.

The 80-acre property had a vast space for the vegetable garden. Each spring, dad would bring the tractor and plow, plow up the area, then bring in the disk to make the soil nice and smooth for planting. We all helped with the planting of the different vegetable seeds and plants. Mom also wanted space for flowers at the very north end. Most of the time, the flowers were beautiful until autumn came around. Autumn was the end of the blooming season. I also spent a lot of time cultivating the garden after the seeds came up. Around the planted area were several black raspberry plants. I spent a lot of time staking and pruning these plants before they began to bloom in the spring. Mom showed me how to do this. They produced a whole lot of excellent fruit. We ate some, mom baked pies with some, and we sold some.

Along the west side of the garden was a large strawberry patch. It also produced a lot of strawberries. We picked every other day after the berries were ripe and ready to harvest. Sometimes we had help harvesting the berries, and if someone helped pick berries, mom would send the berries they picked home with them. We also sold some strawberries to Mrs. Byrum. I remember putting the boxed strawberries and the boxed raspberries in the basket on the front of my bicycle and riding it over to Mrs. Byrum's house in Bartonia. Mr. Reich helped us pick several times. Mom would make strawberry jelly for him to take home. He was a farmer, plus a pretty nice guy. He had an Indian girlfriend, a lovely lady, who helped pick the strawberries too.

There were about 25 apple trees in the orchard north of the house and a large crab apple tree next to the chicken house. There were about ten peach trees along the east side of the garden. About four plum trees were on the garden's north side, next to the fence. On the north side of the barn bank was the white peach tree and plenty of wild roses, both red and yellow. We usually sprayed all the fruit trees to help with some diseases that decrease the trees' productivity. We also gave away lots of apples when apple time harvest came around. Along the east side garden fence, there were some hop vines. They were planted there by someone who must have made their own beer. They were pretty, but we never did anything with any of them.

After we moved to the 80-acre farm, dad changed the setup of the fields. There were five square or rectangular fields when we moved there, with a lane to allow access to all the areas. After a year or two, dad removed all the old fences and made five long narrow fields with access from the front of the farm. It eliminated the need for any lane. The lane area land could have been more productive because it had to stay open to allow the farm equipment to travel from one field to another. The route also allowed the cattle to move to different areas. Dad wanted as much land as possible to produce income. I helped dad do some fence work, but dad did 90% of the job because I was going to school during the day. I helped on the weekends and when I could. Changing the setups of the fields and aligning the fences was tough. Dad never steered away from hard work. Dad did it all, driving the "T" posts and stretching the new wire. I tried to drive a "T" post, but I was not tall enough to raise the steel "T" post driver high enough to drive the "T" posts into the ground. Doing all this fencing and making these changes took over two years.

The most help I could do was connect and disconnect the fence stretchers. After dad changed all the fence borders, each year, dad mowed all around these fences by hand with a mowing scythe. A couple of years later, he purchased a mower to do this work, but that mower took a lot of work (with and operating). Our dad was proud of his 80-acre farm and was right to be proud. These reorganized fields were almost ½ mile in length but not very wide. But they still contained about 15 acres each. After planting, Dad prided himself on his straight rows in each field. Today they use a laser, but dad's rows were just as perfect. How he did that, I will never know!

Before, dad changed the field setups and made the new fields in 1952, he planted soybeans in the backfield. Dad planted corn and clover in the other fields. But in this backfield, the prior tenants had planted corn in this field the year before. When they harvested their corn, they left behind several ears of corn. After dad's soybeans came up and grew taller, the weeds and leftover corn began to become increasingly taller. As a result, dad wanted to remove all the weeds and corn because most would reach 5 to 6 feet in height. His reason was his International #62 combine did not handle weeds and corn very well. It would plug up the inside of the machine after the weeds and corn got inside. Then dad would have to stop and clear it out. It took away valuable harvesting time. So dad told us, kids and mom, that if we would go back to this field and clear all the weeds and corn, he would buy us a new TV when we finished. Dad said we could pull the weeds out of the earth, place them on the ground, and cut the corn off with a corn cutter. I do not remember if my sister and brother helped do this work, but I know mom helped for a couple of days. But I was back there as much as possible, after school and on weekends, doing one row at a time. We finished doing this, but it took three weeks. I always helped with the chores around the farm when I came home from school, and then I would go back to this field and try to finish another row. Dad was pleased after we finished this project. He said the beans had a pretty good yield that year. And dad kept his word. After we had removed the weeds and corn, dad took the whole family to Greenville, Ohio, one evening to a Sears Roebuck store. Dad purchased a new 17-inch Silvertone TV. He also bought a swiveling table for it to sit on. Now we could watch TV from the kitchen and the living room. We thought we were in the big time now. I think back to the time before the TV came into our house; we read some, listened to the radio, etc. but we were extremely happy after we got the TV working.

Dad had to put up an antenna, connected to a 1 ½ galvanized pipe outside, to get the TV reception needed to operate the TV correctly. Using a pipe, we could turn the antenna around with a pipe wrench to get the best possible reception. The antenna had to reach above the house roof and needed support wires to protect it from the winds. To adjust the TV reception, someone would watch the TV's reception, and someone else would stand at the window and tell us if the reception was good or bad. Then one of us would rotate the pipe with the antenna and turn it until the picture was good using the pipe wrench. We thanked dad, all of us, for getting the family a TV. We all were happy. Now, dad could watch wrestling on Saturday nights on his TV. Dad loved that. I still think most of the wrestling was a little phony then.

Before dad changed the fences, and about ½ the distance from the barn to the back road was sort of a low spot in the earth.

Water would accumulate in the corner of this field, mainly caused by years of cattle going in and out. It was the middle area's entrance on the lane's south side. The water stood there after it rained and stayed very wet while the rest of the land was in a more tillable condition. Dad did not like this and decided to put in a new clay tile ditch, which we did by hand. My job was to use the spade and dig the first step down. Then we used a shovel for the second step down into the earth. Dad and I shared removing this area of the soil. Then dad would level the bottom of the trench and lay in the new tile ditch. Then he would stand on top of the tile, pull a small amount of dirt on top of the tile, and move forward. I had to move backward as I was digging. I had to take two spade's widths, side by side, to make the trench wide enough for the removal of the second step to the sufficient level. As I did this, I removed the dirt along the side as neatly as possible because it all had to go back into the trench when we finished the job. Dad and I worked on this for several days, and I don't know exactly how many feet of ditching we did. I dug as fast as I could, and dad did his part and kept up with me. I think we were able to complete about 50 feet each day. I estimate we put in about 400 feet of the new ditch. As I remember, we worked on this for 2 to 3 weeks before we finished. We could only work on this project for a few hours because we had our other daily chores to care for, milking, bedding, feeding, etc. This new ditch went across to meet up with a giant tile ditch, which ran from the barn area east to the outlet in the open ditch over on the neighbor's property. The open ditch belonged to the County, and they maintained it well. This new ditch removed that wet area for dad.

    We used this procedure at a few other locations around the property to help with the drainage. Dad had a pair of dousing wires that let him know where to connect these new ditches. I remember helping dad repair other ditches in different areas of the farm. Dad was good with the dousing wires because he found many ditches. Sometimes he found ditches for other farmers at various properties. He found terrible ditches on the Shaw farm. Dad also helped grand-dad with some drainage around his house and barn. Dad was good at using those simple wires. I have tried to use the dousing wires too, but I've yet to achieve the accuracy that dad had.

After some time, I estimate three years of living in the 80-acre house; dad decided to install a toilet in the kitchen pantry area. Before that, we used the outhouse built onto the back of the garage. To get the toilet to work, it needed a sewer system. I remember helping dad dig a large hole east of the house. This hole was about 6 feet deep and about 3X6 feet wide. We needed a ladder to get in and out of this hole. At the bottom of this hole, dad and I poured a slab of cement to cover the entire base, at least 5 inches thick. This rectangular hole now contained four large sewer tiles. Dad placed one tile beside the other, and the other tiles sat on top. Each tile was about 3 feet in diameter. The top of the second tile must have been about 18 inches below the soil's surface. The larger tiles were connected by one smaller sewer tile inserted between them at the upper level.

Dad cut a hole in the sides of these large sewer tiles with a cold chisel and cemented the whole thing together, sealing each end of this smaller tile. Dad cut another hole for a small tile, which he also sealed, to run a short ditch over to the house to connect to the toilet. It was about a 30-foot distance. The large tiles had some kind of manufactured covers on top to keep the dirt out of dad's system. As I remember, it was round cement covers that contractors used. These lids fit inside the lip of the vertical sewer tiles. Dad said we always had to keep the tractor away from this area. I wonder how dad came up with this septic and sewer system.

I do not know how dad learned about doing this, but it worked very well. Dad had chiseled a hole through the cement house foundation for this tile to extend through, and then it connected to the bottom of the toilet stool. And the outlet tile from this septic system ran across the garden and connected to another tile ditch which ran completely across the field and emptied into the open ditch about a mile away. Installing a new toilet sure made all the family very happy! This pantry area was minimal, but it worked. And at some time, after I was away in the military, dad changed the access stairway to the basement and remodeled the whole area. Dad designed a completely new bathroom. His recent remodel had a shower, a new sink, and a new floor. Dad changed everything except the toilet. It turned out very lovely, and everybody was happy. Before dad made the new bathroom, we had to shower in the shower area down in the basement. I remember showering down there when it was wintertime. It was something we did quickly. This same bathroom system is still in use today. Dad was a genius.

Dad replaced the kitchen countertop shortly after we moved into the 80-acre house. The old countertop had a linoleum surface, and dad replaced that top with a Formica surface. I do not remember if he put in a new kitchen sink, but I don't think he did. Because each property had to have its well for its water supply, most homes installed a water softener system. Most farmhouses still have a water softener system because the water from these wells is called hard water. The hard water makes it very hard to wash your body and hair. Plus washing dishes too. With the soft water, it was much easier to bathe and easier to dry after showering. It makes ladies' hair much easier to maintain. Most women are concerned about how their hair looks. These soft water systems are a system where the water to be used runs through a salt filtering system as a treatment. The reason I am mentioning this is that this kitchen sink had regular hot and cold faucets, and it also had a separate tap. The hot and cold water through these faucets ran through the water softener system. But the other fixture carried water directly from the well, or hard water. We always drank the water from the hard water faucet but used the other hot and cold taps to wash the dishes. Soap suds up much more and is more manageable with soft water. I also think my sister washed her hair over this kitchen sink.

In those days, some of the older farmhouse's wells would run out of water if the summer was parched. The well at the 80-acre property was about 115 feet deep, with a submersible pump. We also used quite a lot of this well water at the barn. I also remember granddad's well was about 140 feet deep. I wonder how these wells are doing today, now that climate change has made the entire country much dryer.

In the 80-acre house upstairs, you could see out over all the surrounding fields and areas. The biggest wonders to see were the field tilled and planted by our father. When you looked out the windows to the east, you could see the areas of clover, corn, silage, etc. I don't think you could see the soybean field from the house. That field was quite a distance away. And dad only planted soybeans the first year or two after we moved to the 80-acre farm. Dad usually only grew corn, oats, and clovers on the 80-acre farm. Mostly dad planted soybeans at the other farms because dad usually sold those crop yields to help pay taxes, etc. But one year, when dad grew wheat on the 80-acre farm, Mr. Gray had planted wheat on his field across the road. I don't remember the kind of wheat dad usually planted, but Mr. Gray planted Bearded Wheat. I don't think there was much difference in the grain yield of the different types, but Mr. Gray's wheat had these long grain heads, which curled over just before harvest time. That wheat stalk, with that head of grain folding over at ripening time, with its long beards on each head, they were so pretty. That field sort of glowed when the sun was shining on it. Dad's kind of wheat usually stood straight up and also had a pretty good yield. Also, when I looked over the clover fields, they were so green and lush. And when we mowed the hay (cutting the clover), you could see the straight windrows of hay drying in the distance to be ready for baling. And the rows of corn, as far as you could see, were very straight and pretty. At the corn tasselling time, the field looked like a giant blanket. You could easily see the cattle walking and grazing out in the clover fields. From the east and south windows upstairs, you could see the hog barn being built and the barn area too. We could see the plants growing in mom's garden during the summer. It was a remarkable sight to see all that you could vision. Once, after an ice storm had passed, it left its wonders on all the trees. The grass in the barnyard was a true sight with the ice on top. Yes, sometimes the ice's weight was so great that some of the tree branches would break and fall, then we would need to trim them up. But the ice was pretty until it melted away.

Wayne and Spartanburg Schools

My sister and I went to school just down the road from our grandparents Burk's house for my first two years of schooling, Wayne School in Wayne Township, Indiana.. I started school when I was five years old because there was no kindergarten then. If there was a kindergarten, there was none in our rural community. My sister and my two cousins (Aunt Mary's daughters), and I rode the school bus. Other children were already on the bus. We lived about 3 miles from Wayne School. It was a small school, with all 12 grades represented inside. Then in February of 1951, when we moved to a different Township, we had to change schools. Our mother and father had sold their 39-acre farm near Union City. They then purchased an 80-acre farm down the road, about 5 miles south of Union City.

My sister and I continued our spring schooling at Wayne school for the remainder of 1951. The Wayne Township school bus would come as far as the township line and then turn around. My sister and I walked a short distance to the Township line for the remainder of that school year. Then the following fall semester of 1951, we started attending Spartanburg school, about 4.5 miles away. Because the 39-acre farm was in a different township from the 80-acre farm, we had to change schools. Wayne school was in Wayne township, and Spartanburg was in Greensfork Township. Spartanburg school was much more extensive and had more students, even though both were country schools.

We did get an excellent education at Spartanburg school. As I look back, school at Spartanburg was a great experience. Our teaching at Spartanburg school was outstanding. Classes were small, with 15 to 20 students per class. Teachers had time to make sure each student learned their school work. Spartanburg teachers were brilliant and could explain the subjects we were taking. Our education would be about the same as a private school today. Over the years that my sister and I attended Spartanburg school, we became involved in several after-hour school activities, primarily school band. And sometimes, we had to practice after school for an upcoming program. The sad thing about this was when the day came for us to perform, mom attended, but dad never came to see us. I always wished he would have come. But dad did help me with some of my Agricultural projects.

For all the years I can remember, dad never attended anything my sister or I did at our school or became involved with my sister or myself's school activities or anything connected to the school besides learning. My sister and I both belonged to the band. Sometimes we needed to practice after school. Dad never went to watch or participate when the band traveled to other schools or competitions in different areas. My sister belonged to the school chorus too. Our band traveled to several basketball games over time. Our school band also went to the State Fair a couple of different years. We did march and play at a few things happening in the City of Winchester, and I remember dad going with us for that. But those times at Winchester were more like parades on the city streets. They were not competitions, only participation for our school and many other area schools. We kids always had fun and enjoyed showing off our efforts at doing our best playing and marching. Mr. Pipes was our director, and we tried to do our best for him. Mr. Pipes was a patient and very talented teacher. I only wish I had worked harder for him.

I participated in class plays in both my junior and senior years. I did not have the lead in either play. However, I am trying to remember whether dad went to watch us. Participating in school plays was fun and challenging.

Several times I drove the tractor to Spartanburg school. I want to remember why. I also drove the '54 Dodge truck to school two times. I had been learning how to weld metal and do woodworking in our classes for the shop. That day, I welded a piece of metal on the back of the truck's frame. It was a hitch to connect wagons, to pull them through the field, or to the grain elevator. It worked well, and dad used it frequently. I also used this truck to haul sawdust from the lumber mill to fill in the sawdust pits at the school, which were used at track meets. I mentioned before that I had driven dad's car and trucks up and down the roads before I could legally do so. I also drove my car to school sometimes, but only after I had my driver's license. I suppose it was because something needed to be taken care of after school. I did this not more than 4 or 5 times during high school. Dad and mom trusted me.

At Spartanburg School, we needed to raise money for our class trip during our Junior and Senior year. About half of our class of 20 were dependable. It was too bad that all the class members did not help with the work because the money we accumulated helped all of the class members. Our class planned on going to New York City and Washington, DC, for our class trip in May of 1961. We arranged to pick tomatoes to take to the Farmer's Market in Indianapolis to make a few dollars. To do this, we needed a tractor to get out in the field to pick up our baskets of tomatoes after the baskets were full. I asked dad if I could use his tractor and trailer, and he said ok. So I used dad's tractor and trailer to accomplish this.

I also asked dad if I could use his pickup truck to haul these tomatoes to Indianapolis to the Farmers Market. Dad said ok. Sadly we were unable to sell any tomatoes there. I also arranged for some of our class members to pick up knocked-down corn one Autumn. The corn was free. I had found a person who wanted the corn, so I used dad's tractor and trailer to do that job too. All the use of dad's tractor and trailer required fuel and wear and tear. Dad never complained or said anything about me using his equipment. And as it turned out, when we were ready to leave for our class trip, we earned enough money that our parents did not need to help pay for our trip expenses. Dad was a Super Dad. I was never able to tell him just how much I appreciated him. There were millions and millions of things dad did for me.

Once, I asked dad if he would take our class on a hayride in his big truck. He agreed; there were about 16 kids who participated. Our class sponsor and her daughter rode in the cab with dad. But this left me in the back to try to control some of the wilder boys. It did not work, and I just gave up. Some of the boys started smoking, and I did not think that was good because they could catch the hay on fire. That could result in a disaster. One time, dad had to stop at a stop sign. Some of the boys jumped out of the truck and grabbed corn from one of the corn fields along the road. Dad waited for them to get back in the truck. Then they shelled the corn and started throwing it at cars as they went by, and they also threw some of the hay at other vehicles. But we all enjoyed the ride and what dad did for us. I arranged the hay for the back of the truck for this hayride, and

I cleaned everything up after arriving home. That was the end of the hayrides for our class. Dad did not make that decision, but I did; I did not want to put dad in that position again. All of us kids enjoyed this ride. It was too bad a couple of guys tried to spoil the evening. But they didn't!

Some Distant Neighbors

For the many years I was in school, and living at the 80-acres, I would stand next to the road and watch for the school bus in the mornings. I watched for it, and after I spotted the bus, I told my sister that the bus was coming. My sister always seemed to be running late when catching the school bus. While waiting and watching, I saw several neighbors regularly drive by our house at about the same time each day, around 7:30 am. I always saw the school teacher mentioned earlier, who was in an automobile accident. She was the mother of some of our classmates at school. Then there was another car that was driving by on a regular basis. I do not remember the make of the automobile, but I believe it was a Buick. It was always clean and had the same people riding in it. It had an older African-American woman driving and an older African-American man riding in the passenger seat. Then in the back seat were two younger African-American female ladies. They never went fast, always drove by at the same speed, and never hurried. Their speed was about 30 MPH. I say this because some drivers would be going very fast, and others would take their time. And you could set your watch because this car always went by at almost the exact time each day. After a couple of years, I discovered who these people were and where they traveled. This African-American family lived about three miles from us, close to Ohio. Our 80-acre farm was one mile from the Indiana/Ohio state line. The State Line road, which was 1 mile east, did not run straight through to Union City, but the highway we lived on (#227) ran straight from Richmond, Indiana to Union City, Indiana. This is why people use this road. This older lady and her husband drove their two daughters to the factory where they were employed in Union City. They drove by in the morning to work, then back home. Then, in the evening, the car would go back to Union City and then drive back down the road, taking the daughters and their mother and father home. I always saw these same people, with the same seating, do this day after day. The lady driving must have been the only one in the family who knew how to drive then. But sometime later, one of the daughters must have learned how to drive and purchased her own car, and then the two daughters would drive themselves to and from work. I would see them, and we always waved at each other. These young ladies were much more friendly than their mother and father. My sister knew these two young ladies. They were from our school.

    A couple of years passed when this same older lady and her husband stopped. They drove in the driveway at the barn. I was in the barnyard when they stopped. I learned who they were and why they drove past our house. The lady asked if she could talk to my father. I said yes, and I went and found dad inside the barn and asked him to come out and speak to this lady. Dad came out and talked for a time to the lady; the husband never said a word. The husband never did say anything in all our experiences. Come to find out, she wanted to buy some seed oats from dad but only had money to pay for them later. She promised dad she would pay for these oats at a specific time. Then dad told me to get this lady some burlap bags and oats. I did, and I gave her a guessed amount of oats out of the granary that she had requested. Dad checked my amounts. It was three bags.

    Everything seemed to be okay, and afterward, that car would drive by our house each day, just like before. It was before the daughter started driving. But this lady never returned to pay dad for the oats, not at any time. I don't remember the date she was supposed to pay. Dad never said anything about their agreement. The following year, this same lady returned and asked dad for more seed oats. Dad did not want to give her more oats, but dad gave in again. Again, dad told me to sack up some oats for her, but not quite as much as the last time. And again, she promised to pay, but dad warned her that he was not in the practice of giving away oats. She never paid anything at the time. But before she left, dad asked her for her address and where she lived. Later in the year, long after the date for payment had passed, dad told me to get in the truck. I did. Then dad and I went to the lady's house. Dad took me along as his bodyguard and witness, I think. We never stepped inside the lady's house. She came outside to talk to dad. Dad requested payment for the oats and told her that she owed for both years, of which he had given her the oats requested. The lady argued with dad and said he was wealthy enough to provide her with the oats. That did not go over very well with dad, and he argued for payment. It ended with her giving dad a couple of dollars. Nothing close to what she had agreed to pay. And, of course, dad told her never to stop by our house again. And they never did. But afterward, when that car drove by, the occupants just looked straight ahead and never turned their heads to look at any of us. But I would still wave at the daughters when the two sisters drove by. They always waved back. They were pretty girls. They both worked at the same Union City factory. I remember the daughters being adorable and kind—soft talking. I had a chance to talk to them a couple of years afterward. They were nothing like their mother. But I still had my duty of standing next to the road. I always watched for the school bus to tell my sister the bus was coming. I did this every day until I graduated. My sister and I have always argued about her catching the school bus!

The reason I always argued with my sister about catching the school bus was, my sister always had to have everything perfect before she would get on the bus. She would stand in front of the mirror and look and look to make sure every hair was perfect and her clothing was neat and just the way she wanted it. I argued because I always felt it was ok to check yourself, but it was more important to be on time for the school bus. I wasn't so concerned about what I looked like. If you like me, it would not matter what I looked like. My siser was such a perfecttionists, but I love my sister, and brother.

My mother was not like my sister concerning being a perfectionists. Our mother was more concerned about doing things. Our mother was a hard worker like my dad. And she was more concerned about the cost of supplies, food, clothing, etc.. Mom took care of the farms checkbook. Mom usually gave us a little money to spend, when we went on school trips. Mom always attended our school activities, and helped supply cakes for the ice cream socials. Mom attended to all our needs at school. And for these activities after school or on weekends, mom would always make sure we were on time, and had the required dress for that occasion. Our mother took very good care of us children. Our mother was a very good mother.

Dad, I sincerely thank you for everything you taught me and for all the kindness you tried and did teach me. So many of these things I did learn, and I also use and remember to this day. Dad was quite an Angel to me. It doesn't seem long ago, but it has been well over 50 years ago. Wonderful memories! Again, I must say, I hope I was always worthy of dad's trust and love.

Garage

The 80-acre property had a one-car garage when we moved there. And there was no inside toilet. The original builders built the outhouse on the back of the garage. It eliminated having to get out in the weather if a person needed to use the toilet. However, we no longer needed the outhouse after dad installed the new toilet inside the house. In the autumn of about 1955, not sure of the exact year, mom and I drove to Richmond, Indiana. I was about 11 years old. Mom had seen an advertisement about a company in Richmond that said they could remove your existing garage, haul it away, and build a new two-car garage, with extra storage space, at a reasonable price. The area was plenty big enough to handle a larger building. I am still determining what the cost was, but it was affordable. And as we later found out, the materials were pretty good, but the workmanship could have been better. Dad had no idea what we had done, and mom told me not to tell dad. But I had listened to the salesman in Richmond, and I knew what mom wanted to happen. Mom gave the salesman a check and signed a contract. Mom wanted a new garage without dad having to build it. Then the day came when the workers came to remove the existing building and install a new one. Of course, this is when dad found out they would get a new 2-car garage. Dad did not say anything and did not interfere. The workers tore down the old garage, leveled the earth, and poured a new foundation and floor made of cement. The workers returned a day later and started forming the new structure. I learned a lot about buildings, but the workers also needed to gain more experience. After a few days of work, they finished the job, and mom paid them in full.

Dad looked over this new structure and started criticizing the whole thing. He was correct. Then dad took some of the redwood sidings off and put in some new bracing, additional wall studs, and more roof bracing. After dad was finished with that work, dad reinstalled the redwood siding and repainted everything. Dad was correct to do this additional work. I never knew what dad said to mom, but her intentions were excellent. She just wanted to improve the garage and not need to have dad do it. The new garage had two roll-up doors, which could have worked better. Then dad adjusted both of them, and they have worked well since. Dad also built a chimney inside and put in the old wood stove, the stove from the back porch at the 39-acre house, to heat the garage when someone was working there during the wintertime. Then dad, mom, and I moved the freezer from the basement to the garage. We moved all the egg washing machines with all the ingredients for washing the eggs. Then the clothes washing machine from the basement and everything they wanted to put into the new garage space. There was a designated space for these machines next to the south wall, and they still had plenty of room to park two cars. It was a lovely change and convenient. It was a good addition, which made it easier to perform all our necessary tasks and still have plenty of space to park two vehicles. A breezeway connected the garage to the house. This area was great for us barn workers to take off our dirty clothes and shoes/boots, especially in the wintertime, with the snow and ice outside. This new garage was a great addition, made dressing the barn clothes much easier, and kept everything cleaner. The breezeway we used to use was never heated during wintertime. Now we could change our farm clothes inside the garage. They built the new garage with a drain in the floor and all necessary lighting, plus it had a running water spigot to supply any essential water. Now we could wash our hands if we needed to. Mom had made a good idea come to life!

Fanny

This 80-acre property has a county road, which runs north and south behind it on the east side of the farm. Because there are families who live on this road, these properties need access using this road. One time when I was about 12, dad wanted the clover hay mowed in the field east of the new hog barn. That afternoon I started the mowing. As I cut around the fence along this road, heading south, I turned back west towards the barn area. I saw that there were two little dogs there. The one dog had a worm in its mouth, so I knew they were pretty hungry. They were puppies, both female, very small, and probably about five weeks of age. They were only there a little while, probably about a day. Someone must have abandoned them there. I knew they could not stay there because they could get killed by the mower. They could never survive there. They would probably starve to death. So I got off the tractor, picked up both of them, and placed them on my lap. Then I continued mowing back towards the barn area while holding these dogs on my lap with my left arm. When I reached the end of the field up by the barn, I shut the tractor off, took these puppies to the house and garage, and explained to dad and mom how I found these two animals. At first, mom said we could not keep them.

I hoped we could. We did keep both of them for a day or two, fed them, and gave them a safe and clean place to sleep. Then mom and dad decided to keep the smaller of the two, and mom took the other dog to the shelter in Richmond. Mom said there was someone there that was looking for a puppy and took it home right away. The little dog we kept we named Fanny. This little dog stole everyone's heart. No animals were allowed inside the house, that was the rule, but Fanny changed that rule. This little dog would sit on your lap while driving the tractor, rode in the truck and car all the time, and was the sweetest dog. She sat on dad's lap when he was sitting in his easy chair in the house. She was never in the way, but always close. This dog never caused any problems. Mom always said Fanny was my dog. After I entered the military, Fanny stayed inside the house all the time when I came home from leave. She always went to the bathroom outside. She was such a good dog, and everyone became attached to her. Watching Franny put her head out the window and look out of the car and truck windows while driving was very comical. She was always looking intently, even though she had been up and down those roads hundreds of times. Fanny lived to old age and eventually lost her hearing. Sadly she was killed when she was accidentally struck by a car.

Dad loved this dog too! While Dee and I lived on the corner farm property, I built a unique little dog house for Fanny. It was insulated, had a metal roof, and was as deluxe as I could think of, special for Fanny. But Dee always liked kitties. And most farms have several cats. So Fanny and some cats would all sleep together in this dog house. (We have a few pictures showing Fanny and the kitties.) Of course, Dee had given all the kitties names.

Hunting

Over the years, we had different raccoon-hunting dogs. We called them coon dogs. At first, dad had black and tan hound dogs. The first was "Old Sport," and the second was "Boston Blackie". We also had a little fox terrier dog. This dog (Andy) was more of a watchdog for the family than a hunter. Andy was a great dog for hunting rats. But you had to watch Andy, and sometimes he would bite. And he scared people when they came to visit. We would need to hold him or pen him up. Sadly Andy ran away one night, and we never saw him again. A short time later, my Uncle Artie gave me a small Redbone hound dog, which I named Reddy. Shortly after

Blackie died, dad purchased a trained redbone dog to hunt raccoons. The two Redbone dogs chased pretty well together. Dad's dog did not run the track from raccoons very well and rarely barked but would bark when the raccoons ended up in a tree. My little dog Reddy ran the track of raccoons very well. He barked a lot, but when the raccoons got up in the tree, he would not bark. Therefore they made a good team. Dad and I didn't hunt often, only during the hunting season (November 15 to January 15); we went out 4 or 5 nights a week if the weather was good and not raining. I think we may have captured about 15 each season. I specifically remember when we were in the woods a couple of miles north of Bartonia. The dogs had barked a lot and ran around the tree, a sign the dogs thought there was a raccoon up in the tree. Dad looked and shined his flashlight to the top of the tree but said he did not see anything. Dad said we needed to go, thinking the dogs were wrong, but I told him I saw something at the top of that tree. Then dad looked again and shined his flashlight at the top of the tree again. Sure enough, there were two raccoons up there, which dad had not seen the first time he looked. Dad took his rifle and shot the two raccoons, and we brought them home to show mom. Mom and dad took a picture of me holding these two raccoons in the kitchen of our house. I don't know what my age was, but it was all I could do to hold those two raccoons up.

After I was older, maybe 13 to 16, we changed our hunting routine. Dad would drop the dogs and me off on one road, and the dogs and I would hunt through different wooded areas and meet up with dad at the next road, which was about a mile away. This way, we did not need to backtrack, to get back to the truck. Sometimes dad would walk back toward us if he heard the dogs tracking something. I hunted like this with cousin Charlie many times. Then dad would sit in the truck and talk with Uncle Artie while we were hunting through from one road to the next road. We never did catch anything when we hunted with cousin Charlie and Uncle Artie. They kept talking all the time. The raccoons knew we were there. I felt sorry for cousin Charlie. He was so afraid of the dark. As we walked, he would walk very close to me. When raccoon hunting, there was nothing to be scared about, but you had to watch out for cattle. The reason is that the cattle would chase the dogs, and the dogs would come back to us. We always carried a lantern.

We always had the lantern lit, and the cattle ran after the dogs and the light. Several times, I had to get into the creek because the young steers would come charging after the dogs and me. The black Angus calves liked to play, and chasing dogs must have been fun for them. We only hunted in a few wooded areas if the wooded area had cattle roaming in it. Raccoons usually do not stay around cattle or sheep. One other thing that is still a mystery to me about dad was that we would often run across Opossums when hunting. Each time we saw one, they played dead, but dad said they were no good. Dad did not like them. Many times dad would kill them. And no matter who we were hunting with, or just dad and myself, we were home by 10 to 11 pm.

On the evening of December 25th, 1959, I had just turned 16, I took the dogs out by myself shortly after dad finished the milking. Dad was going to catch up with us later. I walked to the west of our house, down to Greenville Creek, down around the fencerows, and the dogs and I ended up at the Dismal area south of the 80-acre farm, about a mile away. It was around 6:30 pm when the dogs started fighting with something, which I could not see at first. But there was quite a fight going on and lots of barking by both dogs. After a few minutes, I discovered this grayish animal. I had no idea what it was. But I could see it had long toenails and a mouth similar to a small dog's mouth. I knew it was not an opossum. We captured and killed this animal after I shot it nine times. I carried a 22 rifle. There were seven bullet holes visible after we were able to look closer. Three in its body, and four shots in its head. This animal started chasing me during the fight because the dogs kept coming back to me. That was the main reason I felt I had to kill it. I thought it was going to attack me. It did chase after me, and I am sure it would have attacked me if it had not been for the two dogs constantly grabbing its attention. But this fight went on for probably 20 minutes before its life finally gave out. During the battle, its toenails sliced the neck of my little dog Reddy, and it was bleeding. After the fight, I gathered all my belongings which I scattered behind me and headed home. But before I had gotten very far, dad showed up with his truck. Dad asked me, what did you get? He commented about hearing the dogs barking and fighting so much. I said, "I don't know; I think it may be a bear." I had no idea what kind of animal this was. We went home and looked over the dogs and the animal we had captured. Reddy needed attention for his neck. We called a veterinarian we knew, who was also a hunter and took the dogs and the captured animal to see him. He patched up my dog, checked out the other dog, and then went to the truck to see the captured animal. None of us knew what kind of animal it was. It was days later that a fur trader told us it was a Badger, which was rare in this area. They suggested I have the animal stuffed by a taxidermist, which I did. The veterinarian was surprised to see the Badger. He said most dogs that are wounded like this, the animal that caused the wounds are usually never captured. I suppose I was lucky. I had told dad that I thought it was a bear, but I had no idea. I only said this kind of animal could really put up a fight. The Badger was a female and weighed 18 pounds, and its front toenails were about 2 inches long. Dad had such a big grin, and happiness showed on his face when he saw and heard the story. I have always wanted to make my dad proud. I think we did. Dad said he listened to the dogs fighting something and was happy none of us were seriously hurt. I recently gave the Badger to a facility, a Mr Miller's collection in the midwest, who has many other stuffed wild animals on display similar to this one. I had contacted a few wildlife museums locally, but they already had many badgers. Mr Miller has several school children observing and learning about different wildlife animals at his collection...

Aunt Mary and Uncle Bill

Aunt Mary and Uncle Bill lived just down the road while we lived on the 39-acre farm. Uncle Bill was my mother's half-brother. Mom and Uncle Bill both had the same mother but different fathers. Uncle Bill's mother's first husband died, Moore was his name, then she married my mother's father, Mr. Gibson. I will talk a little more about Uncle Bill later. Aunt Mary was his wife. They lived closer to Union City, Indiana, than we did when we lived on the 39-acre farm. My sister and I walked past their house every Sunday to visit Union City Methodist church. Aunt Mary's daughters walked with us a few times. But my sister and I went to church about every Sunday in the summertime if the weather was ok. We walked to Aunt Mary's house almost every other day, to deliver her milk and eggs, and sometimes fruits and vegetables from mom's garden.

I have mentioned some about Aunt Mary's cooking and baking earlier. When other people visited them, we usually spent most of our time in their kitchen. They had a large kitchen because I remember someone remodeled it, but it was not Uncle Bill. Most Family Christmas dinners were at their house, and everyone always enjoyed themselves. They had a nice living room with a large window to let viewers see outside. I do not know how long they lived in this house. The house was a small two-bedroom house. It also had a nice garage, which looked like a small barn. They had about an acre of land, too. Dad plowed and prepared the ground for planting a couple of times for Uncle Bill. I know they planted some corn, and there was also space for growing other vegetables. But that did not last very long because none of their relatives wanted to do any work tending them. The acreage had been planted in clover, which dad mowed and baled. I suppose dad took the hay home for our cattle. Uncle Bill had no farm animals but a couple of dogs and cats. In their backyard, Uncle Bill also had a medium-sized garden and an area for burning wood for hot dog roasting and other barb-b- -que get-togethers.

We spent many picnic days at their house, cooking food over these fires. Aunt Mary was a wonderful hostess and always had juicy gossip to talk about, plus lots of excellent food and drinks. Most of the talk was good-natured and really was not gossip. As I said before, she was always at Bingo. And Uncle Bill was always doing his own thing. He was a pretty good backyard mechanic. One thing I always remembered about Uncle Bill, he always rolled up the sleeves on his long sleeved shirts, all the way to the elbow. I thought, why not put on a short sleeved shirt? When their oldest daughter married, they purchased a new 1951 Chevrolet automobile for her and her new husband. But they did not check the oil and ruined the engine.

Uncle Bill had kept that car and replaced the engine with another Chevrolet engine. After he had it all finished, I purchased it from him for $125. I bought this first car when I was 15 years old. When I went to get the car, mom took dad and me to Uncle Bill's house, and I drove it home with dad as my passenger. At that time, I only had a permit. I say this because, on the way home, dad had me stop at the gas station, and he put in $2 worth of gas, that filled the tank to almost full. I always remember how much and how big of a gift it was from dad. This car was great. I was the only boy in my school class with a car that ran and was dependable. Sometimes I had nine kids in that car when we went to Richmond to look around and have a coke and burger. For $1, we could see a movie, eat a burger and drink a coke, or soda at the popular drive-in restaurant. It was called Carter's Drive-in in Richmond, Indiana. Other school kids and I occasionally went to other towns and school activities. Of course, we always went in my car.

Aunt Mary and Uncle Bill had two daughters and later had a son, but that was after the daughters had married and left home. The big thing about getting together with Uncle Bill was that dad and Uncle Bill would play their guitars and sing songs they knew, especially when they came to our house. Because years earlier, Uncle Bill had played his guitar and sang over the local radio station to earn enough money to afford their home and lifestyle during the Great Depression. They lived in Richmond, Indiana then. Uncle Bill could have been better of a singer, but he had a great heart and knew lots of songs. My sister sometimes played the piano with them after she was a little older. We all tried to sing along, but I did not know the words to all those old songs. Dad told us that he was into music before he met our mother. Dad always had an ear for music. Dad could have been a good musician if he had practiced more. Dad could whistle very well too. Dad could whistle a complete song if he had time and wanted to. But when these two musicians played together, those evenings were very memorable for all involved. I can remember some of the songs, and I am sure my sister remembers some of them, too, probably more than I do. Our mother took several pictures of them playing music together. The sad thing is I do not remember either of Uncle Bill's daughters being around. We all enjoyed their music and efforts. And I do not remember their son being there, but he was pretty young. I imagine they all got together and played and sang after I went into the military. Their son may have been involved then.

And after Uncle Bill's son got older, he listened to his father, and got into go-kart racing. There was a group of young racers and a small race track close by. Then Uncle Bill was a go-kart mechanic too. Dad told me he saw Uncle Bill's son race his go-kart at that local go-kart track. Their son had collected some trophies. The son never went into automobile racing later on, not that I know of, but they all had lots of fun with the go-karts.

Uncle Bill later purchased a milk truck and route, a similar milk route to what dad used to have. I helped Uncle Bill do this route two times when he was not feeling very good. And one time, his truck broke down, and he needed to use dad's truck. Dad's truck sat much higher off the ground than Uncle Bill's truck. By then, I was probably about 15, and I could put the full cans of milk up into the truck for him and up into dad's truck. Dad went with Uncle Bill to run his milk route two times. We liked helping Uncle Bill. He was a very good-intentioned man. The funny thing was Aunt Mary asked me to come and work on her car for her. Maybe Uncle Bill didn't want to be bothered with it. But I fixed her car for her. She was very appreciative. Aunt Mary and Uncle Bill had a different relationship than most married people, because they seemed to argue about almost everything. Aunt Mary was always going to "bust" Uncle Bill just like she told many other people, especially her children. She threatened to "bust" me too. But they really loved each other. Afterwards they would be laughing. They were very great people, I admired both of them so much.

Over the years, Aunt Mary always wanted to have a hot dog roast for just about any occasion. We had a lot of hot dog roasts. Aunt Mary also talked about opening her own burger restaurant with all the juicy gossip, but she still needs to do so. We talked a lot about opening a burger place but just never tried to open anything. Usually, mom made a big pitcher of Kool-Aid to drink at these occasions, and potato salad, baked beans, and many other dishes to go along with the hot dogs. Mom was very good at making deviled eggs. Because of needing a fire to cook the hot dogs, burgers, or whatever mom and Aunt Mary wanted to cook, I built a brick bar-b-que away from the buildings, down in the yard by the garden. It was just a bunch of bricks stacked together. When planning a cookout like this, I would start the fire early to enable it to burn down to hot coals by the time we were ready to do the roasting. These evenings were delightful. Especially if the mosquitoes did not invade us. We usually had this get-together at our house because we milked at about 5 pm, and we could all eat when we were finished, around 6:15 pm. Dad and mom were the only farmers in our entire group of relatives. All the other relatives worked in factories or shops in town. Everyone respected mom and dad and their way of making a living. And as I look back at it, mom and dad's farming business was more successful in the end than any of our other relatives. But everyone was happy and got along well. Sometimes dad and Uncle Bill would play music after darkness settled in, after these hot dog roasts. After we ate our food, we usually toasted marshmallows. Sometimes I made homemade ice cream if I had some ice.

Dad and mom liked to play Euchre card games. Euchre is a typical card game for midwestern people to play anytime. They usually played at Aunt Mary's house, but sometimes we played at ours. When I was home on leave/vacation, I usually went to visit Aunt Mary and Uncle Bill. The one time I remember very well was when I was home on vacation for a short time; dad, mom, and I went to Aunt Mary's house to play Euchre. While there, Uncle Bill asked me if I wanted to drink a can of beer with him. I was 21 years old, and I said yes, I would. I didn't really want it, but when would I ever have a chance to drink a beer with Uncle Bill again? And besides, Mom was dead set on anyone drinking any kind of alcohol. But this was her brother. I thought I'd show her that drinking beer is not deadly if you drink responsibly. So Uncle Bill went to his back porch and brought in 2 cans of beer. The beer had not been refrigerated, and carrying it probably shook it.

Then, when Uncle Bill set the beer cans on the card-playing

table and popped the tops. Beer exploded all over the place. It even hit the ceiling. Of course, everyone cracked up laughing! Now we had to clean everything up. There was beer on the table, all over the floor, on the kitchen cabinets, and on us. I don't remember if we ever drank the beer. But it was a night to remember. And that was the only chance I ever had to do anything with my Uncle Bill. After Dee and I had returned to Indiana, we played cards at Aunt Mary's house, but there never was any mention of beer to drink. But I know we laughed a lot about the night I mentioned. Even my mother remembered that specific evening! Mom never commented about me drinking beer..

However, I know that Aunt Mary was a fabulous cook and made all kinds of pies. Aunt Mary's pecan pies were out of this world. Aunt Mary did not use measuring utensils. She just put into the mixing bowl the amounts she wanted. Everything Aunt Mary made tasted wonderfully good. She told me many years later that she always liked inviting me to her house for a meal because I always ate everything she prepared and lots of it. Aunt Mary liked that. Her family was finicky eaters. Aunt Mary was a comical person. When a person entered her house, she would laughingly say, "tell me some juicy gossip." It did not matter, this was her way of getting people to loosen up and talk, but most of all, Aunt Mary always had us all laughing. She was a great hostess, cook, Bingo player, and fun to be around. She went to Bingo games eight times a week, twice on Sunday. I went with her a couple of times. She was lucky sometimes, I have no idea if she won much or not, but she enjoyed herself. I think she may have lost more money than she won overall.

Uncle Bill owned a row boat, about a 14-footer. No motor, it had oars, that was its motor. It was wooden and in perfect condition. He purchased it used, and stored it in grandmother Gibson's barn. It was on a nice boat trailer. I am sure there were no life preservers in this boat. At least, I do not remember any.

When I think about it today, what a risk we were taking by going out in reservoirs filled full with rain water. Many of us would not be here today if that boat leaked. Uncle Bill was a pretty happy fisherman. He fished everywhere. Lakes, rivers, gravel pits, reservoirs, any place he could drop a line. I do not think he caught much of anything. Dad and I went fishing with him several times on Sunday afternoons. The most fishing I did with him was on White River, close to IN #32. We would sit and keep moving the fishing poles but not catch anything. Aunt Mary would laugh when we arrived back at their house. When she asked Uncle Bill what he had caught, nothing was the usual answer. They could always laugh at each other. That was the one thing about our dad and mom. There was never any laughing about things either of them had done, whether good or not. But we all liked Uncle Bill and Aunt Mary.

Harder Park in Union City, Indiana was the city park where people almost always set off fireworks on the 4th of July. Aunt Mary and Uncle Bill lived half a mile from Harder Park. Almost every 4th of July, we would all go to their house after we finished the milking and farm chores. We always had plenty to eat. After eating, we would take some chairs out on their front lawn in the evening and watch the fireworks. Sometimes we just sat on the lawn if it was a lovely warm evening. It was always a fun activity, except when the mosquitoes decided to attack us. But mom always had mosquito repellant handy. Indiana has pleasant warm evenings around this time of year and plenty of mosquitoes.

Uncle Bill's property had about an acre of land east of the house and barn. Further east was a junkyard. Aunt Mary hated that junkyard. A few times, Uncle Bill asked dad to come and mow the clover/grass growing there and bale up the hay. Uncle Bill had riding lawnmowers, but this was much too large to cut with a lawnmower, plus dad could always use the clover hay. Dad took the hay home. Dad paid Uncle Bill something for the hay. Before Uncle Bill had the clover hay growing, dad plowed the property, and I remember working the soil for planting. The next day, Dad planted corn and maybe soybeans the following year.

When dad planted Uncle Bill's property in corn, there was not much corn remaining to harvest in the autumn of the year. That was because many members of their families would pick what they wanted. They wanted to have corn on the cob to eat around the end of July. Uncle Bill sold a lot of corn on the cob to people where he worked too. After everyone had taken the amount they wanted, there was not much left to dry out for cattle food. There was always a section, not very big, along the garage area, for planting a vegetable garden. Aunt Mary did not want to plant and care for flowers. They did have a couple of trees. They were not fruit trees. I don't remember their daughters getting involved with any type of flower or vegetable gardening. But Uncle Bill's family wanted him to save the space in this garden for planting and growing different kinds of vegetables. He did, but that only lasted a year or two. Those children did not want to take care of any garden. And Uncle Bill did not need the extra work. After the garden idea did not work out, Dad sowed the whole area with clover and cut and baled the clover hay during the summer.

My sister recently told me a story about Aunt Mary. However, there are lots more stories similar to this one about Aunt Mary. This story was about Aunt Mary's oldest daughter. Her birthday was in the middle of May, and another neighbor girl's birthday was the next day. These two young girls attended the same school and were always invited to each other's parties. They were girlfriends. Of course, we knew Aunt Mary's daughter, and we also knew the neighbor girl, and her parents, pretty well too. This neighbor girl and her parents lived just down the road from us when we lived on the 80-acre property.

For Aunt Mary's daughter's birthday, Aunt Mary always

baked a birthday cake for her daughter and put candles on it. I do not know whether my sister attended these birthday parties, but I imagine she did. Before these parties, Aunt Mary always baked cupcakes to give the neighbor girl. Aunt Mary gave this young lady a cupcake with a candle at her own daughter's party. Aunt Mary wanted that girl to know that Aunt Mary appreciated her and her family. Aunt Mary never met a stranger and was friendly with everyone. I loved her. We all loved Aunt Mary. Also, Aunt Mary always had her favorite saying, "I'm going to bust you." We loved her.

The Shaw Farm

I do not know when (late forties) dad agreed with Russell Shaw to rent Russell's farm of about 132 acres. Russel and dad's contract were the same as our grandmothers. The agreement was the landowner paid for 1/2 the seed and fertilizer, and dad paid for the other 1/2. And again, dad would do all the work of tilling, planting, and caring for the crops. The landowner received 1/2 of the crop results at harvesting time, and dad received the other half. Of course, dad had to furnish all equipment and care for the land costs, such as fuel, wear and tear, and watching for soil erosion. Soil erosion required making waterways through any area of soil washing away. Dad was responsible for mowing and maintaining these areas. These areas meant there would be no crops planted on these areas, thus a loss of actual farming ground. The Shaw farm had enough storage space to store most of the grain harvested for that year. Then dad would sell the grains over the winter when crop prices were higher. Usually, that year's yield belonged to both dad and Russell. I do not know what agreement they had. But oh, how I remember shoveling grain into those bins, then moving that grain back into the truck during the winter. Later, dad purchased a portable grain elevator to help do this work, making it much more manageable.

At first there was no electricity installed anywhere at the barn area. We had to use most of these electric cords originally for the lawnmower for the electric equipment at the Shaw Farm too. I remember it was about 300 feet from the Shaw house to the grain storage building. Several years later, electricity was installed in the Shaw barn, and also this smaller building used to hold the grain, where Russell parked his Buick automobile. But most of these electric extension cords were originally purchased to provide electricity to the electric lawn mower for mowing the barnyard at the 80 acres.

Dad farmed the Shaw farm even after Russell Shaw left. In 1960, Mr. Shaw had a new house built in Spartanburg, and moved away from this farm. Dad kept farming the land. After Russell moved into his new home, he rented this farmhouse to a man who had five children. I met the man, he was a very nice man. The man was a professional parachuter who jumped out of airplanes at different air shows. But sadly, a year or two after he moved his family into this house, his parachute did not open when he jumped out of the airplane. Of course, he was killed. The man was married to a Japanese lady, and left behind his wife and five young children. Then the lady and children moved.

I visited Russell and Josie at their new home in Spartanburg because I had my car and wanted to say hello. Of course, Josie gave me cookies that she had baked. But about two years after they had lived in this new house, Josie passed away. Russell died off a broken heart about a year after Josie. Then Russell's son owned the farm. While I was in the military, dad purchased this Shaw Farm property in November 1967, all 132 acres, from Russell's son.

This Shaw farm had many large rocks scattered out in the fields, and I mean lots of stones and rocks. Many small ones, but probably at least a hundred large ones. They required digging around them and using a tractor and chain to pull them out of the ground. Then slide them over to the edge of the woods. When the equipment struck one, these rocks would do a lot of damage to the farming equipment. I remember dad repairing and replacing many plowshares. The Farmall "M" tractor pulled a three-bottom plow, and losing plowing time to repair equipment could be costly. So one-year, dad had talked to Russell, and they decided to remove as many of these rocks as possible. 1954 was the year we did the most rock removal. .

There was an area beside the wooded area where we could drag these rocks. So the three of us spent several days digging and removing these rocks from the fields to the wooded area. Some of these rocks were so large that it took both tractors to slide them across the fields to that wooded area. I wonder how much some of them weighed. But Russell helped dig, and dad and I drove the tractors, and we finally removed as many as we could. I remember we only got some of them, and we pulled a few more after dad had harvested the crops. Years later, while I was in the military, dad had a contractor dig a gigantic hole and push all these rocks into it to bury them. There were lots of big rocks and gobs of small ones altogether. Dad and Russell had an excellent farming relationship, and there was never an issue with crops or yields. Now, I am so happy to recall removing all these rocks. Also, the many memories of the times we raccoon hunted in these wooded areas. My sister owns this property now and has made many improvements to this property since she acquired it.

The one thing I remember specifically, and I am not proud of, happened at the Shaw farm. The fields were all arranged differently during those years because this land had farm animals living and grazing in different areas before dad took it over. But there used to be a small field, just west of the corn crib, granary building, which held about 3 acres. There was also a big tree in the middle of this field. This field was planted with corn, and the corn was about 8 inches tall. Dad always cultivated his corn and soybeans to keep the weeds down. We had just put the cultivators on the Farmall "H" tractor. Using this tractor, it could plow two rows of corn at a time. Dad showed me how to operate this tractor with the cultivators. No problem for me, so I proceeded to cultivate the entire field.

After we had eaten our lunch, dad told me to go to the field closer to the woods and cultivate that corn. I said I would, and I did. But after some time, I got sleepy and drove too fast. I plowed out a lot of the corn which had already been planted. When dad returned and saw what I had done, he became very angry. I thought I had done everything correctly until dad explained what I had done. I tried to push some of the corn back into the row. I would like to know if that helped any or not. I know this represented a loss of crop value come harvest time. But before we went home for that night, dad made me tell Russell Shaw what I had done. I am glad dad made me do that. I made a mistake, and I still feel guilty about this memory. That was the only time I drove the cultivator; dad never trusted me after that. I felt terrible about what I had done, even today, I wish I could change that memory. Even today, I cannot watch things moving across in front of me. Cultivating crops made me dizzy watching the row all the time. Just watching a train go past at a railroad intersection makes me dizzy. I learned my lesson the hard way. I still regret what I did. Was I worthy of dad's trust in me? I know I disappointed dad many times. Because of doing the things I did before thinking about right and wrong or good and evil.

I need to tell you something about Russell Shaw. Russell was a very kind man and stood about 6ft +tall. He had a soft voice, and I listened to everything he had to say. I would have done anything Russell asked me to do. His wife, Josie, was maybe 5 feet tall and always gave me cookies, cake, etc. They had a son, but he was some years older than me and was never interested in becoming a farmer. Russell was brilliant. He even started the local bank. That bank helped so many of the local farmers. Russell's son worked in this bank. Dad never wanted to open an account at this bank, and I do not know why. I have an account with that bank now, some 60+ years later. After Russell moved to Spartanburg, he retired from the bank. Russell turned over the bank's operation to his son, but remained on the bank's board.

Russell had a 1949 Buick automobile. It always looked new. This car had a straight eight engine with the Dina-flo transmission. Russell always had his Buick parked inside a building when he lived on his farm. The building had a corn crib on one side and soybean and wheat bins on the other side. His car could get dusty, but no rain or snow could get on it. The driveway from the barn, where Russell parked his car, to the house driveway is about 150 yards. That area of the road is slightly uphill. When Russell and Josie wanted to go to town or the store, Russell would drive his car up to the house to pick up Josie. There was an area of gravel in front of the house. And when he pulled out onto the road, the engine sounded like a race car. It would be revving too high RPMs, but it always moved slowly. That was how those cars with this type of transmission worked.

Russell also had an area inside the wooded area of his farm. A grassy lane connected the wooded area from the living area of this property, approximately ½ mile away. Russell could drive his car into the wooded area and then turn it around inside the wooded area. It was a nice smooth grass roadway with many trees and a large oak tree leaning over the drive. He and Josie would travel in the Buick back into the wooded area and have lunch. Russell had a small table and benches positioned there to dine on. They ate their lunch many times there. And as I think about it today, what a relaxing way to eat, with all the trees, wildlife, and beautiful wildflowers. While dad and I were working out in the fields, we occasionally saw Russell driving the Buick down the lane and disappearing into the woods.

This wooded area had lots of trees. There were about 20 acres of this wooded area. There were many large Oak trees and other kinds of trees too. Dad and I hunted raccoons in this wooded area often during the winter. It was a clean woods; you could walk through it quickly, with not much bushy shrubbery or dead trees on the ground. We also used to look for mushrooms in these woods in the springtime of the year. There were several Beech trees too. Grandpa Burk told me about one of these Beech trees in the northern part, where he had carved his initials many years before. I can't remember what they represented, but I found the tree and looked at it every time I was in that wooded area, whether raccoon hunting, mushroom hunting, or just wandering around. After Russell moved from this property and passed on, his son sold most of the Oak trees and other trees of any size for logs to be cut into lumber at the local sawmill.

Along the east side of this wooded area was an open ditch. Many years earlier, part of this open ditch had been rerouted into a 16-inch clay tile ditch, which now belongs to the County. The open ditch dried up because of that change, except for a short time after heavy rains. The open ditch had been on the east side of the wooded area. Several trees had grown up on the east side along this open ditch area for many years. Some of these trees were several years old and probably 20 inches in diameter. There were a lot of trees along this strip of land. For some reason, dad and Russell talked and decided to remove all these trees on the east side of this ditch to make room for planting more crops.. Dad purchased a 17-inch chainsaw, I bought a new ax, and we went to work cutting and burning these trees. All wood of stove-burning size, about 12 to 14 inches in length, was kept and placed in an area down by the rocks. Dad usually ran the chainsaw, but I could have after I was big enough. Dad would cut the trees, and I would burn the leaves and branches that were not large enough for firewood. We did this work during the wintertime. Some days it was frigid, and getting a large fire going was appreciated, especially if the snow was on the ground. Our clothes sometimes got wet from the snow. We usually would take dad's trailer with us, and I would load it with wood at some point, then we would take the trailer loaded with the wood home when we finished the day. When home, I would put the wood in the basement area of the house. The wood furnace in the basement, centralized heat, used this wood for heat. This wood would be used in the furnace/stove to heat our home during the winter.

Along an east and west fence, along the north side of this farm was a large dead Elm tree along the newer houses built there. They had purchased the land from this farm sometime earlier to allow these new houses to be built along a State Highway. At first, there were two houses, but more people purchased the property and built more houses along this highway. Russell asked dad to cut down this Elm tree because it died. This tree would eventually have fallen on one of these houses, so Russell and dad decided to cut it down. I realized it was a tough job because the tree was huge. I remember driving the tractor, connected to this tree by a long rope, out in the field to hold tension on the tree to ensure it fell out toward the field. It worked out; dad kept sawing. Finally, the big tree came down. Then we had the job of clearing this giant tree and hauling it away. It took a couple of days to accomplish this. I remember how big this tree was; dad's saw was only a 17" cut. Dad took on a hazardous project. But Dad never shied away from hard work. This tree provided a lot of good firewood for our furnace.

One year at planting time, around May, dad had Pleurisy badly. By this time, I was old enough to be responsible for working all the ground to prepare for the planting. I could connect all the equipment after dad told me what equipment to use. I could check the oil in the tractors and fill them with fuel for the day's work. But I needed to be taller or bigger to use the planter. I needed help to reach the top of the containers which held the seed and fertilizer. So dad asked Uncle Roy to operate the planter. I had everything ready to use, seed, fertilizer, and all, placed on a wagon. I worked the ground in front of the planter with the Farmall "M" tractor, and dad pulled the planter with the Farmall "H" tractor. But this particular year, Uncle Roy drove the tractor and planter, and we planted the field that day.

Uncle Roy's rows were not very straight. He did his best, but dad always commented how crooked the rows were after the seed came up. I do not think it mattered. I think there were still the same amount of rows in that field. Dad always thought a person could get more straight rows in an area than crooked rows allowed. And believe me, the successive rows in the fields on the 80-acre farm were something of a marvel to see. You could see a long way to see the straightness of the rows of corn or soybeans. I do not know how dad could drive the tractor so straight. I know that a lot of farmers now use lasers. Lasers were not around for farmers in the 50's.

Baling Hay

Farmers who have cattle in Indiana usually need some kind of clover hay to feed their animals over the winter months. In Indiana, most cattle generally graze out in the fields during summertime. There are many different types of clover used for cattle feed. Dad planted a lot of alfalfa and said it helped the cows produce more milk. Directly east of the 80-acre barn was the alfalfa field dad used for cattle feed to cut and store in the barn for the wintertime. It mainly was alfalfa but had some clover mixed in too. Dad and Uncle Roy had cattle and milked cows, so they both needed to cut and store hay for their cattle.

Probably about 1952, dad and Uncle Roy purchased a new International #45 hay baler together. Dad paid half, and Uncle Roy paid half. And the agreement between the two brothers was Uncle Roy would help us bale hay, and dad and I would help Uncle Roy bale his hay. Each year, they talked and coordinated between them as to which one would cut their hay first, and then the other would cut his. We could not be baling hay at two different places simultaneously with one baler. It worked out well. Some days we were at our farm, and the next day we could be at Uncle Roy's. When the equipment supplier brought the new baler to our field, it took quite some time to get most of the adjustments made for the machine to operate correctly. Mostly all of the first afternoon. But the next day, everything was working well. Of course, I drove the Farmall "M" tractor that day while dad, Uncle Roy, and the mechanic would walk alongside the baler to see if any new adjustments were needed. It was working pretty well after a few hours.

After some time everything worked out well, and productivity went much better. From then on, it was mostly me driving the tractor pulling the baler. Uncle Roy usually stacked the bales on the wagon pulled behind the baler. Dad and granddad would pull the wagons of baled hay close to the elevator and stack the grass/hay inside the barn. Sometimes dad hired extra people to help stack the hay inside the barn. And sometimes Uncle Roy hired extra help when we were baling his hay. This was the procedure for many years. I don't remember how they did things after I went to the military. But I know mom said she drove the tractor, pulling the baler sometimes.

When we baled hay at Uncle Roy's, he was supposed to supply a tractor to pull the baler and another tractor for moving the wagons around. Most of the time, this worked out, but sometimes dad had to help with one of his tractors. One year Uncle Roy had a Case tractor with a hand clutch. I never operated a hand clutch before, but it only took me one instruction, and I had it. The funny thing is, I liked that tractor. It was great for pulling the hay baler. It was easy to shove the gearbox out of gear while the PTO (power take off) was still running at the regular speed, and then the land travel would ease to a smooth stop. Neither dad nor Uncle Roy had tractors, which had a live PTO in those years. I don't know what happened to that Case tractor. I know it was not a very strong tractor. Uncle Roy also had an old Farmall F-20 tractor. You had to hand-crank it to start it. Similar to granddad's tractor. I do not know where Uncle Roy found this tractor. It worked pretty well pulling the baler, but sometimes the engine would stop running. Then Uncle Roy would take out a wooden match stick, sharpen it with his knife, and put it into the magneto, crank the engine, and away we would go again. Dad never used the F-20 for pulling the wagons around, probably because you always had to hand crank the engine to get it started.

Uncle Roy was a character! One time he and I were baling hay in one of his fields. We did not have much to bale, but to give Uncle Roy a break, I said I would pull some of the bales out of the baler chute and place them on the wagon. These bales weighed as much as I did, but I could stack one on top of the other. That was as much as I could do. Uncle Roy started driving the tractor, pulling the baler, and I was on the wagon, and I had pulled out about 20 bales from the baler when suddenly, the wagon bed fell off the chassis. Uncle Roy had never bolted the bed down. I had pulled too many heavy bales behind the rear axle of the chassis, and the bed tipped up and off. We both laughed and laughed about this episode. We had to remove all the bales, back the chassis under the bed, push the wagon bed up on the chassis, and then put the bales back on the wagon. Then Uncle Roy said, "I guess I will have to fix that." No harm done. That reminded me of the old Ma & Pa Kettle movies.

Several times I had to drive the F-20 tractor, pulling the baler and empty wagons down the road. This tractor had a road gear, and it could speed along. But when using the road gear, the differential would whine after picking up a little speed. It was a good tractor, but it needed a lot of TLC. I think dad or my brother purchased that tractor at Uncle Roy's farm sale after Uncle Roy had died in 1966. I mentioned driving Uncle Roy's F-20 tractor down the road from Grandmother Gibson's farm.

The Original Burk Place /Our Great Grandparents

Our Great Grandfather, William Burk, lived from 1855 to 1941. Our Great Grandmother, Barbara Ellen Price Burk, lived from 1858 to 1944. They were married in May 1874, just a few days before our Great Grandmother turned 16 years old. Our father never said much about his grandparents. He mentioned his grandfather, but I never knew what or how he felt about either of his grandparents. On what is now the Base Road is the road where they lived. Out in the field north of the existing barn is where the original house sat. When Uncle Roy and I were baling hay, we stopped, and Uncle Roy explained why those rocks were there in that field. The rocks that are there, if they still are, were the rock foundation for the original Burk house. Most country buildings built during that era had rock foundations.

I have yet to learn how old or when it was built. But from what I have been told, that original house caught fire in the late 1920s or early 1930s and burned completely. Then they built the house that is there now. I am curious how long our Burk Grandparents lived in this new house before they passed. I believe our Burk Grandparents had seven children. Two died at birth. Uncle Artie was the oldest of the boys, our grandfather was in the middle, and Uncle Elmer was the youngest boy. I have no idea when any of the girls were born, their names, or much of anything about them or the rest of their children. Some of their grandchildren were living with our great grandparents too. And it seemed some neighbor boys lived there for a while also. Our Granddad Burk always complained about his sister, Cora, who was several years older than him, for calling and complaining to him. It seems she found complaints about anything and everything, according to granddad. We visited Aunt Cora a few times, but only sometimes. I remember going to her house at Christmas one time. Granddad said he stopped to visit her when he was going into town. I do not remember Granddad visiting Uncle Artie, but he visited his youngest brother, Uncle Elmer.

I mentioned Great Grandfather William Burk was born in 1855 and died in 1941. He was a farmer and had some cattle. Great-grandfather must have used a couple of workhorses to till his soil. He milked a couple of cows, and I believe he had a few pigs. They also must have had some chickens because there was an old chicken house. In the 1950s, Uncle Roy tore the old chicken house down and built a garage for his new car while he lived there. I don't know the acreage of that property then, but another parcel was added later. Somehow, an additional farm was added: a green shingled house, a barn, and an underground fruit cellar, located across the road from the original farm. It was never clear to me concerning this house, but Bill and Barbara Burk moved into this green shingled house for a while, right after the old original house burnt. It was on the westside of Boundary road. Maybe it belonged to another relative; I do not know. But when Uncle Roy owned it, he would drive his cattle across this road to graze out in the fields of one farm or the other farm. We also put hay in that barn when we baled hay for Uncle Roy. But Uncle Roy owned the property with the green shingled house, plus the original Burk property. Around the green shingled house, they had planted several trees, some for shade and many fruit trees. Our Uncle Ira and his family lived there when I was young. Uncle Ira had a large vegetable garden and he picked many fruits from the different trees. Cherry was the one I remember most. There were some Cottonwood trees around for shade too.

My only information about our great-grandparents is that Great-Grandpa William died in 1941. And listed in his obituary are the six names of the Pallbearers. They were Carl Armstrong, Aunt Edith's husband; Charles Burk, Uncle Artie's middle son; Alva Yoder, I think he was a neighbor; Leon Green, Aunt Cora's son; Fred Burk, Elmer's son, and Elvin Burk, our father. Our great-grandparents are buried at the Union City Cemetery. They have a large stone on their gravesite, and the name Burk is carved on it. No dates that I recall. I have no information on Great Grandma's obituary, only that she died in 1945 and is buried beside our Great Grandfather William.

Our Uncle Ira worked at a glass factory in Winchester when we were young. He and his family lived in this green shingled house. And Uncle Ira also loved fishing and camping. Uncle Ira had a camping spot reserved at Lake Celina in Ohio. Uncle Ira and his family went there about every weekend during the summer. When I was 10, I also went with them a couple of times. I remember I did not enjoy it very much, only because it was very different. I do not remember Uncle Ira catching many fish, but he did have a small boat. I never went out in the boat with him. I only remember how hard his wife, Aunt Grace, had to work when they were at this camping place. There was no running water, and shared bathroom facilities were far away.

Aunt Grace had to prepare food on a little camping stove. But Aunt Grace, Uncle Ira's wife, liked to converse with many other ladies around the campgrounds. Years later, Uncle Ira had a pontoon boat, and we went to ride around on it two times, but it only moved about two miles per hour. I do not think Uncle Ira had any life jackets on any of these water vehicles.

But sometime after I joined the military, Uncle Roy rented

out the green shingled house. My sister and I went to school with the people who rented it. Later, after Uncle Roy passed, the property was sold, and the house, barn, cellar, and trees were all removed.

After I was old enough to remember, Uncle Roy and Aunt Marguerite lived in the newer Grandparents Burk's house sometime around 1940. They were married, and they had one daughter. Our great grandparents' more recent house was charming and designed very nicely. I am not sure how large it was, but it had a large kitchen, a music/library room, and a living room. I think it had about three bedrooms, but I am not sure. It had to have been large enough for all those Burk children when it was first built. At the back, it had what they called a fruit cellar and a large back porch. When they built the house, they enclosed the back porch at that time. The back porch had a sink with running water; we could wash and change clothing before entering the house. Aunt Marguerite was a clean fanatic, so I was not inside this house but only a very few times. As a small boy, I was always outside and always had much of the farm dirt on me. I liked Aunt Marguerite, but I was sort of afraid of her. And, of course, I was timid at that age, which probably didn't help. But we did celebrate Christmas there at least a couple of times. Another day, dad, me, and another man were working on something outside, and we all ate lunch in the kitchen. I think dad was combining oats, but I am not sure. As I remember, Aunt Marguerite was a pretty good cook. Their daughter helped prepare the lunch.

At the southwest corner of this Burk house was an apricot tree. I suspect our great-grandfather planted this tree, as it was of good size. Aunt Marguerite made a few pies, even though we ate at their house a couple of times. This apricot tree was the one I remembered most of all. Mainly because, when we baled hay at Uncle Roy's place, we would take a break from baling and pick and eat these apricots when they were ripe and ready to eat. We ate many of them because they were so good, and of course, we took several home to mom, and she made pies with all that we did not eat on the way home. Our family ate lots of fresh ones too. These apricots were delicious. They were sweet and had never been sprayed with any chemicals. And rarely did any have any bugs or worms inside. And if they did, we would just throw it away.

According to records from other relatives, Uncle Roy lived on the original Burk property. The road it was on is now called Base Road. It was our Great Grandparent (Bill + Barbara's) property for many years before our grandfather was born. Our great-grandparents were farmers. Our great-grandparents were married in 1874 and probably moved on to this property around that time. Our grandfather was born in December 1889. Uncle Roy, granddad's oldest son, was born in May 1911, Uncle Ira, their middle son, was born in 1915, and our father, their youngest son, was born in June 1917. Our dad mentioned visiting our great-grandparents at their farm, but dad never went into detail about any of his relatives.

We know seven children were born to our great-grandparents. Probably some of them lived in this house, I don't know when the children were born, or their ages, but in those days boys moved and went to work for other people. Plus some of the William Burk children may have been married while our Great-Grandparents were alive, and they probably lived in their own homes. We know our granddad was married in 1910, but I don't know when he moved to the RR4 address. Leon Green also lived in this house. He was their nephew. There were a couple of other children who also lived with them. I never knew who they were or why they lived with our great-grandparents. The builders built the original house on a rock foundation, which was quite a distance from the road. The barn sat between this house and the county road back then. Late 20's or 30's that house caught fire and burned completely down. Then a new house was built closer to this Base road, with a large back porch and apple cellar. It was a large, lovely house. There were a couple of other small buildings there, too, one for the chickens and one for the pigs. The fire never damaged the barn. Uncle Roy added an addition onto the barn later on.

Down the road lived a disabled gentleman. His name was Tip because his last name was Tipple. He helped Uncle Roy some. He helped us bale hay when we were baling hay at Uncle Roy's farm. Tip had no regular job. And across the road from Uncle Roy's house was a family who had built a fishing pond behind their barn. Uncle Roy took me over there to fish two times. We didn't catch much. Several times I helped Uncle Roy do other farm chores. He had sheep, pigs, and cows. He sometimes needed help to trim sheep's toenails and move the pigs around, and I milked his cows for a couple of weeks once when he made a trip to California. But dad wanted me to be helping him and mom instead of assisting Uncle Roy. Dad and Uncle Roy sometimes had slight differences, but they always worked things out. I said before that we all worked together when baling the hay. Dad also combined Uncle Roy's oats and wheat for him. Uncle Roy had no combine at that time. Uncle Roy was a good guy.

When we baled hay for Uncle Roy, usually the temperature was pretty warm, often hot! We always carried a large Thermos of drinking water containing some ice when we started baling in the twine holder box on the baler. We usually had a drink from it when we needed to change wagons. But the refreshing thing was Aunt Marguerite, Uncle Roy's wife. Aunt Margueite would bring sandwiches and cold drinks out into the field for us in about the middle of a hot afternoon while we were baling hay. She drove a beautiful 1951 Kaiser automobile, green and white. It was a wonderful break for us. She notified dad and the other helpers to come out to the field after they finished emptying the wagon they were unloading to enjoy these refreshments. The refreshments were a real treat. Then I mentioned to mom what Aunt Marguerite had done, so mom started bringing out refreshments to us when we were baling hay for dad at the 80-acre farm.

   We all worked together like this for many years. But after I graduated from high school, I worked for a construction company and only helped with farming when I could. And later, I had to go into the military. Mom told me a little about what was happening in her letters after I left. Sadly, Uncle Roy died while I was in Vietnam, at 55 years of age. I said before that I had milked Uncle Roy's cows. But when Uncle Roy died, dad had to come and milk all of Uncle Roy's cows until they could sell the cows. That was hard for dad to milk his own cows and then go to Uncle Roy's and milk his. Dad did not finish milking until 10 am. And then he had to start early in the afternoon, doing the milking to get all the cows milked. And this was seven days a week. Dad said he had to milk Uncle Roy"s cows for about a month, after Uncle Roy had died. And dad milked about 38 each morning and afternoon. Dad's milking setup was much more convenient and more manageable than Uncle Roy's. Luckily dad and Uncle Roy both had mechanical milking machines. Dad told me that milking all those cows exhausted him.

   Another thing I remember about Uncle Roy was when dad and I worked with and for him one day. When it became time for lunch, Aunt Marguerite was unavailable and could not prepare lunch for us. Usually, Aunt Marguerite would prepare lunch for us while working in the field or whatever we were doing. But this time, Uncle Roy took dad and me to the bowling alley restaurant in Union City for lunch. That was the very first restaurant I had ever eaten inside. Eating in that restaurant is something I will never forget. I liked Uncle Roy. He taught me a lot too. Granddad taught me many things about working metal and how to enjoy life.

   By helping with the farming with dad and mom, I only

slightly remember how things worked out after I went to work for the construction company. I helped when I was home, but I was on construction jobs during the warmer months for two years and was only home on weekends. I had a younger brother who helped dad and mom when I was away. I do not know how dad and mom got things done after I joined the military. I hope my brother helped some. I wanted to be on the farm but needed a weekly paycheck to acquire cash or savings. Indeed I would have purchased land and farmland after saving enough for a down payment. Working on construction was the only way to enable me the opportunity to gain a future. But, the Military Draft changed many of my ideas for the future. I knew at the time of my graduation that the Military would be coming for me. I was healthy and had a younger brother who could help with farming. There was no excuse for me to avoid any Draft notice.

Tractors

Dad purchased a Farmall "H" tractor in the late 1940s. While we lived at the 39-acre property. Farmall "H" tractors were manufactured from 1943 to 1952. I know it was a used tractor when he purchased it, but I do not know the manufacture year of this specific tractor. It was considered a two-bottom plow tractor. Around the early 1950s, when dad took on farming the Shaw farm, dad purchased a Farmall "M" tractor. It was a more significant-sized tractor than the Farmall "H." The Farmall "M" tractors were also manufactured from 1943 to 1952. The Farmall "M" was considered a three-bottom plow tractor. I used the "H" for many of the usual farm activities in my younger years, such as hauling manure, working some plowed ground, etc. Dad used it for many daily things, even pulling the hay baler. The farm hay mower would only fit this tractor.

Dad used the "M" for plowing the ground, and I came along driving the "H" with the drag and other equipment to level the dirt because big clods could develop as the land dried out. The clods of dirt could become rough to drive over when preparing the soil for planting. Plus, this process helped the earth retain some of its moisture. But when planting time came, I used the "M" to pull the disk, cultipacker, drag, and harrow to break the soil and make it easier for the new crops to be planted. Preparing the land like this was necessary for planting, cultivating later on, and reducing weed production. Then dad used the "H" to pull the seed planter. Dad used this piece of equipment to plant corn and soybeans too. I was not tall enough to get the fertilizer and seed into the planter. It sat too high off the ground for me. And I am sure I could never have driven the planter, making the straight rows like dad wanted. But nowadays, this type of planting and tilling of the soil has all changed.

I do not remember the exact year, but dad had taken the Farmall "M" into the shop in Fort Recovery to rebuild the engine so it could produce more power. If I remember correctly, the "M" had about 30 horsepower when it was new. The shop somehow increased that to 44 horsepower. When dad and the mechanic were working and tuning it, I was allowed to go into the parts counter to get some of the needed parts to complete this job. We would never be able to do that today, probably because of insurance. I do not know if they entirely rebuilt the engine completely or not. But when they finished, I drove that tractor home from the shop, about 25 miles. The engine definitely had more power, and they increased the RPMs it put out. The ground speed was breakneck. Everything worked pretty well until the "M" broke an axle not long after they had done the work to the engine. Dad had that fixed, and then the axle broke the second time. The increased horsepower was more than the axles were designed for. Now, dad didn't want to gamble on having more problems because repairs took more valuable time than dad wanted. So dad and I went to a field where the Farmall company was using a used Farmall "400" tractor to plow the ground. This "400" was a more powerful tractor than the "M." Dad traded the "M" for the "400". The Farmall "400" had newer options on it, but it used much more fuel to operate than any of dad's previous tractors. Dad complained about this. But the more recent tractor was great for pulling the hay baler, although we rarely used it for that. We almost always used the "H" or Uncle Roy's F-20 to pull the hay baler. The "400" had a live PTO, which meant the baler would keep running when the land travel stopped. The other tractors did not have this option. The hay baler did not need such a powerful "400" tractor to pull it. The Farmall "400" was the primary tractor dad used when I entered the military. But one time, when I came home on leave from the Navy, dad had just purchased a new International "706" tractor. I think he traded the "400" in on it. I do not remember driving the "706" on the farms. But I know dad really liked that International "706" tractor. While I was in the military, dad traded the Farmall "H" for a Farmall Super "M." I said these tractors were Farmall until the International Company purchased Farmall. Now International has become part of the Case manufacturing company.

The Ford 8N

I am trying to remember my age, or the exact year, but one day, dad and I went to Cincinnati, Ohio, to pick up a load of fertilizer. And on the way home, we saw a Ford "8-N" tractor for sale. It looked good and already had a manure loader installed on it. I have no idea what the price was, but it seemed fair. Then we went home and unloaded the fertilizer off the truck. A day or two later, while I was in school, when I came home, dad had gone back, purchased that Ford tractor, and hauled it home in his truck. I remember helping dad unload it off his truck.

Dad purchased this tractor chiefly for cleaning the lower barn area and loading the manure spreader. This area under the barn is where the cows slept and had a limited distance between the concrete floor and the bottom of the main barn floor up above. This sleeping area used by the milk cows usually built up fairly quickly during the winter because each evening, we would need to add more straw for the cattle to sleep on to keep them as clean as possible. All this buidl-up of straw, and cattle waste, meant we needed to clean this barn sleeping area about every fifteen days. It required most of a day, about 25 manure spreader loads. When we first moved to the 80-acre farm, dad had a horse-drawn manure spreader. But it was pulled by dad's tractor. It was pretty old, but it worked. It was not long before dad purchased a new manure spreader. It was bigger and spread the manure much better out in the field. It was pulled by the Farmall "H." After we started using the Ford tractor to load the manure, this little tractor made it much easier to operate to clean the waste out of the lower part of the barn. Before purchasing the Ford tractor, dad and I had been loading the old manure spreader by hand but loading it by hand was a tough job. Several times dad and I cleaned the barn and loaded the manure spreader by hand with pitchforks.

Dad sometimes had other things which needed to be done. I had no complaints, I could load the spreader myself, but it was hard work, and the manure was heavy. I remember breaking many fork handles because I would try to pick up too much of a load each time. But I appreciated this new mode of using the Ford tractor for hauling manure. I very much enjoyed it. After getting used to this little tractor, I could move 30 manure spreader loads from under the barn in one day. That was usually enough to clear all the manure inside the barn sleeping area, where all the cows slept. Dad always wanted the barn to be kept reasonably clean because sometimes the weather would rain for a long time and would not allow the tractor and spreader to get out into the fields for a few days. The cow's sleeping area had to have new straw bedding placed every night to keep the cows as clean as possible. The buildup of bedding, and cattle waste, needed to be removed periodically. We could haul it out onto the field, and the manure spreader would scatter it over the land in a somewhat equal amount over all the area. It provided a large amount of natural fertilizer for future crops.

We usually cleaned the chicken house manure only about once a year. We had to carry all the chicken manure out of the chicken house to the manure spreader outside by hand. There was no way of getting a tractor inside this chicken house. We also applied some chicken manure to the garden area, as it has more fertilizer value than ordinary cattle manure.

When we moved to the 80-acre farm in February of 1951, it had a large, beautiful house, a chicken house, a large 40 ft by 80 ft bank barn. A bank barn is sort of like a two story barn. It has a flat lower level, and then a ramp of approximately 6 in height to reach the upper part of the barn, which is about six feet above the lower floor.. These ramps widths depended on how large the barn was, and how long the owner wanted. This farm had an older building, which had corn cribs on each side for holding ear corn for the animals. The other building was the brooder house that dad had slid down the road from the 39-acre farm. All buildings were painted white and were in good condition. The big house had gray asbestos siding with white trim around the windows. It was an attractive farm property.

Combines

Dad always used the Farmall "M" to pull the combine. The first combine dad had was a used International #62. Then he traded it for a new International #64. The #64 could handle the weeds much better and was operated totally by hydraulics. I never operated either of these combines out in the field. I started the combines a couple of times so that dad could make adjustments. I remember crawling inside the #62 to change the grain screens because that required a small person to straddle the straw racks, I think I was about 10 years old. I tore my clothes doing this because the straw racks inside were worn very sharp from use. It required a couple of hours to complete this change. The screens needed to be changed because dad was going to combine Sweet Clover for a neighbor. I rode in the grain hopper while dad was harvesting the sweet clover. When dad was about half-finished, the chain broke on one of the elevators and carried dirty seed back into the grain hopper. I stopped dad and showed him the problem. Dad fixed the chain and proceeded to finish harvesting the seed. Then we had to change the screen inside again. I will never forget this. We needed to start and run the #62 combine a few minutes before I could get inside, because rats had made nests inside it. There were no rats inside when I climbed in. I was about ten. Later, dad traded the International #64 combine for a self-propelled International #406 combine. We never needed to change any screens in the #64 combine. I remember driving the #406 a lot during the summer harvest that year. I do not remember driving it for the harvesting of soybeans. But I remember dad doing extra combining for neighbors who did not own a combine. It was an excellent machine to operate. As I mentioned before, I think it was 1972 when dad purchased another new combine. It was a different manufacturer. I believe it was a New Idea combine. I know it had a lot of automatically controlled devices for its operation. Dad had become very ill about the end of 1972, and was unable to operate this new combine but only a few hours.

In the fall of that year, after the dealer delivered this new combine, dad tried to adjust this piece of equipment, but then he became much more ill and could no longer operate it. I returned to Indiana to help with the harvest in the autumn of 1972. I made several adjustments to this machine. It worked well before I had to leave to return to California. It had snowed quite a lot one day, and I did not think I could combine any more grain for several days. That is why I decided to return to California. I felt I needed to get back to my work there, and I was worried about my wife being alone and caring for all our responsibilities at our home in California. Sadly, dad passed away about two months later. I do not know what mom did with dad's farming equipment after dad died.

The Old Corn Crib

This building was a little small. The size of each crib for corn was about 6 ft wide, 28 ft long, and about 12 ft high. Between the corn cribs was an area for storage, about 12 ft wide and the length of the building. Dad usually stored his big truck in this area. Earlier, I had mentioned dad replacing the 41' Dodge truck with the 54' Dodge truck. Before dad traded trucks, dad had built a new truck bed for the 41' truck. The new truck bed had a 3" angle iron all around the outside. These angle irons held the contemporary sideboards and protected the flooring from getting damaged from use. The new truck bed was 8 ft wide and 16 ft long. It could hold about 300 bushels of corn. Dad also saved the wood from the old truck bed. Later, dad wanted to build a bin to hold oats in the upper portion of this old corn crib building. We used the old truck bed flooring for the bottom of this oats bin. I remember helping dad get that lumber up above the cross joists. Then we put the old sideboards up there too. I helped nail some of the floorings in place. I cannot remember how the sideboards were held in place, but the front, back, and sides were from the old truck bed. It made a nice, reasonably large bin for storing oats. We filled it with oats at harvest time. We used a grain elevator to carry the oat grains into the bin. But the dust was terrible, and lots of it. Dad was harvesting out in the field, and I was up in this bin, shoveling the grain to the back of the container because the grain elevator could not reach that far. Mom was watching the wagon as it was unloading for any problems. These oats were used for the cattle's feed later on and usually mixed in with the corn. But this corn crib building did not hold enough corn for all dad's animals. Dad put up a temporary corn crib once, but it was hard to get the corn out of later on. Plus the temporary corn crib exposed the corn to all the foul winter weather. But this old corn crib building had doors on each end. We needed the doors to the west to allow access to get the truck in and out and also access to the corn. The doors to the east were going to be used to allow animals to enter and exit. Dad made a cement ramp going down out of these doors. But the ramp proved too steep for any animal to climb up or down, or even dad or myself. Then we only opened these doors periodically to allow fresh air to flow through. This building was pretty old and maybe older than the barn. Dad had cut areas in the roof on each side to allow for the filling of the corncribs by using the grain elevator. About 15 years ago, 2007, our mother had new metal siding installed over the old siding to protect the building and installed a new front door.

About 1952 dad purchased a hammermill somewhere, and for quite some time, dad and I would use some of the corn and oats from this supply to enable us to grind feed for the milk cows' food. The hammer mill was connected by a big flat belt connected to the tractor's belt pulley. The tractor engine would run at top RPM engine speed, turning the hammermill as fast as possible. Corn and oats were put in the back of the pickup truck and backed up as close as possible to the hammermill. Dad would feed the corn and oats into the hammermill, and I would bag it after it was ground. We usually ground about a five-day supply each time. It did not take much time, approximately 45 minutes. Dad always wanted the cows to have fresh ground food to eat during their milking time.

I mentioned the oats being stored in the old corncrib, up above the truck, which was usually parked there. Also, up in the big barn on the northwest corner was an area made to hold more oats and other small grains but no ear corn. It had an entryway to access the storage bins. There were three storage bins in this area. Dad used these to store more oats for the cattle. Dad needed lots of oats for the cattle feed. Filling these bins at harvest time was very difficult at first. Then dad cut holes in the tops of these bins to make them easier to fill. We stored oats in each of the three bins, and sometimes we filled the entranceway by shoveling the oats into the walkway. After dad cut the holes, we could use the elevator to move the grain to the upper floor to fill these three bins. It made life much easier for us. And if you know anything about oats, they create lots of oat dust when handling them. It was tough and dusty to get into any oat bins and push the oats back to the unreachable corners. I would tie a handkerchief over my nose to keep the dust out of my lungs. After an hour, the handkerchief would be black from the dust. Mom wanted to get into the bins and do this, but I would never let her. It was hard work, dusty, and dirty. I would not let mom do it.

The Hog Barn

Dad wanted to build a new building. There was plenty of space for this, just northeast of the big barn. Dad wanted a large corn crib on one side of that building and room for animals on the other part, with some storage up above the animals. We put hay and straw on the loft above the animals' sleeping area each year because we needed it for the animals during winter after we completed the second part of this building. Dad had all the measurements in his head. He had no blueprints. I marvel at how dad knew how he wanted to build and utilize such a building. Dad was a genius! To this day, I still wonder how he decided to put up part of this building one year, it was 1952 when dad started the construction, and he put up the rest later in 1953. And I wonder how he knew to use the three boards nailed together rather than using 6x6s or 8x8s as most builders used. The wood that dad had cut at grandad's place a year or two before was used to construct this new building. But almost all the construction wood in this building is Elm, a hardwood after it has dried. How did dad have these figures, measurements, and ideas in his head? I wonder when and how he learned this.

I never found any measurments for this building or anything else dad built in all of dad's notes and papers. Uncle Roy, dad, and I poured a slab of cement about 6 ft wide and 40 ft long, with recessed bolts in the cement to bolt the bottom wood structures for the corn crib part, the first year. Grandad had a cement mixing machine that we used. The mix was five shovels of gravel, one shovel full of sand, and one shovel full of cement. Dad purchased the cement material from a store in Greenville, Ohio. I don't remember where dad bought the sand and gravel for the foundation, but it may have been from the same store where he purchased the cement. I only remember it being there in a big mound.

For the second part of this building, the following year, we mixed all the cement with the same mixing machine for the foundation and floor for this section. I think Uncle Roy helped with this part of the building. After the cement was dry, dad laid cement blocks up for part of the walls and wood above the cement blocks to reach the roof. And on the insides of the cement block walls, dad installed bolts to partition off different areas for the other animals to keep them separated. On the outside walls on the animal side, dad had left two 8-foot regions to allow being able to get the tractor inside to help clean the area. A cement block wall was inside to keep the animals enclosed and out of the center part of the building. Openings on this inside wall permitted entry to the animals for feeding and bedding from the center area. We used this center area, the space between the corncrib and animals, to store farm machinery and tractors. Sometimes, we used it to hold extra straw. Also, most of the time, the very east end usually had baby calves in a pen for a couple of months each year. Because this building had a cement floor, the floor could be washed if needed. But even with animals in this center section, we usually had enough room to store the manure spreader. But all cement for this building was mixed by us, using grandad's mixer. Dad also used grandad's mixer to mix the mortar between the cement blocks.

Uncle Roy did help build the first part of this new corn crib. I helped dad build as much of this new structure as possible, but I had difficulty driving nails into the hardwood. At least I could hold the wood in place while dad nailed it. The interesting thing, which was genius on dad's part, was that he placed three 2X8s, fixed together, across the top about every 16 feet, and they extended out to the south about 2 feet. Dad was planning to use these beams to support the roof and the beams to hold the building together for the 2nd part. They worked perfectly to tie the top together after completing the 2nd part. He slanted the roof just the way he wanted. When dad finished the corn crib part, the first year, we filled it with ear corn for the animals.

Dad always had pigs too. So the following year, Uncle Roy came to help us again, and we poured a new cement foundation to increase the size of this building to house the pigs across from the new corn crib. This extra part was connected with the corn crib part, built the year before, by connecting to the 2X8s at the top of the corn crib. The two sections, the corn crib and the animal side section, were joined by nailing more 2X8s together and extended across the center aisle section. Then dad covered the entire structure with a metal roof, matching the previous year's corn crib roof. Construction of this newer part of this building used more of the wood dad had cut from grandad's trees the years before. I had never seen anyone do any structure like this, but nowadays, manufacturers use laminated lumber for construction. Dad did this 50 years earlier by nailing the wood together. That was dad's style of lamination. Dad was certainly innovative. And doing it this way, he could build this new building all by himself and did not need a contractor. Yes, I helped as much as I could. Uncle Roy helped, and maybe granddad too. This new structure had a loft and storage space above the pig's area for hay, lots of straw, grain, and other farm supplies. This new building had cement block walls about 4 ft high to house the pigs and could easily be washed down when needed. Dad had made allowances for partitioning off the area for different needs. This way, we could separate the baby pigs from the larger pigs. Because the larger pigs would eat all the food, and the little ones would get very little. Any manure accumulated in the partitioned part of this building had to be manually loaded into the manure spreader.

The cement we used for the building's foundation we mixed by hand with grandad's cement mixer. But the cement floor in the center was poured later, and dad used Redi-Mix Concrete inside. Doing things this way saved a lot of time and labor.

Redi-Mix made the job so much easier. I helped screet the extra cement and level it off. The year after this building was completed, dad made holes in the corn crib's roof to enable the use of the grain elevator to fill this corn crib. Dad truly knew how to manage, accomplish, build, and plan for his future needs. Dad was the most competent man I have ever known.

The 80 Acre Barn

The big barn on the 80-acre farm had moisture damage and rot on the south end of the building, especially on the 12'X12' beam, which runs from east to west. This beam is 40 feet long. It runs from one side of the building to the other side. It was damaged because the siding on that side was old, leaking, and dad wanted to replace it. The exposure to the weather had rotted the wooden beam. Dad hired Art Dull to come in with jacks to jack up the barn's end and help dad put in a new replacement beam. They had to order a particular order from the sawmill for one piece of wood, 40 ft long. It required a specific straight tree to get a log that long. It took some time, but they finally got one. Then the day came, and they started to install the new beam. Well, they could not get that beam in place for some reason. It just would not fit correctly. I was there helping but did not know what they were talking about. They had to cut the new beam in half and then bolt it back together. It worked out well. Then we had to put the cross woods up the end of the building to hold the siding. These were bolted into place. We did not have electric impact drills then, only wood-bit drills, which had to be hand-cranked. I remember cranking, drilling holes, and tightening bolts. Dad and someone else installed these, as it was dangerous work, and dad would not let me hold the ends, only the two lowest ones. But I could pass up bolts and new pieces of wood.

After this was completed, dad installed all new siding on that end of the barn. I am amazed at how dad did all this. And the south end of this barn, being a bank barn, is very tall. Dad had a set of 40ft wooden extension ladders. To reach the top of the south end, up by the roof, dad had to park the big truck there and put the 40ft ladders on the floor of this truck to reach the top. Forty feet up like that, and on top of the truck, dad had nerves of steel! That is a long way up, and dad used no safety protections. Then, after dad got finished, dad painted everything. There was no paint-spraying equipment being used at that time. Dad had to hand brush everything using a 4-inch brush and oil-based paint. And two coats too. This was a big job.

Below this beam at floor level and down to the cement foundation, it was about another 7 feet. Before removing all the jacks, dad replaced the walls with cement blocks. Cement blocks would never rot or need replacing and could be painted. And when dad dropped the building back down onto the cement blocks, these walls were very strong, much stronger than wood. I marvel at how dad knew about these things and how he knew how to do all of these things by himself. Yes, I helped some, but I was a kid. I could mix mortar, handle some hand tools, and help with supplies, but I would like to know if I was much help. I could never lay cement blocks as dad did. Dad worked every day on these things while I was in school. And we also had to set some things aside when it came time to milk the cows and farm in the fields. Dad was a super patient person. Especially with me. Because he tried to teach me many things, But I was hard-headed, which probably caused extra stress for dad. Dad replaced all these lower walls around the big barn building with these cement block walls. Finishing all this work took at least two years and some of the third year.

I just remember how nice it looked and how much easier it was to clean the manure out of the bottom of the barn after removing all the jacks and equipment. Dad painted all these block walls green and white, with some kind of special paint, in the milking parlor. I don't remember the dates and years, but I know some jacks were still under the barn for some time, around 1955. Sometime after I was in the military, dad removed a small old wooden wall in the middle of the barn, which ran the whole width of the barn. This old wall held up the hay manger in the middle part of the barn. He replaced this old wall with a new one made up of cement blocks. He had also installed a hopper wagon bed on this wall to hold a more significant amount of cow feed for the milk cows. By then, he was taking the milk cow's feed to the grain elevator to have it ground. Doing this was easier for dad, and he could haul more considerable amounts of feed for their food, which would last longer. Using the hammer mill was hard to do if there was only one person. Having the feed ground at the elevator did away with needing to use the hammer mill. Dad had installed a hopper wagon bed under the upper barn floor because it was slanted, and the food would automatically slide down to the feed door. Dad also cut an area on the upper floor that lifted, and the food could be dumped directly from the pickup truck into the hopper bed below. Dad was constantly upgrading his business and making things easier for himself and my mom's future. Dad was always thinking and working.

This big barn was 40' X 80' at the foundation sight. And as I had mentioned, it was pretty tall, with the typical sloping roof for barns. There were man doors at each end of the feed way. It ran through the middle lower part of this barn. In the cement feed way floor, at the south end of this feed way was a hole about 3 feet deep. At the bottom of this hole was the water pipe, which ran outside the building to fill the cattle's drinking troughs. Also, at the bottom of this hole was a pipe valve with a little drain tap on the side. This valve could be turned off at any time but was always on in the summertime. But during the cold winters, we would reach down to this valve, turn the valve off, and open the little drain on the side to drain the water out of the pipe above the floor. Failure to do this during the cold winters could cause pipes to freeze. And usually, the lines would burst if they were frozen hard. Dad showed me how to do this shortly after we moved to the 80-acre property. Dad would ask me if I drained the pipe on cold winter nights before we went to the house for the night. I never failed to do that.

This big barn had several doors. Below were two person doors, about 4 feet in width, one at each end of the feed way. There was another man's door in the milking parlor to go in and out of the milkhouse. The east side had a 3-foot wide door to allow the milk cows in for milking. Then on the south end of this barn, there were two 10 ft doors to enable the tractor to enter when necessary. Of course, we used the door going into the bedding area of the milk cows, most of all because that was the door where we used the tractor to remove the bedding and waste excreted from the cows. These entrance areas had doors on each of them, which helped keep some freezing cold air out during winter. The upper part of this barn had two big doors, 20 ft wide by 14 ft tall, as I remember the approximate sizes. The back side of the barn also had these big, same-sized doors, but they were rarely opened, only when we had put fresh hay in the barn. One of the front doors had a small man door cut into it to allow going in and out without needing to open the big doors. These big doors at the top of the barn bank were tough to open when the wind blew. Sometimes it took two of us to get them open. And during the wintertime, when the wind was blowing, and we needed these doors open, the wind would force a tremendous amount of wind current to the lower part of the barn. That is where we were milking the milk cows. But usually, we did not need those doors open at milking time. But I loved this barn. When we first moved there, there were lots of Bats in the upper part of the barn. They were filthy because they defecated all over the straw and hay. Dad did not like this, so I tried to force them out of the center part of the barn, but that did not work out. Somehow the Bats moved out of the barn on their own later on.

Dad painted all these buildings all by himself. Everything was painted white, and dad kept everything painted well. The roof dad also painted with aluminum paint. Dad had nerves of steel to climb all over these buildings and never had any fall protections. I marvel at how dad could do all that he did. I never knew of anything dad may have been afraid of.

A year or two later, after the hog barn was completed and dad completed the work on the big barn, dad wanted to pour cement around the big barn. Dad purchased cement from Redi-Mix companies, as I mentioned before. It was to help keep the animals cleaner, especially during the wintertime. We poured the first section of cement after the hog barn building was all finished. Dad had been wanting to sell Grade "A" milk. There were three grades of milk that the creamery purchased from farmers. Grade "C" milk was from farmers that had no refrigeration. Grade "B" milk was from farmers with some type of refrigeration, but their milking area was not as clean as the grade "A" milk. Selling grade "A" milk meant that the milk cows had to be washed every time they came into the milking parlor before milking. The entire milking parlor had to be cleaned after each milking and inspected every so often for cleanliness. Daily spraying of an insecticide to ensure there were no flies or bugs. It pretty much fumigated the area. No animals could be close to the milking parlor unless a concrete wall separated the two regions. There were many requirements for farmers selling grade "A" milk. The area outside the big barn was mostly mud at first. The excessive mud and dirt issues were why dad wanted to pour the cement. The cement kept the cows' feet and legs much cleaner.

The first section dad poured was about 10 feet wide along the north/south wall on the east side of the big barn. Dad and I spent a lot of time leveling and shoveling dirt. Dad had to purchase some gravel from Clyde Byrum to help with the leveling. Then a Redi-Mix truck came, backed up, and put their loads along this area. Dad and I leveled it off using 2x4s. We did not use a trowel because dad did not want the cement to become slick. After all, the animals could slip. And this cement worked out well. After we finished that section, we leveled the barn's south end, the east/west area. And we poured another 10-foot wide section with Redi-Mix there. Then the following year, we went around this area with another 10-foot section of cement. Over the next couple of years, Redi-Mix cement covered the back lot area used by the cows. As a result, the cows only required less time washing them when they came for milking.

I am thinking between the lines. I wonder where our father learned his building construction knowledge. My dad's older brother, Uncle Roy, knew about construction because he built a new garage and a large extension onto his barn. I think it was in the late '40s. And as I had mentioned earlier in this book, Uncle Ira, dad's middle brother, built the house across the road from dad's farm west of Union City, which was in the mid-'40s. Uncle Ira also had construction knowledge which he learned from someone. And as I have mentioned, dad had construction knowledge about how to build this new hog barn. All three of the Burk brothers learned construction knowledge from somebody.

All three Burk boys probably helped build the new house after the old one burnt down on the original Burk property. The road now is the Base Road. I do not know and never will because all of them are deceased, but I have come to this idea. Across the road from dad's childhood home, which Anis and Ollie Burk owned, lived a man; dad called Uncle Johnny Price with his wife. Our great-grandmother was Barbara Ellen Price Burk, I am sure there was a connection, but I do not know what it was. I think Johnny Price and Barbara Ellen Price Burk were brother and sister. I did not know much about Uncle Johnny Price, but I think he was a farmer. I only remember meeting him twice. One time we went to their home around the Christmas Holidays. I am trying to remember why dad, mom, and us kids went or if we ate there. The other time, dad and I drove to their house, and dad and Uncle Johnny talked extensively. It may have had something to do with building the new hog barn. It may have had something to do with crops, seeds, and fertilization. Maybe Johnny Price purchased some fertilizer from dad; I do not know. I am sure the Burk boys helped Uncle Johnny Price construct barns and other buildings that farmers wanted to build around the area in their earlier years. It will always be a mystery to me!

Dad's automobiles and trucks

When we moved down to the 80-acre farm, mom and dad owned a 1939 Plymouth automobile. Dad had a two-wheeled trailer for hauling feed and other farm supplies, and dad needed to use the car to tow it around. Not very convenient. We had lived on this farm for about a year when Uncle Hank had a 1949 Dodge pickup truck for sale. Uncle Hank had his own automobile body shop business at that time. I do not know how Uncle Hank acquired this truck, but he sold it to dad. It was a great little truck, and we used it for everything. It always ran well, hauled gobs of things, and was so convenient all around the farm.

Someplace dad had found an air compressor that fit into the head of this engine. When you take out one of the sparkplugs and screw the threaded end of the compressor into the head, where the spark plug was, it would pump lots of air. Then start the engine. It would run on five cylinders and provide enough air to inflate down tires. We had to use this many times. On this little truck, we put a canvas over the backend to haul the raccoon hunting dogs around during the hunting season. One time when we had come home from hunting, dad had left the parking lights on all night by accident. No matter, this little engine started the following day. Dad had to pull grandpa's F-12 tractor to get it started once, and he used this little truck. That was a massive job for this truck, but the tractor finally started. This little truck was a jewel! We must have used this little truck a million times to pull wagons and trailers. I am still wondering how many miles we put on it. For a few years, before I was 16, I drove this little '49 Dodge truck around the local roads many times. I never went any distance driving this truck. When I hauled grain to the elevator in town, I always pulled the wagon with a tractor because I was not legally old enough to operate any automobile or truck on the roadway.

When I was 16 years old, our school raised money for our class trip. One method to help raise money was picking tomatoes and taking them to Indianapolis to sell them. I used the "H" and trailer to work in the field, gathering the tomatoes, cleaning them, and placing them in baskets. Then we put them in the back of this little truck, and I drove it to Indianapolis to sell them. This idea was our teacher's, and she went with us to Indianapolis. Everything went well, except when we arrived at the selling place, our teacher wanted more money for the tomatoes than anyone would pay. People looked and asked but would not pay that much. So we ended up bringing them back home with us. Then I had to take them home, put them in dad's other truck, and take them to the tomato canning factory in town. We could have sold them, but the teacher made a mistake because she wanted a higher price than others were willing to pay. I learned a big lesson. But this little truck was a workhorse!

Later, Uncle Hank found another pickup truck that needed some repairs. Uncle Hank made the required repairs, and then dad purchased it. It was a 1957 International manufactured truck. The truck bed was a little bigger than the '49 Dodge truck.

Dad acquired this truck while I was working on the construction jobs, and I was not home then. It was ok, but it did not have the personality of the little '49 Dodge truck. And later, while I was in the military, dad traded that pickup truck for another International pickup truck. It was able to haul larger weights than either of his other pickup trucks. This truck also came from Uncle Hank because it also needed repairs before dad could buy it. We have a picture of this truck. A long time after dad died, we gave this truck away to a school teacher, who said he would restore it. We don't know what happened to any of these trucks, except the last International.

I had mentioned the 1939 Plymouth automobile dad owned when we moved to the 80-acre farm. Dad had to tow the trailer with this car. Dad also owned the 1941 Dodge 1 1/2 ton truck when we moved. That truck moved us. We had not lived on the 80-acre farm very long before dad traded the '39 Plymouth for a '48 Plymouth automobile. Dad never pulled the trailer with the '48 Plymouth. It was shortly after that time when dad purchased the '49 Dodge pickup truck from Uncle Hank. And then about 1957 dad traded the '48 Plymouth for a 1955 Dodge automobile. This '55 Dodge was a beautiful automobile, blue and white. My mom and dad owned this automobile when I enlisted in the military in 1964. I know dad traded the '41 Dodge truck for the '54 Dodge truck in 1956 because the '54 truck was only two years old then. Not long after we had moved to the 80-acre farm, dad had built a new truck bed on the '41 Dodge truck. The frame on the '41 truck was the same width as the frame on the '54 truck. I have a picture of the '41 Dodge truck with dad and grandad standing beside it. Mom took that picture the day the '41 Dodge truck left our home, and dad and grandad came home with the '54 Dodge truck. And because the frames were the same size, it was pretty easy to move that truck bed from one truck to the other. The '54 Dodge truck was more powerful than the '41 Dodge truck.

But this specific '54 Dodge truck needed many repairs before it was a dependable truck. The previous owner used this truck on a milk truck route, which had a lot of hard use before dad purchased it. But dad worked on it, and then it worked pretty well. Dad never had many problems with it after that. Later, Greg and I sanded and masked everything, and then Greg painted the cab. I had already scraped and brushed the frame and wheels and hand-painted them black over the winter months. It ran and looked pretty good after that for a long time. Sadly, the '54 Dodge truck engine blew a connecting rod as dad was coming home with a load of fertilizer from Cincinnati. Dad had the engine repaired and rebuilt. Dad liked Chrysler products, but I wanted Chevrolet products. He also seemed to like these International pickup trucks. Dad took excellent care of all the trucks, cars, and tractors. We regularly changed the oil in each tractor, checked the coolant/water levels (anti-freeze) in those years, and greased grease fittings each morning before use. I do not remember how the oil got changed in either of the trucks. Dad had the Sinclair garage change the oil and service the cars.

Dad and I lubricated all farm equipment each morning before use. Dad took excellent care of his farm equipment. When we finished planting, we would take the planter and grain drill apart, clean all parts, lube them to keep the rust away, and have them ready for the following year. During the winter, we would check the disks for wear and replace any blades necessary. Plowshares would be changed or sharpened, and we checked the cultivator shovels and changed any bad ones. Mower and combine sickles were sharpened during the summer, but we usually replaced some of the worn mower sickle bar sections during the winter. Dad said doing maintenance was a "money maker." I learned so very many things from my father! I sure wish he could have lived longer.

One of my favorite memories was when dad had the "41

Dodge truck. And when he was going to Cincinnati to get a load of fertilizer. Yes, I went with him at least a half dozen times. We would leave the farm early in the morning to get to the fertilizer plant a little early because if you got there late, the line would get very long with trucks to pick up their loads. Dad always wanted to be as close to the first as possible. That way, he would get home earlier. Usually, dad would drive down #227 to Middleboro, Indiana, and then take a small country road over to the main highways. And on this country road was a small wooden bridge. I never knew why that bridge fascinated me, but it did. Dad always came home via different routes. The little wooden bridge could not support much weight. That was around the early '50s. I have been down that little country road several times since then, and I am sure the creek is still there, but the little bridge has been replaced. After dad purchased the '54 Dodge truck, I do not remember him going that specific way to Cincinnati. But I liked that '41 Dodge truck. It was what is called a cab over. That truck design means that you sit above the engine when driving. I guess I liked that. Plus, as I am older, I like older vehicles. I like going to old car shows. I never went to any with dad.

Racing

I was about 10 years old when dad and I started going to the automobile races at Pleasant Hill Racetrack, north of Union City. Dad drove his '49 Dodge truck to get us there, about 8 miles each way. It was an oval ¼ mile track. There was no banking around any part of this track. A lot of dirt and dust was created by all the race cars. We usually had quite a bit of dust on us when we got home.

Dad and I always went by ourselves. But later on, I asked dad if I could ask granddad to go with us because I knew he was sitting at home and doing nothing but listening to the ballgame. Our grandmother was in Aunt Edith's nursing home. I thought granddad would like to get out of his house. I enjoyed doing things with him, just like I enjoyed doing things with my dad. And granddad liked going with us too. I loved my granddad and my father very much. There is a picture of the Pleasant Hill race track at the back of this book. Most of these races at Pleasant Hill Racetrack took place on Saturday nights.

After dad and I had been going to Pleasant Hill Racetrack for some time, dad somehow heard about another racetrack not too far from our home. Dad wanted to check it out. It was much more extensive, had a higher class of race cars, and paid more money to race winners. Most of these races took place on Sunday afternoons at a $3/8$"s oval dirt track, Eldora Racetrack at Rosssburg, Ohio. I think this was between 1954 and 1960. Dad and I had gone a couple of times, granddad went a couple of times too, and mom wanted to go with us because she did not like sitting at home alone. There could have been a little jealousy or something on mom's part because she never cared for our granddad. Then dad had to drive his car because now he had four passengers. Mom did not like granddad much, but everyone had a good time. Granddad and I sat in the back seat of the car. But if mom wanted to go, she had to agree to take granddad with us. I remember saying that I wished granddad go with us. Mom decided he could join us, and we went many times and to another different track once in a while, New Breman. And later, mom involved her sister and brother-in-law.

The first track dad and I went to; the races took place at Pleasant Hill on Saturday nights. I do not think mom ever went with us there. There was a lot of dust and dirt. Somehow dad knew of the man who owned this track. We never formally met him, but we would see him there every night they had automobile racing. We always said "Hi" to him. Ironically, years later, this man's daughter became one of my wife Dee's wonderful friends. And she remains an excellent friend today. One of the pictures in this book was given to me by her; which her Uncle had taken at her dad's racetrack, Pleasant Hill. The Pleasant Hill Racetrack was sold and is now a cornfield. But there were other automobile dirt racing tracks around that area in those years. Eldora Racetrack still has racing nowadays. This lady (whose father owned Pleasant Hill Racetrack) now lives in Arkansas. A great young lady and family too. We talk on the phone frequently—beautiful memories of all those experiences.

For a few years, we went to automobile races every weekend. Dad never wanted to go to any of the Nascar-type races or the Indy-type races. He wanted to spend the money on something other than tickets that allowed entrance. The older dirt tracks had a very reasonable ticket price. And we just liked going to these racetracks. We went to Eldora, New Breman, Winchester, Ridgeville, and others. I followed some of the drivers but could never personally meet them. Most drivers were local and were the same drivers almost every weekend, and the racecars were the same. The race cars usually had a sponsor—an auto dealer or a gas station. A few other businesses sometimes sponsored them with many different names. In the early months of the year, they most all had pretty paint jobs. Later some had many dents, which they had obtained from the weekends before. There were some wrecks, but rarely was anyone hurt, just shaken up. But I do recall, one time at Eldora, a wheel came off of one of the racecars and bounced up into the audience. Sadly, it struck a little girl who died from her injuries. We were always careful to sit in seats far enough from the race track to avoid any problems.

Eldora racetrack was close to where Aunt Icy and Uncle Bob lived. We all started going to the automobile races together, usually on Sunday afternoons, at the Eldora racetrack. We all liked automobile racing. Dad and Uncle Bob always talked a lot about automobile engines. They always spoke about horsepower. We all, Uncle Bob, Aunt Icy, grandad, mom, dad, and I would go on these Sunday afternoons. We all enjoyed our outings.

At another time, a friend we called Stumpy had purchased an old Plymouth from our Uncle Roy, and he tried racing it one Sunday at the Winchester track. He drove it in 2 races, but he didn't do any good. The old car wasn't fast enough.

Aunt Icy and Uncle Bob

Aunt Icy was my mother's younger sister. They lived in Rossburg, Ohio, pretty close to the Eldora racetrack. Mom asked them to go to the automobile races at Eldora with us, and we all went about every Sunday for some time. This was in 1958. We all liked that family. Aunt Icy worked in a lawnmower factory, and Uncle Bob worked for Fram filters manufacturing in Greenville, Ohio. We had a lot in common, because we all liked playing Euchre together. Each time I was home from the military, we visited them and played Euchre, and Aunt Icy usually baked me a cake for dessert to eat while we played the game.

Aunt Icy and Uncle Bob lived on a small property of about 20 acres. Uncle Bob tilled the soil for a while, and then ended up renting the land to a neighbor. They had a few farm animals, but sold the animals after they rented out their property. It seemed dad and Uncle Bob had a lot in common, because Uncle Bob was always asking dad about farming practices. But Uncle Bob gave up farming after dad died. They had a few farm animals but no more livestock after they rented out their property. At one time, Uncle Bob had a tractor but must have sold it because it was gone on our next visit. And at one time, Uncle Bob had a team of pulling horses. We went to see him pull his horses one time. That was a terrible challenge for the horses. We never went to watch his horses pull again, and I think he sold them when he found out they could have been a better pulling team. And lots of competition at these pulling activities. Poor horses.

Pigs

Ida was Uncle Bob's sister who lived close to Aunt Icy and Uncle Bob. She was married to a man named Carl. Carl had several brood sows. Carl was the man who raised baby pigs, and dad purchased these feeder pigs from Carl. Dad arranged to purchase some of Carl's baby pigs. Carl was a nice guy, and had a very nice facility for the brood sows. The feeder pigs were about four weeks old when dad purchased them. Every spring, dad would arrange to purchase about 40 of Carl's baby pigs. We took the pickup truck to Carl's house to haul them home. It was a profitable farming practice for dad. Dad fed the pigs his corn and oats, which fattened the pigs. After about five months the pigs weighed around 200 pounds each. It was then dad would sell them to the pork market. The pork market would supply the slaughterhouses with hogs for the pork meat markets. We slaughtered 3 pigs every winter for our family's consumption. I had names for many of these pigs, and I was sad to see them go away, but later in the year, dad would buy more feeder pigs. This was one of the ways dad made money to keep his farms going and keep us kids with our needed supplies. The raising and selling of the pigs, and the milking of the cows, was dad's best way of earning money. Care and feeding of all dad's animals were why he farmed the land and raised the corn, oats, hay, and wheat. Dad always had it measured out. The hay would be gone by June when the hay-making time rolled around. The oats bins would be empty by July 1st. About all the wheat straw would be used up by July 1st. The corn cribs would be empty around the first of October. Dad had it all figured out!

When Working at Dad's different properties

When dad and I were working at any other property, at lunchtime, when we were working at planting and sowing time, we would need to fill the gasoline fuel cans for the tractors. We had to go back to the 80-acre farm to fill these containers. At first, dad had a 200-gallon gasoline tank sitting on top of the ground. But later, dad dug a big hole and buried a 500-gallon gasoline tank with an electric pump outside to draw the fuel out of this tank. Then it was just like going to the automobile service station. The gasoline pump was furnished by the local Sinclair fuel dealer in Winchester, Indiana. Dad always used Sinclair products from this dealer. And we also knew the fuel dealer's family personally. My sister and I went to school with some of the dealer's children. But dad never put this gasoline in any car or truck; he said this was strictly tractor gasoline.

Of course, we loaded all the gasoline storage cans in the back of the pickup truck to take home for us at lunch time. After lunch we would fill these cans with fuel for the tractors, then take them back with us for the afternoon's work. Some days, mom made sandwiches for me while driving the tractor. I would continue preparing the ground at lunchtime because it took more time to prepare the soil than it did for dad to plant the crops. I could eat the sandwiches while driving the tractor. Dad would fill the gas containers and bring them back after eating. Dad showed me how to take the gasoline from the cans and put it into the gasoline tank on the tractors without needing to use a funnel. I learned how to avoid spilling any, and we could not risk having gasoline drip down on a hot engine. But sometimes, when we went home for lunch, we would need to pick up more seeds or other supplies for that afternoon. Dad knew precisely what was required, and his timing was always perfect. The only thing that got in dad's way was if it started raining, which presented problems. If it rained, dad always had some other work for me to do.

Dad never kept any books or memo pads that I knew of, only the Agrico and the little black book. I am amazed at how dad could remember and organize everything we were doing. And what we needed to get done for the family's benefit. Dad always told me what to do and how to do it as if I was learning something new. Our father was the most intelligent man I have ever known. Our society did not have computers in the 1940s and 1950s, but our dad's brain was just like an organized computer. From one day to the next, he knew what to do and what he wanted to accomplish. He may have stopped working physically, but his brain never stopped. And when it came time to milk the cows, everything would stop in the fields or whatever we were doing, and we would do the milking and other daily chores. Then the farming out in the fields could begin again. Of course, we would work on many other things in the wintertime, such as cleaning, repairing equipment, improving livestock areas, etc. Sometimes in the spring, I would get out in the field for an hour or two before going to school to plow or prepare the soil for planting then do my chores. After finishing my tasks, I would go to the house, grab a bite to eat, wash my face, and then catch the school bus. Some days, I was embarrassed at school because I had farm dirt on my clothes, and I probably smelled. Some days, I stayed home from school to work out in the fields, and mom would write a note for me to take to school the next day, stating that I stayed home to work for my father. Because dad was a farmer, it was an automatic excuse for farmboys if they skip school to work on the farm. I stayed home from school 3 or 4 times each year to help dad with the crops and farming. I always ok'd it with dad the evening before. And he would assign me what needed to be done, if dad was not around that day.

At about 13, I could connect the equipment, fuel the tractor, and do whatever dad had assigned me to do. Even though we milked the cows around 5 pm each day, we sometimes would go back out and work in the field for another hour after we finished the milking. Sometimes dad would go out to the area, but usually me. I took the farming industry very seriously and constantly studied agriculture and how to improve our actions. As a result, it could yield more profit for our labors. Dad did not agree with many of my suggestions, but he at least listened and decided to try some. Some of my tips required more cost to accomplish, but I had studied them, and they could be more profitable after we perfected them. Today many farmers use ideas similar to the ones I had. I was ahead of my time. They would have made dad more profits. But dad always kept many of his ideas the same. Dad had good ideas.

Dad and I saw a neighbor working the ground with that farmer's tractor and equipment. Dad could see the kind of disk, cultipacker, harrow, and drags connected to prepare the earth for planting. I remember looking at the soil after this equipment had done what they wanted it to do. That land was as smooth and refined and almost like powder. Undoubtedly ready for any type of planting of crops. Dad connected his equipment, similar to how we saw, and it changed how he prepared the soil for planting. This change was a big help. Not much of this type of equipment is used today.

Dad and Cousin Fred

Our Great Grandparents' youngest son was Uncle Elmer. When I was around 8 or 9, Uncle Elmer and his wife, Aunt Gertie, lived just down the road a short distance from our Great Grandparent's home, and the green shingled house. Many years before Uncle Elmer lost his left arm in an automobile accident. Uncle Elmer was a farmer, and Aunt Gertie worked at the Union City Memorial Hospital. They had two sons, Richard, who was killed in the military, and Fred. Fred was about ten years younger than my dad. Fred never had to go into the military because farmers were exempt from military service if they were the youngest son of a farmer. At least, this is what my dad told me. Fred was a farmer and took over the farming responsibilities after Uncle Elmer passed away in the early 50s. Uncle Elmer owned a 40-acre farm. He had a few farm animals some of the time.

Around 1953, not long after Uncle Elmer passed, Fred was responsible for farming their farm. Fred wanted to clear a wooded area on this 40-acre property. Fred said it was about 3 acres. It had some large trees and several small ones but many overgrown bushes. Dad and Fred (dad called him "Freddie") cut all of those trees down with dad's two-man crosscut saw. I was helping as much as possible, but I was never big enough to pull the saw to cut anything. I just piled brush on the fires to burn part of the brush and collected firewood. But I did try to pull the saw. Dad laughed and said we needed to wait for Fred. And after the more giant trees were down, they cut the logs with the same saw. And they cut most of the wood, so it could be handled by hand. Dad had a buzzsaw that fit the front of the Farmall "H." It could cut up lots of firewood in one afternoon. I know dad took some of the firewood home with us when we finished for the day. Fred pulled the trailer and wagon back to the worksite with his tractor. I remember them working at this for a couple of months during the wintertime. And I remember there was a lot of water, which we had to work around because of the snow and cold winter. I do not remember how Fred removed the leftover stumps. Of course, later, both Fred and dad invested in chainsaws. They were much faster and easier to work with.

At some point, Fred built a charming small living space above the garage close to the house on this property. I was told it was going to be the space where Aunt Gertie was going to live. Her grandson mentioned that Aunt Gertie never lived in this apartment, but Fred and his wife Wilma lived there for a while. It was a nice place, but small. I do not know how much dad helped Fred build this addition, maybe none, but I think some. I do know for sure.

The main things I remember about Aunt Gertie were two things. First, when dad and I went to work with Fred, she always had me come into her home. Her home was next to the garage. She baked cookies and cupcakes, and I am sure she baked other things too. She always wanted me to come and talk to her and eat cookies and drink a glass of milk. We celebrated Christmas at Aunt Gertie's home. I do not remember how or when.

Another thing I remember about Aunt Gertie was when I was 14. I had my tonsils removed at the Union City Hospital. While she was working there, Aunt Gertie brought me ice cream, jello, and lots of both. They were little cups. But she did not realize that my throat hurt so badly I could not think of eating anything. But I appreciated her for trying to help me. I also remember our family going to their house for other occasions, but I cannot be specific about what they were.

Some years later, after Fred was married and had children, he and his family visited us at the 80-acre property. I saw a picture of him and his family sitting on the sofa in our living room. I do not remember visiting with Fred and Wilma at Christmas after their marriage. But I remember seeing Fred and Wilma at their home just to visit. I remember Fred talking with dad concerning some farm issues.

A couple of years before our mother died, it was 2009, we three children wanted to clean and clear up the barns and around the barn area of the 80-acre property. Our mother moved to another property she owned, and our brother was now living in this house. It took us some time, but we cleaned up and disposed of all the excess trash. There was that 500-gallon fuel tank that dad had buried in the ground. I remember helping dig the big hole by hand, and then the local fuel company installed the pipes and pump to fuel the farm equipment. No one was using it now, and the tank was full of water. We tried digging around it to remove it because we did not want it to begin to leak and contaminate the earth. It was a much bigger project than I thought it would be. But luckily, Fred had a backhoe on his tractor, and he and his son came down and dug the tank out. Then they backfilled the hole.

When we finished doing this, Fred mentioned that if anything ever happened to our mother and the property came up for sale, he wanted his family to purchase it. Fred's family was renting the farming ground and grain bins then. Sadly, our mother passed away in 2012. And because my sister, brother, and I inherited the property, we decided to sell it in 2013. We called Fred's son and asked if they still wanted to purchase the property. They did buy the property, and we did what Fred had asked us to do. Unfortunately, in 2016, Fred accidentally fell to his death while working at the grain bins on this property. He was alone, so no one knew precisely how Fred fell. It is so sad that Fred lost his life there. I remember Fred well and the projects he shared with dad.

One other subject I want to mention, along with this Burk family, is my name. Just south of Uncle Elmer and Aunt Gertie's house was a property owned by Raymond Polley. This is my father's story. When I was born, dad and mom did not have a name thought up. They probably did not know if I would be a boy or a girl then. Somehow dad remembered Raymond Polley, so they named me after Raymond Polley. Dad always called the man Ray. I met Ray a couple of times. He seemed like a lovely man. I am happy to be named after such a good person. My dad's middle name was Leon. I wonder why his middle name was Leon. But anyway, dad and mom made my middle name Leon also.

Dad's Towing

A couple of other things that dad did for me, or rescued me may be more appropriate words, were concerning automobiles. One time I had driven my '51 Chevrolet to Indianapolis for something. I do not recall why I needed to go there. It was the summer of 1959, and I was 16. When I was leaving Indianapolis, it was late evening and almost dark outside. I had taken a couple of friends along. John Ward was one, and I think Dick Watson was the other. But along highway #40, the timing gear went out of the engine on my '51 Chevrolet on the way home. We were able to get the car pushed to a gas station along the highway to get it off the roadway. I called dad, and he and mom came to tow us home. We took the '51 Chevy to Dick's house, where Dick and I replaced the timing gear after a couple of days. Dad had pulled us with his '55 Dodge automobile that evening. Then in late 1961, I sold the '51 Chevy to my sister and purchased a 1955 Plymouth. Dad found this car and wanted me to buy it. It was a good car, but the engine threw a rod on my way home from Fort Wayne, Indiana. I had never hot-rodded that car. We thought someone had worked on the engine before I purchased it. That was in 1961. I called dad, and he came and towed that car back to his house, where we later had it repaired. He had towed me then with his '57 International truck. Then late in 1962, I traded the '55 Plymouth for a 1959 Chevrolet Impala. Several months later, I was working construction in Fort Wayne, Indiana. And once on the way home, I had stopped and cleaned the sediment bulb on the engine and then started driving. I was on highway #67 heading for Muncie. I must not have gotten the glass part sealed adequately, and gasoline leaked down on the hot engine. The engine caught on fire. Of course, I stopped right away. The local fire truck came and put white stuff all over the engine. Of course, it would not run. Then I called dad again, and he came and towed me back to the farm with his '57 International truck. Thank goodness, I never needed him to tow any more vehicles for me. I was not a hotrod driver. I should have checked the sediment bulb for a leak, but I did not. All these things happened from wear and tear, not hot-rodding or rough use.

Dad taught me how to take good care of my vehicles. Dad taught me many things about caring for automobiles. Dad also taught me a lot about caring for farming equipment and tractors. Plus, I spent hundreds of hours driving them and working out in the fields. Dad always said he would rather have good farming equipment with an older tractor pulling it, than have a new tractor pulling old farming equipment. Our father was a brilliant man. He may not have had much schooling, but he sure knew how to manage with what he had. Caring for the equipment was extremely important. Before starting work, we checked each tractor's oil, water, and gasoline and fully greased all the equipment. Sometimes it took close to an hour to grease the combine and the corn picker, even with dad and I both working the grease guns. Sometimes we needed to run the equipment slightly to turn some parts over to reach the grease fittings.

Thinking along the lines of towing, I want to mention some other instances. I mentioned needing to pull grandad's tractor to get it started earlier. Then there were times when we had to pull Uncle Roy's cars, tractors, and machinery to get them going. But the ones I want to tell you about were the ones that happened during the winter when snow was all over the land. And sometimes, the roads were covered with ice. Next to our 80-acre house was a road on the township line, which ran east and west. There was only one family who lived on this road.

When they built this road, whoever made it, only surfaced the road to these people's house and did not extend the surface ½ mile more over to the next road. But they built a nice bridge across Greenville creek on the roadway section they never finished. However, no one ever used this bridge for automobile traffic. The farmers tilling the fields along this road used it some. The roadway had been graded for continuing the gravel surface. Regular gravel was on the surface of the part of the road which had been finished. But the contractor never covered this western half of the road with gravel. During winter, when it snowed pretty often, the snow would cover this section of roadway with deep snow.

A few times, young people would try to get down this road in their car. They mainly wanted to do their parking, necking, etc.! Well, they would get their vehicles stuck in the deep snow. Dad's 80-acre property, about ½ mile away, had a bright night light on a pole that showed all night. It had a photocell that turned off and on according to the light source. After getting stuck, the driver would walk to our house, and wake up dad as they knocked on the door. Dad's bedroom was next to the front door. They would ask dad if he had a tractor and if he could pull their car out of the snow. Yes, he had a tractor to pull them out of the snow. But within a minute or so, dad would call me, wake me up, and say to come downstairs. Then he would tell me to get my winter clothes on, get the tractor out, and pull their car out of the snow. So I would drive around the highway, go down this partial road, hook a chain to their car, and pull them back to the asphalt roadway. I remember doing this probably 5 or 6 times over the years after I was old enough to operate the tractor. Some nights were frigid, especially driving the tractor through the cold air. But I did it and saved dad from needing to get out of his warm bed. And other times, when there was ice on the asphalt highway, vehicles would slide off the road surface and end up in the ditch. They also came to our house for help.

Then I would take the tractor, pull their vehicle out of the ditch, and back onto the roadway. The last time I did this was when dad was very sick, shortly before he passed. A man's car had slid off the highway and into the ditch. I took the tractor out and pulled his car out of the ditch. He proceeded forward about 50 feet and slid back into the ditch. The road surface had a pretty large amount of ice accumulation. I then told the man to leave his car there and come into dad's house, and I would pull him out after about an hour when the road was more clear of the ice. The man went with me, mom fixed him some coffee and toast, and he talked with dad for a while. After about an hour, the man and I went to his car, I connected the chain and pulled him out, and he went on his way. Most of the ice had melted by then. That man would have continued sliding into the ditch as long as the roadway had that much ice covering it. The man needed to wait for some time until the ice melted. I even slid a truck into the ditch once because of the snow and slickness of the road surface. There were other incidents over the years when people had problems with the weather conditions on the roadways. Luckily, no one ever had any injuries or damages to their vehicles.

Other Critters

I remember a couple of summers down by the barn. I made a connection with a crow. I would stand at the south end of the big barn and call him with some sound that I had come up with. It must have resonated a little with this specific crow because it would come and sit on the fence and make its crowing sounds. Dad would laugh, probably at me, but it was an exciting experience. There were gobs of birds then, but not nearly as many nowadays.

Another thing I never understood about dad, most farms have many kinds of snakes and rodents, and most are beneficial.

I do not know if dad was afraid of them or not. I was not, but I did not want to get close to several of them. Many snakes around the waterways on farm properties are poisonous, especially Water Moccasins. But when dad and I were working the land with the tractors, if he ran across a snake, he would stop and chase it toward the tractor I was driving and want me to steer over it and kill it. I really did not want to do this because snakes are very helpful in controlling rodents and unwanted critters. But this one time, he had come across this beautiful, large Blue Racer snake. He kept chasing it toward me, and I finally drove over it and killed it. I have always regretted doing that, but that was what dad wanted me to do. Around our garden were Garter Snakes. Most of them around our garden were no problem and went their separate ways. When we were out raccoon hunting, if we ran across opossums, dad would always kill them. I never knew why. I always thought they were pretty, especially the smaller ones. Most opossums were large during wintertime. They had plenty to eat during the summers. Maybe they killed chickens. I do not know. Shortly after we had moved to the 80-acre farm, dad and I sat out in the field for a couple of nights at night. We sat back to back, holding our 22 rifles. We were watching for a fox. Dad said the fox had killed a baby pig. We never did see any fox. I don't think the fox killed any baby pigs after that because dad put the pigs inside the barn. Dad never cared much for cats, but we always had a few kitties. Most of our kitties had a bad case of distemper (sore eyes). We only fed the kitties milk from the cows. Dad said he did not want to provide food for the kitties. Dad wanted them to be hungry enough to catch some of the rats. They did kill a lot of the mice. We always had plenty of rats. I understand killing rats because they eat up everything. They are destructive by eating the wood frames of barns and buildings and the grains and hay in storage. And there were always many living in the ear corn cribs. And some lived inside the hay. I tried shooting some of them in the corn crib with my gun, but that was useless. There were just too many living off the grain and the excess animal food spilled by the cows, pigs, and chickens. But I think everything has a purpose. I do not know how rats are beneficial.

Holidays

We recently celebrated the Christmas holidays. It reminds me of the several wonderful Christmases of the past. The thought makes me smile inside. I am trying to remember a lot about the Christmas holidays when we lived at the 39-acre farm and house. Did we have a tree? If we did, I am trying to remember where it was sitting. Somewhere in the living room, I would imagine. But I do remember some of the gifts I received for Christmas. I remember Uncle Roy giving me a pair of red knee boots. I was around five years old then. I remember wearing them outside and tracking through the mud and water. They extended up my legs just short of my knees. And actually, I needed them because I needed dry feet in the wintertime to feed the chickens and pigs and do all the other farm chores. Always before, I would have dirty shoes, wet feet from the barnyard, and plenty of damp everything else from the snow. I have no idea what happened to those boots. I just remember how happy and fun everyone was around the Christmas holidays. And most Christmases were white with snow. I also remember Aunt Mary coming to our house. She came often, and her family came to our home at Christmastime. I know her daughters were there quite often.

Most of the time, Aunt Mary came for milk and eggs, or she sent her daughters to pick up the milk and eggs for her. Aunt Grace came a few times and gave me a Disney Cell, which I have always kept. It hangs in our bedroom on this day. It used to shine after dark, but now that it is probably 70+ years old, it doesn't shine after dark anymore. Both the Burk and Gibson families used to draw names at Christmas time. The Gibson family stopped doing this about the time we moved to the 80-acre farm. But the Burk family continued. One year I drew Uncle Roy's name, and mom or dad purchased a 10-inch Crescent wrench for me to give to him.

Uncle Roy was good at being fun to play around with and tease. Mom had the idea to put the wrapped wrench in a large box. The wrench was a little small, so we wrapped it in a newspaper, put in another box, and all other kinds of wrapping paper that we could find. Then when Uncle Roy opened it, he kept looking and pulling out all this extra paper, extra box, and everyone laughed hysterically. We also celebrated Christmas at Granddad and Grandma Burk's house until grandma had her stroke. Then it was too much work for granddad, and the rest of the family, so the Burk Christmas thing ended. But we continued giving gifts to our grandparents. Grandmother Anis usually gave us kids a silver dollar. I know Christmas, with purchasing gifts to exchange, can be a little expensive, but I like the Christmas Holidays. Lots of good memories.

At the 80-acre house, Christmas was great. I remember dad teaching me how to shave one time at Christmastime. One year mom and dad gave me an electric train. What a treat that was. I played with that train for hours that day. Then I had to go to the barn and do my farm chores. When I returned to the house, my brother was playing with my train. I did not care, except my brother always liked to pull the wheels off his toys and mine.

For this reason, I did not want my train out of the box if I was not playing with it. So each time I had my train out to play with it, I always put it back in the box before I went out of the house to do my farm chores. And I would tell mom, do not let my brother play with my train. She did not let my brother play with my train. Then my brother received a new electric train the following Christmas. I still have my train stored in my garage.

I have not had it down to put it all together to let it run for some time, but it has always been dry and clean. It should work if I put it together. Plus, I have collected some other train sets over the years. At Christmas in Indiana, I almost always received clothes. Most of the time, it was the things I needed: socks, pants, underwear, shoes, and other garments.

One year dad purchased a 22-caliber single-shot rifle for me at the Sears store in Greenville, Ohio. The same store where dad bought our first TV. Dad taught me how to use it properly and always to be careful with it. I carried that gun with me for several years for hunting and trapping furs. I had it tied with twine to sling it over my back as I walked. I only remember using it a few times. But I needed it the night I captured the Badger. All the times we were raccoon hunting, I had it across my back. I could climb through or across wire cattle fences by having it secured with twine. I had it wrapped in an old jean pantleg to help keep it from getting scratched. But it did get scratched some. I refinished the gun stock years later. I have since given it to a gun collector. I am not fond of guns. But dad always had his own rifle, which he used when we were out raccoon hunting.

When we moved to the 80-acre farm in 1951, there was an old sled in the top of the old corncrib. The farmers of the past used it. It was pretty old, but it worked well for what we used it for, mainly hauling straw. You could carry bags of grain on it and other supplies around the farm. Originally it was built to be pulled around by horses. Of course, we did not have any horses after we moved to this farm. The fun thing about this sled was that when there was snow on the ground, dad would attach the sled to the back of the Ford tractor on the holidays. And pull it around the field on the top of the snow. The floor of this sled was about 12 inches above the ground and about 3 feet wide and 4 feet long.

The fun thing was jumping on and off this sled as dad pulled it around the snow field. He would drive fast, so you could roll in the snow when you fell off. I remember some of our cousins riding a little, but they did not seem to be impressed with this type of fun. But I enjoyed romping in the snow and jumping on and off this sled out in the snow. We only played with the sled, usually during Thanksgiving or Christmas. It was usually about the only time of year when there was much snow on the ground, and we had some time to play around. The area used to get more snow around the holidays than it gets nowadays. The old sled was broken up and thrown away a few years ago. I do not know of any other people who may recall this sled and the fun times it gave us. But dad always seemed very happy pulling this sled around the snowy field and watching me fall off and jump on this sled. Dad and I had fun together.

When we moved to the 80-acre farm in 1951, the previous owner had planted some juniper bushes and a fir tree around the front porch of this house. The fir tree was 5 feet tall then. At first mom had purchased some lights to decorate this tree with. As the tree grew, I purchased more Christmas lights to decorate this outside tree. Dad helped me decorate the tree with the lights for the first few years. The tree kept growing taller and taller. Each year, when I was about 14 years old, I had to come up with different ideas for how to decorate it. The last time I decorated this tree was the Christmas Holiday before I went into the military in 1963. By then, this tree was pretty tall. I had to use dad's 40-foot wooden extension ladders to reach close to the top, and then I would try to climb up the tree a little more using the branches. At that time, the tree was at least 45 feet tall. But I reached as high as I could to hang the lights as high as I could on it. I do not know how many bulbs lit up, but several. I used the larger Christmas light bulb strings. They lit up pretty nicely. I loved decorating this tree, and many neighbors commented on how pretty it looked. On clear nights, you could see the lights on this lit-up tree; for a few miles, I never measured any mileage distances. However, Indiana has many trees, which could block your sight when trying to see this tree from a distance. That tree is no longer there.

The 80-acre Barnyard

Some other things that were lots of fun at the 80-acre farm included the big lawn in the barnyard. It was south of the big house. It was pretty big, and we mowed it with a lawn mower. I often did the mowing, but we did share some. Most of the time, we used an electric mower. We could not use the reel-type mowers. And we frequently, accidentally, mowed over the electric cord, which stretched all over the lawn, close to 300 feet. That cut the electrical cord in half. We would need to put a splice in the cable. Somehow, dad had acquired a reel to wind all the extension cords on for storage until we needed to use these cords again. We used these same electrical cords for lawn mowing, and supplying electricity to run the grain elevator.

The previous property owners had this lawn area fenced in, allowing their cattle to graze and wander around. Why did dad not want animals on this lawn area? They would have kept the grass down but probably made the area more uneven and more brutal to mow. Plus, entering the barnyard from the highway would have made it very difficult. We would have needed a gate to control the barnyard animals, to keep them off the road. A white wooden gate was at the entrance from the roadway to the barn when we moved to the 80-acre property. But it required stopping on the road to open this gate. Dad did not want to stop on the State highway, so dad took the gate away, and never allowed any animals to roam anywhere in the barnyard.

And it also took quite a significant amount of time just to mow all the grass on all the lawn areas. Dad also planted a couple of Maple trees in the yard in front of the house. Plus there were some Cedar trees, one next to the road and two on the east and west fence, just south of the house. And there were some on the east side of the barnyard. When the ice damaged any part of them, dad had to saw part of the Cedar trees. The saw cut smelled excellent. I am sure that is why people line their clothes closets with Cedar. All the Cedar trees died from some kind of disease. There were some plum trees and a smaller lawn area east of the house. Mom had her clothesline in this lawn area.

But the fun times in this barnyard were worth it. They were mostly playing baseball. Dad was so funny when he played. Dad played like a crazy man. Dad was so hilarious. Dad could throw the ball all around, and he could throw it around behind his back. He could be looking at you, and you were thinking he was going to throw the ball at you, but instead, he would throw it behind himself to someone else. Many times that person would not be ready to catch the ball and drop it. And dad was so very accurate with his throws. Dad would run around, sort of like a dog acting crazy. Dad made everyone laugh and have fun. Somehow, he would hit the ball with the bat, but he never threw it in the air before he hit it. I am curious to know how dad did this. And when he hit the ball, it would come straight to the person he was aiming at, to have them catch the ball. Dad could have taken the game seriously, but dad just liked to play around.

Anytime any of the young male relatives, and some girls too, showed up, we were ready to get out and play if it was not raining. Where dad learned how to play so very well, I don't know. I'd like to know if several Burk boys and some neighbor boys also played baseball together. They may have played some at the Haysville Diamond. It was easy to find, and everyone knew where Haysville was located. Dad and I watched some local men play baseball on that diamond on Sunday afternoons. They had Mr. Mote as the umpire. They must have belonged to a league because they played several games there. I do not remember any uniforms.

We used this barnyard for many other things. We had Badminton games. We played Croquet with wooden mallets and wooden balls. Sometimes during the summer, we would have a table set up to hold sandwiches and Kool-Aid too. And maybe potato chips. For any people participating in any of the sports. We usually had the hot dog roasting out in another section of lawn, closer to the chicken house and garden, on the lawn area east of the house. And with a table set up holding the condiments and drinks. And if we were baling hay, sometimes mom had a table on the lawn under the Cottonwood trees. She would have our sandwiches and Kool-Aid there to allow workers shade while we took a break.

Cottonwoods & Garden

When we moved to the 80-acre property, along the road were about eight cottonwood trees, with a fence next to the trees and a side ditch between the fence and roadway. After we lived there for about five years, the electric company trimmed the trees first, then started cutting them down. The electric company removed all those trees, but only a couple at a time. They did it over a period of time, probably six years, because the branches were reaching up and into the electrical wires. The trees must have been relatively old because they had a lot of dead limbs. Those trees were slowly dying. The limbs would frequently fall because of ice buildup during the winter ice storms. We would need to pick up the broken limbs. We would cut them up and put them in the basement to burn in the furnace. Eventually, all of the cottonwood trees were cut down by the electric company. They cut the logs into sections. Then we could split the wood with an ax. I do not think dad sawed any of them, but he may have. I know we saved most of the wood to burn in the furnace in the basement. Cottonwood could be better for heat, but we used it anyway. The leaves were tough to deal with, during the fall of the year. We had to hand-rake all the leaves before we could mow the grass.

On the east side of the barnyard, and west of the garden, was a line of peach trees. I do not know how old they were because they never produced much fruit, and eventually, they were cut down and burned in the furnace. And there were two Cedar trees along that area too. They were damaged by the ice, and died. Dad cut them down and burned the wood in the furnace.

A couple of plum trees were on the east side of the house along the east/west fence. They must have been pretty old because they only produced a few good plums. These plum trees were cut down and burnt too. Also, at some time, someone had planted peach trees along the east side of the garden. They never produced much good fruit, and were not producing any fruit any longer, because they had caught leaf curl disease, and died. I had purchased a new handsaw and had to try it out. I remember cutting 3 or 4 of the old peach trees down on one Sunday afternoon. I cut the branches short enough to finish cutting them up with the buzzsaw for firewood. Along the east side of the garden also was a long strip of lawn which we mowed with the lawnmower. Along this strip of lawn and with the garden just to the left, we planted black raspberry plants and staked them up. Mom helped me do this to allow them to grow well and make it easier to harvest the fruit. They produced lots of good fruit. I remember picking lots of black raspberry fruit, and eating several while I was picking them. They were naturally very sweet. Mom sold some of the extra fruit to Mrs. Pat Byrum at Bartonia. Mrs. Byrum purchased strawberries from the strawberry patch on the other side of the garden, plus she purchased some black raspberries. I remember putting the basket fulls in my bicycle basket and riding them over to Mrs. Byrum's house.

The strawberry patch was huge and produced many beautiful berries. Mom baked many peach, black raspberry, and strawberry pies during the summer. She also put some in the freezer. Mr. Reich and a lady friend of his, who said she was an American Indian, used to come and pick strawberries several times during the summers. Mom always sent all the berries they picked home with them. Mom made some strawberry preserves too. Mr. Reich loved strawberry preserves.

Chicken Houses

To the north of the 80-acre house dad had the chicken's brooder house. And east of the brooder house was also a chicken house. It was a long building divided in the middle, making it equal in size for the two sides because dad had built the newer westside shortly after we moved to the 80-acre farm. There was a water line in one area of the chicken house. One side had the older chickens, and the other had the younger chickens. The chickens were separated like this because of the eggs mom was selling. The more senior chickens on the east side produced larger eggs. The younger chickens on the west side produced smaller eggs. But after some years, the older chickens would go away. Older chickens die. I don't know why. Primarily, the older chickens were used for food for the family and some for other relatives. Then dad and mom would move the west side chickens to the east side. The chickens were allowed to be outside during the summertime but always had to be inside at night and most of the wintertime. Chickens are a draw for wild animals, like foxes, opossums, raccoons, and weasels. Mom usually had about 200 to 250 grown chickens all the time. The chicken house area had a fence to keep the chickens from traveling too far. The brooder house, to the west, was for raising baby chicks.

Mom purchased these baby chicks during the wintertime. I never knew why mom bought them at that time of year. But after the chicks came, mom had an electric heating mechanism hanging from the ceiling. As the chicks grew, the heating mechanism would be raised higher to ensure they could not get their backs burned while eating. Yes, the feed for the chicks was directly under this heating mechanism. This brooder house also had watering containers for the chicks to drink. The brooder house had no running water and did not have any electricity. Dad had to connect an electric cord over from the chicken house to provide electricity to operate the heating mechanisms. When the brooder house was not in use, the electric cable would be disconnected and coiled up.

Corn on the Cob

One of dad's and my favorite meals contained corn on the cob. When soft corn was available, we always had corn on the cob to eat for our noon and evening meals. This was when the corn was ready for us humans to eat. Later, after a couple more months, the corn would be more mature and dry. Then it would be ready for the animals and harvesting. Mom raised sweet corn in the garden, which was pretty tasty. But dad's and my favorite was the field corn. The ears could sometimes be 12 inches long. They were a meal in themselves. Mom boiled all the corn for a meal in a large kettle on the kitchen stove. We never roasted any ear corn over an open fire. This field corn was entirely filled out on the cob and was sweet. No wonder the cows liked it so much. So often, we would go to the field, peel back the shuck a little, and pull the entire ear from the stalk. We left the shuck on the ears until mom was ready to prepare them for a meal. Then I would help mom shuck the ears and clean all the silks off each ear. Several ears were so large they had to be broken in half to allow them to be small enough to get into the boiling kettle. Mom usually boiled about five ears at a time. And sometimes mom cooked corn for the meals twice a day. I could easily eat at least one by myself and sometimes more. Dad ate his share too, and he liked it. I could eat tons of mom's corn and mom's homemade noodles. The most prominent ears of field corn came from the 160-acre property. Of course, mom and dad owned it then. And also we planted Kentucky pole beans, which climbed up the corn stalks. When we harvested the ears of field corn for a meal, we usually pulled off several of these beans too. Like the corn, these beans grew to a very long filled-out size. Dad and I would sit at the kitchen table; we thought we were typewriters!! Dad and I always worked hard, and our bodies burned many calories. We loved those beans and the corn on the cob!!

Equipment

All farming requires some type of equipment to be pulled behind or in front of a tractor to till the soil for planting or sowing. In the early spring, dad would top-dress the wheat with fertilizer and usually add grass seed. Dad always planted winter wheat. Winter wheat was not used by the cattle but was ground and used by humans for baking, but was produced as a money crop. Dad planted wheat to grow during the winter and spring. Then it would be harvested, usually around the 4th of July, and the grain sold for the profits it made to help pay for other farm expenses. That meant that dad sowed the wheat seed in the Autumn part of the year, and the wheat grains would sprout and come up before the cold winter set in. The wheat grains would grow and could get moisture from the winter rains and snow. Cold and freezing weather does not affect the wheat grains if they have sprouted and grown beneath the soil before wintertime sets in. The wheat plants could get extra nourishment from the fertilizer, whether natural from the earth or chemical.

In the springtime of the year, dad would take out his grain drill and make sure it was ready to do the work of top-dressing the wheat field. As dad was top-dressing the wheat, I often rode on the platform on the back of the drill to make sure the fertilizer was feeding down properly. Grain drills also usually have containers to hold grass seeds. They have a shaft under the bin, which turns and deposits a small amount of the seeds. These seeds fall into the soil and grow to produce the clover, which will be used later as hay, and cut for the cattle's feed. Also, this grain drill needed to be used for sowing the oats and dropping some grass seed into the soil. Dad planted the oats in the springtime of the year. These oats, after they were harvested, usually around the end of July, would be used for the milk cow's feed. Chickens also consumed a large portion of the oats too.

Dad planted several acres of oats each year. Dad tried to do the top-dressing of the wheat, just as close as possible to the sowing of the oats. After dad had finished that work, dad and I would take the drill apart and wire brush to clean all the metal parts. After dad and I cleaned all the pieces to his acceptance, he put them in a bucket filled with old tractor motor oil. Chemical fertilizer is very corrosive to any metal parts. We would always take time to do this, and after the pieces had drained of excess motor oil, usually a couple weeks, we would put the drill back together. Then it would be ready for the next season for the top-dressing, sowing of the wheat seed, and later the sowing of the oats.

This specific grain drill had three containers on top. One larger one to hold the seed grains (wheat, oats, or rye), one to hold the fertilizer, and a small one to hold the grass seed. Each container reached from one side of the drill to the other. A long shaft connected each of these gears underneath the containers to drop out the specific amount of product that dad wanted to be applied to the earth. The grass seed had a little lever to open and close the amount of seed to feed into the shaft to allow that certain amount of grain to fall to the ground. As the drill moved forward, the gears rotated the shaft controlling the sowing process. The speed of flow of the grain dropped to the ground was operated by the speed of this shaft. The fertilizer container was utilized very similarly, ran by the shaft underneath, and controlled by the speed of this shaft. This specific drill had rubber tires. These tires were connected by gears and chains that turned these three shafts as the drill moved over the earth. To control the speed of these shafts, they were controlled by another two chains at the center of the drill. These chains were connected to one of three sprockets at the center of the drill. The smallest sprocket was aligned and used if you wanted more product to fall. The larger sprocket, if used, meant a lesser amount of seed or fertilizer would fall to the earth. The middle sprocket, if used, meant the amount of seeds and fertilizer dropped would be about someplace in the middle of using the small or large sprockets. The drill was developed to allow each farm owner to make their own decision about how close together they wanted to plant their crop. When the drill was new, it took us some time to adjust everything as dad wanted. The grain drill dad had before he purchased this new drill was pretty old and was driven by the wheels too. But it was mounted on steel wheels and was made to be pulled by horses. Using it required it to be loaded on a trailer and transported from one farm to another. The new drill had rubber tires and could easily be towed to the next property. All of these shafts and moving parts on this new drill had grease fittings, which we greased each day before use.

    Dad originally had a horse-drawn corn planter. It planted only two rows at a time. Dad used it for all his corn planting up and through the 1951 season, and then he purchased the new four-row corn planter. This new piece of equipment could plant corn, and dad could change the grain plates to plant soybeans. This planter had eight containers on top. Four containers for the corn or soybean seeds and four to hold the fertilizer. The grain containers were controlled by a shaft running through the four containers, similar to the grain drill. This shaft was also controlled by the speed of the turning shaft and by the speed of ground travel. These gears on this planter were also turned by a chain connected to a sprocket connected to the wheels. Adjusting the amount of corn dad wanted to be applied to the earth was determined by the speed of the shaft connected to the seed containers at their bottom. To adjust that amount, we had to put the seed into the seed container, drop the planter down on the earth, and pull it forward. We usually did this on the driveway to quickly measure and count the grains. The gear sprockets on the front of this planter also controlled the speed of the shaft. Dad would pull the planter forward and then take a tape measure to measure the distance between each grain. Dad was very particular about the amount of seed he wanted to be applied. We kept adjusting until dad was pleased with the amount of corn or soybeans applied to the earth. The fertilizer containers were also connected by a shaft connected to the wheel. And like the grain containers, it was controlled by the speed of the shaft. Different grain plates were put inside the grain containers for planting soybeans, and again the amount of soybeans applied was controlled by the speed of the turning shaft. And just like the grain drill, the four fertilizer containers were taken off, cleaned out, wire brushed, put into the motor oil for some time, removed, and then we put everything back together. Then the planter would be ready for use the following season. Dad had the planter adjusted to 40 inches between rows. And each grain of corn would be about 7 inches apart. The soybean plates had large holes, which allowed the soybeans to be planted in an almost continuous flow. There was not much space between each soybean grain in the soil.

And another thing I have discovered about soybeans. Dad raised soybeans and stored them in his storage areas at harvesting time, usually around August. We kept the soybeans inside. Then we would shovel them back into the truck and haul them to the elevator to sell, usually in January and February. The soybean prices were higher during these months than at harvesting time. Dad usually sold one truckload each month until they were all gone.

But at planting time, dad would always put the seed soybeans in a tub or large metal container. Dad would sprinkle them with water, plus some kind of black stuff. I just recently found out why dad did this. This process was an inoculation of the seeds. Someone had discovered that doing this inoculation would make the seeds set more nodules to become fixed to the roots of the plant after the plant sprouts and grows through the soil. This process helps the nitrogen fixate to the roots of the plants. Nitrogen makes the plants grow bigger and produce more soybean pods on each plant. Now I know why dad did this. Dad may have explained this to me then, but I do not recall his explanation. I have not been around soybean planting for many years; however, a farmer friend recently told me farmers still do this inoculation to soybean seeds at planting time, some 60+ years later.

I mentioned before that dad wanted to have new equipment pulled by an older tractor rather than a new tractor pulling older equipment. He said this because more unique equipment was invented and improved to better care for the earth than the older equipment. I know dad purchased several pieces of new equipment after I left for the military. But before I went, each year, especially during the winter months, we would be working on different pieces of equipment to enable it to do an excellent job for the next season. Of course, the daily farm chores always came first. Some equipment components needed new bearings, blades, and plow shares, plus fresh paint to help them look better, and new paint gave better protection. But even when we used the equipment at planting or harvest time, we greased it daily. Therefore, the grease improved the equipment, and dad's equipment lasted longer. Dad always said, "We would not lose any time for planting or harvesting because of taking the time to lubricate the equipment for the day." Meaning breakdowns could cost much more time and money. Plus, some of the newer equipment had sealed bearings, which did not need daily greasing.

The Farmall "M" tractor pulled a three-bottom plow, 14 inches for each plowshare. This set of plows had a spring hitch. If the plow hit a rock in the earth, the spring hitch would break loose, and the tractor and plow would separate, and then they could be re-connected. Then the plow would be backed up and raised to get up over the rock without damaging the plow. I would often walk behind the plow, in the plow furrow, mainly because it was so smooth from where the plow had turned up the soil. I think dad usually plowed the earth down about 10-11 inches. Farming has changed over the years, and most farmers do not use plows anymore to till the soil for planting. They use a no-till system. The earth is prepared with a disk/harrow, which prepares the ground for planting. After dad had plowed the field, I used a drag to level the earth, especially if the land was to lay idle over the winter. Doing this helped prevent some of the soil erosion.

We used a disk to break up the soil when planting was close in the spring of the year. Usually, a cultipacker would be connected behind the disk to break up any clods of earth, along with a spiked tooth harrow pulled behind the cultipacker or another drag. Usually, this made the ground pleasant and even and loose for the new grains to sprout and grow. At planting time, I would use the "M" to pull the disk and connected equipment, and dad would use the "H" to pull the drill or corn planter. I was not big enough to fill the drill or corn planter containers. And I know I never could have made nearly as straight of rows as dad did. But dad and I worked well together, and we could get much work done daily. Between the three farms, and the need to transport equipment, we usually had most crops planted in about two weeks. Of course, we had to deal with the weather conditions. Rains coming at the wrong time would mess up dad's schedule. Rain could also interfere with harvest times. Dad must have paid close attention to the weather reports. Dad never complained.

The one essential thing about Dad's equipment was; that he never wanted to leave anything outside; or overnight. When we were working with any tractor, after using it out for some time, we would park it close to one of the barn doors and let the engine cool down for some time. Then, just before going to the house for the evening, we would start the tractor and park it inside the building. We always left the disk and other equipment out in the field overnight. But the planter, drill, and tractors had to be inside overnight. Sometimes the truck would sit out overnight if we did not have room to put it inside. Of course, the big truck always stayed inside the old corn crib. Often the big truck had supplies on the back of it. But we usually made enough room to get everything under the building's roof. Dad always had the same idea for his automobiles. The car always had to be in the garage if it was not in use. Of course, in the winter, it helped to have your vehicle where the frost, ice, and snow could not accumulate on it.

Almost every day, when we were going out to plow, work ground, plant, or sow any crops or seeds, I would ask dad what he planned to do and what he hoped to get done that specific day. Dad had it well worked out in his mind, and he would explain what he expected to get done. Then we would be working together to accomplish what he wanted to do. Dad and I made a good team. When dad was doing something, I knew what the next move was, and I would work towards that. When it was summer and time to get the hay into the barn, I knew what steps were needed and worked to get all those different jobs done. First, I would get an area of the barn cleared and get the tractor and mower greased, fueled, and ready to go. We often only cut part of the clover in the field at a time. Because if the rains came, dad did not want all the hay to get wet because rain on cut hay causes the grass to lose some of its value. That is why dad always planned ahead. The weather was always on dad's planning mind. Dad was almost always happy with what we accomplished. Dad taught me how to work hard, just like him.

Mowing hay took only a short time unless we were going to be baling hay in someone else's big field. We would mow one day or afternoon, and depending on how hot the weather was, we may windrow the hay the next day or the second day after we had mowed the hay. Then probably, the hay would need to dry for at least one more day, but usually two days after windrowing, and then we would come in with the baler and bale the hay, haul it into the barn, then stack and store it inside for the winter. Dad liked alfalfa clover hay. Dad said it produced more milk from the milk cows than other clover hay. I want to remember how many wagonloads of hay we would put into the barn each summer. Each wagon load had 72 bales of hay. Each fall of the year, when all the hay had been cut and stored, it would fill the entire end of the barn to the roof. Plus, sometimes we kept more hay in the center part of the barn: lots and lots of weight. But when spring came, about all the hay had been used up. As best I can recall, I put about five bales in the hay manger for the milk cows to eat overnight. We also used a small amount of hay and straw for the baby calves, the pigs, and some for the dog houses. I also gave a tiny amount of alfalfa hay to my rabbits.

After dad had combined the wheat and oats, we would go into that field with the mower and hay rake. We would cut the stubbles, windrow the straw and stubbles, and bale the entire windrows of straw and stubbles. We stored these bales of straw at the other end of the barn. We usually used 4 to 5 bales of straw each evening to scatter in the sleeping area for the milk cows and some for the other animals. So, as you can see, it took quite an amount of time each evening to do all the feeding, bedding, milking of all the milk cows, and caring for all the other animals. Dad always wanted to keep as many animals as would fit into an area but not be overcrowded because they all represented money to him. Dad was smart! And all of this straw that was used for bedding of the animals, would get dirty from feces and urine, and turn into manure. That is why we needed to haul the manure out of the barn every few days. This is when the Ford tractor and loader was used. The manure would be hauled out of the cows sleeping area, and deposited into the manure spreader parked outside the barn. The spreader would be connected to the "H". After the spreader was full, we would take it out to the field and scatter it with the spreader. This was a wonderful way of creating manure, and using it as a natural fertilizer for the land and future crops.

Earlier, I mentioned the hay track attached to the upper inside of the barn on the 39-acre property. The big barn on the 80-acre property did not have any hay track. However, inside the big barn, someone had left the mechanisms used for the hay tracks. We stored them on a loft above the straw area. Dad kept them, but he must not have found anyone who wanted them. Dad never wanted to install a hay track in this big barn. Probably because people did just what dad did. Dad purchased a portable grain elevator built on rubber tires and was easily moved around. It was an excellent piece of equipment because you could put the upper end above where you wanted the grain or hay to be stored. Then you could place the wagons of corn, oats, or hay at the bottom, turn it on, and it would carry the product upwards to where dad wanted it stored. Most farmers who had a grain elevator used a small gasoline engine to power it. Dad did not like that. Instead, dad had a ½ horsepower electric motor on his. This motor was a 2-stage motor and was strong enough to carry most products to their location with no problem. Once in a while, we could get too much corn on it. Then the motor would stall, but we learned not to overload it. And by using an electric motor, there was no chance of any sparks from the engine causing a fire. Over the years, and by using this grain elevator, dad had cut some holes in the corn crib roofs. Then the corn or oats would fall from the end of the elevator directly to wherever dad wanted them stored.

I purchased a new wagon chassis a year or two after my high school graduation. I built a wooden wagon bed on my chassis, which could be removed by two men, and then set it aside. Dad had two wagons. Because the fall corn harvest was coming closer, dad and I took one of dad's wagon chassis', and my wagon chassis to Fort Recovery, Ohio. We purchased two new hopper beds, one for each chassis. Dad paid for his, and I paid for mine. These specifically designed wagon beds would allow the grain products to slide down to the opening using gravity. They worked so very well. All we had to do to unload a wagonload of corn or oats was pull the wagon next to the bottom of the grain elevator, crank open the door, and the product inside would slide out with little or no problem. It sure made storage of the corn much easier. I no longer had to shovel the truckloads of corn into the corn crib.

During my four years of high school, I took all the Agriculture classes offered. I asked dad to try some ideas I had learned that differed from dad's procedures. I wanted dad to try planting soybeans in 20" rows instead of the 40" rows he had always used. I had purchased a set of cultivators to fit the Ford tractor to cultivate these 20-inch rows of soybean fields because dad always wanted to cultivate crops to help keep the weeds away. The distance between the rows did not matter when harvest time came. Dad tried about half of one field with my idea. It took some time to get things adjusted. But dad tried, and then he told me that my concept took too much time, which was the end of my thoughts about crop plantings. But dad did tell me that when he harvested the field, which we had planted my way, it produced many more soybeans per acre than the other areas planted the way dad wanted. I never wanted to cost dad anything extra, but he would have made more profits if he had planted soybeans my way. I am sure that the time required to plant 20-inch rows would have decreased after we became more accustomed to planting this way. Now most farmers grow rows relatively close together but do not cultivate.

One other mention: I was always so happy to go to the sales room, when dad went to the equipment company to purchase equipment and parts. Because it was so fun to imagine sitting on some of the little tractors on display. Little tractors were like little toys to me. And when I went to the county and state fairs, I always wanted to look at all the farm equipment on display. It has been amazing how much farming machinery has changed. I enjoyed doing this.

Mr. C. Reed

One winter afternoon when I was 16, I was hauling manure out of the milk cow's sleeping area. I had the tractor and manure spreader sitting outside the barn, and I was using the little Ford tractor to haul the manure out of the barn and deposit it in the manure spreader. To fill the manure spreader usually took about 3 or 4 dumps from the loader on the Ford tractor. Then I would take the other tractor, with the loaded manure spreader, out to the field and spread the manure over as much of the field area as possible. By using cattle manure, it produced a natural fertilizer. As I was working on this project, a man I knew (Colby) drove into the driveway at the barn area. Colby was the Agricultural Agent for our county, and state. His office was in Indianapolis. I do not know how Colby acquired this position.

   Colby walked down to where I was working, and asked me, if he could speak to my dad, out in his automobile. I told him yes, but I needed to go to another area of the barn to find dad and have dad talk to him. I saw dad and told him a man wanted to speak to him in his car. I think I told dad the man's name, but I cannot remember. Anyway, dad went to the man's car, and they sat inside it for over an hour. I wondered what they could have been talking about, but that was none of my business. At least, I did not think it was. Later, dad just explained that they were talking about Agriculture. I paid no attention, and everything went on as usual. Colby's son was in my grade at school too. That is where I learned about Colby, the position he was working in for the State, and how he was trying to improve the farming conditions for every farmer he represented. I remember talking to Colby at Colby's home about Agriculture and some of his ideas, when I was visiting his son. I made A's in Agriculture class at school. Dad never told me anything about the conversation he and Colby had that day. Many years later, mom told me that Colby was talking to dad that day about me going to college. I suppose Colby wanted me to go to Purdue Agricultural College. But dad refused Colby's help for me to get to college and refused to talk or think about me going to college. I never knew why dad did not want me to go to college. I have often wondered where or what my life would be like now or how it would have changed if I had attended Agricultural College. Applying those college learnings, could have helped dad and his farming practices. But I am happy, and I hope dad was always happy too. I do not think dad knew, but several years later, I took classes studying Architecture using my GI Bill. I enjoyed it and graduated, although I never became an architect. I have used the knowledge I learned from that class many times. Dad had already passed when I took those classes.

Uncle Artie and his family

Uncle Artie Burk was an older brother to our grandfather, Ollie Burk. Uncle Artie lived with his son Charlie, Charlie's wife Marie, and Charlie and Marie's daughter, Barbara. I mentioned cousin Charlie living in the house across from the 39-acre farm, but that was many years later. I think Uncle Artie was supposed to have been a farmer, but dad never said that Uncle Artie owned any land. Maybe he owned the ground where they lived, but I am not sure; that was never clear to me. But Charlie had an old Farmall F-30 tractor and a couple pieces of equipment. Charlie used this equipment to work the small patch of land around their home. As I remember, it did not produce much of a crop. I remember them saying that another local farmer cared for this land after Charlie let someone else take care of it. Sometimes dad would take mom and all of us kids, and we visited them on Sundays. Uncle Artie and Cousin Charlie always had raccoon-hunting dogs too. And Charlie always said they were the best hunting dogs in the country. But when dad and I went hunting with Uncle Artie and Charlie, their dogs never impressed me. We never caught anything, and my dog was the only dog barking as the dogs were following a raccoon's track and scent..

Uncle Artie had three sons. Uncle Artie's wife must have died several years before I remember visiting Uncle Artie. I estimate we visited them around the years of the mid-'50s. Uncle Artie had three sons. Dean was the oldest, Charlie was the middle child, and Cecil was the youngest. Although Cecil and his family lived in Union City, I don't remember visiting them, maybe one or two times. I have no idea what happened to any of Cecil's family. We visited Cousin Charlie and Uncle Artie many more times. Cousin Dean was the oldest and had been in WWII. Dean's talking was always a little hard to understand. He always said it was because of a war injury. I thought he just tried to talk too fast. Cousin Dean must have worked for some businesses around the area for some time. It must have been about 1954 when Dean married Sarah, who lived in Portland, Indiana. Sarah was originally from Georgia. Her mother, in Georgia, had a lovely property and raised lots of tobacco and pine tree syrup for turpentine. I was able to visit Sarah's mother's property one time. This was when I was 16, and on my trip home from Florida with Stanley.

Sarah had two daughters from a previous marriage. They were close to my age. After Dean and Sarah were married, Dean asked dad to move Sarah and her daughters to Union City. Dad and I went to Portland, where Sarah lived, with dad's '41 Dodge truck. We loaded all of her and her daughter's possessions in the truck and moved them to an apartment in Union City. After they had lived in Union City for a while, Sarah found a job at a local factory. Dean somehow purchased a milk route similar to the milk route dad had years before. Dean also bought a new 1955 Ford truck to haul the milk cans to the farms on his route. I know dad and mom were on his milk route for a year or two. After a couple of years, Dean and Sarah purchased a house in Union City.

Shortly after Sarah and Dean were married, Sarah became pregnant and had a baby girl, but this was after they had moved into the house they had purchased. Dad, mom, and we kids visited them quite often. Dad and Dean liked to talk. I don't know what they talked about. They never had any business dealings between them that I knew of. Sometimes we played a local card game, Euchre. I wanted to visit those girls, but they usually were busy doing other things. Probably because we always called in the evenings or Sunday afternoons. I liked both of those girls and loved to talk with them, even though I was pretty shy.

I did ask the younger daughter to accompany me to our

Junior Prom. She accepted, and we danced, had snacks, and enjoyed ourselves. I remember that evening well, but I never asked the younger daughter on another date for some reason. I wish I had. Many times, Dean and Sarah would come out to our house to visit. But the daughters did not come. They had other things going. I can't say how disappointed I was. I was brokenhearted, for I wanted to talk with them about things of interest to us. I was hoping they would come to our house so we could ride on the sled in the snow, which dad pulled with the Ford tractor. That was lots of fun! All I ever had to talk about was things I had learned about farming. Living in a farming community was all any of us knew to talk about, only farming activities. I did not know much about the current events.

I wanted to know how the other people who were not farmers lived. One of my school buddies asked Sarah's oldest daughter for a date. She accepted. We double-dated, and I had a date with one of my classmates. We went to a movie in Richmond. My friend liked Sarah's oldest daughter but married another friend he had been dating. Sarah's oldest daughter told me many years later that she liked and wanted to further their relationship. But things went in a different direction. Sadly, Sarah's oldest daughter died a couple of years ago. And also sad, my buddy's wife died about three years ago. We just never know the direction any of our lives will go. Dean and Sarah have passed on now, and I think their youngest daughter lives somewhere in Georgia. The middle daughter and I correspond some, and I try to visit her once a year. I don't know anything about the youngest sibling. Sadly, my high school friend has passed too.

Dad's going to the Grocery.

There were two grocery stores in Union City, Indiana, when my sister, brother, and I were young, early '50s. I had mentioned before that my sister and Grandmother shopped on Saturday nights at the Atlantic&Pacific Grocery store. But our mother did not want to shop there, even though it was close to where we lived. Mom said it was too expensive. The prices were a penny or two higher than many other stores. Of course, that made no difference to me. I did not see the value of money. After moving to the 80-acre property, mom arranged to have bread delivered to our house by the Omar Baking Company. The bakery was in Richmond, Indiana. Mom did this for a while but stopped and said it was too expensive. It probably costs more to have deliveries to a person's house, especially out in the country. Richmond was at least 28 miles away.The bread company delivered to other farmhouses the same day they came to our home.

Somehow mom learned about a grocery store also located in Richmond, Indiana. It was called Cutters Supermarket. Mom said it was cheaper and wanted to do her shopping there. Shopping there was okay with dad. On Saturday nights, after we finished the milking and chores and finished the evening meal, plus washed all the dishes, all five of us would get into the car, and mom would drive us to the store. After we arrived there, dad would always sit in the car, and dad kept our brother in the car too. At least when our brother was very young.

My sister and I would go with mom into the store in Richmond. I liked pushing the grocery cart. Mom walked up and down each aisle. Mom filled the cart full of the supplies needed for the month. We only went shopping sometimes. Of course, mom never purchased meats because we had our pork and beef supply in the freezer. But sometimes, in the spring and summertime, mom would buy hot dogs and maybe sliced sandwich meats. Mom bought a lot of bread and would put several loaves in the freezers for later use. Mom usually made her own jams and jellies for us to eat. And when mom finished grocery shopping, we would go to the freezer section in the store and buy ice cream. Mom usually purchased 2 - 2&½ gallon cartons of ice cream. One vanilla and one chocolate. They were large cartons, but she had room in the basement freezer. And if it did not fit, we could eat any partial one left in the freezer. After all, the items were in the cart, purchased, and bagged, we would put them into the car, and mom would drive us all back home. Dad was always so happy to sit in the car. After we arrived home, I would help mom get all the supplies into the house or put the supplies wherever the supplies were stored.

Most of the time, while at the grocery store, mom would purchase maple candy for dad. Yes, she also bought some candy for us kids too. But dad always liked a certain kind of maple candy. It was shaped like a large almond. Dad sure liked that candy; he did not eat much of any other kind. So each time we went to Cutter's, mom would get dad a package of that candy. And there was also a Woolworth's Dime Store in Greenville, Ohio. Whenever we went to the Sears Store in Greenville, we would go shopping at the Woolworth's store. Once in a while, we may go into a different store in Greenville for some specific item. But Woolworth's was always our stop. Dad would almost always stay in the car. Some evenings, when shopping in Greenville, and if the weather was hot, dad may get out of the car and sit on one of the benches in front of the Court House. But that was very rare. It seemed to me; dad just did not want to walk up and down the sidewalks. I do not think he was scared of anything. I think he was always tired and just enjoyed sitting and having a chance to rest his body. When we were with our granddad, he was the same; granddad just wanted to sit. Dad just wanted to sit, look around and talk to anyone who may have walked along. When we tried to buy something for dad as a treat, that maple candy was always his favorite.

One other thought about dad and candy. When we were working at the Shaw Farm, and about the end of our working day, especially on Saturday afternoons, dad would stop me, tell me to put away the equipment I was using, and walk to the Haysville Service Station. It was only about a ¼ mile away. It was the local gas, auto repair, oil change, and tire place for almost all of our neighbors. There was also an area outside where some old-timers could sit and gossip. This station also sold cigars, cigarettes, ice cream, sodas, candies, and a lot more things, I am sure. So, on some of these Saturday evenings, dad would take a dollar bill out of his billfold, which he kept in his breast pocket, and tell me to go to Haysville, purchase cigarettes for him, and a candy bar for us to take home to the family.

Once in a while, dad told me to buy ice cream to take home. I would do this and then walk back to the buildings on the Shaw Farm. By then, dad would have most everything put away and would be about ready to go home to do the milking. Two Reid brothers owned Haysville Station. Their elderly father also pumped gasoline for some customers, collected the gas pump monies, and maybe wash the windshields of the cars. The boys were good mechanics. Dad also did some farm work for the father and his wife, mostly harvesting, as I remember. That was another family where the wife and mother ran the farming and watched everything dad did very closely. All those people are deceased now, but the buildings are still there, but no more service station. When I walked down the road to Haysville station, I walked past a couple of homes. The one home is where the livestock hauler lived.

A couple of years later, I hauled corn for the livestock hauler's father when I was in high school. He paid me for collecting and carrying corn and putting the corn into his barn for his chickens. Some classmates helped me collect the corn out in the fields. That was when we earned and saved money for our high school class trip.

I think dad was always thinking about things that would bring happiness and help to his family. Dad was a wonderful father and was a concerned parent about his children's happiness. Dad always wanted his children to have clean clothes and nourishing food.

Dad and Mom's Wedding Date

Dad and mom were married on May 28th, 1939. They were married at the Harrisville Methodists Church in the little town of Harrisville, Indiana. I wonder why they picked that date. Mom never explained. Dad said they chose that date because both our Grandmother's Birthdays were May 28th. Grandmother Gibson's birthday was May 28, 1888, and she was from Ohio. Grandmother Burk's birthday was May 28, 1890, and she always lived in Indiana. Our mother always told me that, somehow, we are related to the American Indians, but her brother said that he had never heard of that.

We will never know for sure. But my DNA test said there were no American Indian signs in my DNA. And our grandmother Burk was connected to Ireland somehow. Her parents' and grandparents' name was Mullins. It's an Irish name, but I never looked it up because we all are related to immigrants somewhere in our distant past. Dad and mom were married for 33 years when dad passed. I do not remember dad and mom ever celebrating their marriage Anniversary date. But I do know that for their 25th Wedding Anniversary, I gave them an Anniversary clock. It shows up in one of the pictures. I now have that clock. It sits atop our bookcase. I had it repaired to make it work, but I am unsure if it works now.

From what they told me, dad and mom met when dad

played music with some of the local boys when he was young. And maybe his brothers too. Dad never said precisely who was in the musical group he played with. And dad never said what kind of music they played or what instruments were used. I know dad played the guitar, and he also played the violin. He played the violin mostly when his group was performing. And most of the music dad played at home was with his guitar. And when Uncle Bill played with him, it was the familiar music of the 20s and 30s. Dad knew some songs, but Uncle Bill knew lots of songs.

During the depression, Uncle Bill played his guitar and sang live on the local radio station in Richmond, Indiana, to make enough money to provide for his family. Uncle Bill could have been a better singer, but he played the guitar well. Dad was a good guitar player and could sing and carry a tune very well too. Dad could whistle a good song also.

My sister accompanied dad and Uncle Bill when they were playing music. My sister took piano lessons for some time and played very well. I took trumpet lessons, and my brother took saxophone lessons. Our mother wanted all her children to have some musical knowledge. I had to give up trumpet lessons because they conflicted with the school classes that I wanted to take. I do not know what happened with my brother and his saxophone. But we all sang a little and could carry a tune. Mom seemed happy that we had some music in our lives.

John Gibson (mom's father) had something he celebrated at his farm and home west of the Lisbon Church in Indiana. I never knew exactly when this celebration took place. But dad and the musicians were asked to play music for the day's celebration. They were asked to play on some other dates too. Dad said John paid the group to perform. Dad playing at these celebrations is when and how dad met our mother. Mom was one of John's children. Dad and mom liked each other and dated for maybe a year before they decided to get married. So that is how our father met our mother. And I remember dad telling me that he had an old Ford automobile, which he drove around in. I think he mentioned it was a '32 Ford model "A." It had a rumble seat.

John Gibson was several years older than our Grandmother Gibson. John Gibson had been married, but his wife died; I don't know when. John had three children from that first marriage, two girls and one son. They always lived around Dayton, Ohio. Then John married our Grandmother. Grandmother Gibson was also a widow at that time. She had been married to a man named Moore, but he died. Dad told me that Mr. Moore had been hunting. Mr. Moore leaned his gun against the fence and was climbing over the fence, and his gun fell over and went off, striking Mr. Moore. Mr. Moore died from the wound. Grandmother Gibson (Moore then) had two children with her first husband, Mr. Moore, one girl and one boy. The boy's name was Wilbert Moore. The daughter's name was Edith Davenport. This son, Uncle Bill, was the child of grandmother's first marriage and the gentleman we knew only as Uncle Bill. He was our mother's half-brother. Then John Gibson and Grandmother Gibson proceeded to have seven more children after they were married. I remember both our grandmothers and Granddad Burk, but I don't remember John Gibson. There is a picture of him holding me on his lap when I was about one year old. But John Gibson died in 1945. I think our grandmother Gibson died in 1963.

Dad and mom took us kids to visit most of these relatives. Most visiting was done on Sunday afternoons. We went to Dayton, Ohio, to see the one John Gibson's daughter and son, and to Piqua, Ohio, to visit the other John Gibson's daughter. These were from Grandfather Gibson's first marriage. We also visited all of our mother's (Gibson) family at one time or another. But Uncle Bill's daughters and son, we saw probably the most. Maybe because they lived the closest to us. Our Aunt Icy Mae lived close to Edith Davenport. They also had a neighbor named Carl, friends of Aunt Edith and Aunt Icy Mae, they all lived close to each other. This was the man, Carl, whom dad usually purchased his feeder pigs.

Living on the State Line

When dad and mom were first married, they lived on a small farm north of Union City, on the State Line road. This was the place they were living when my sister was born. I wonder how large the property was. And this is where dad and mom lived at the time of some of these pictures. This was when they determined they were going to pursue farming as their way of making a living and raising their family. The first cow they owned is in one picture, and the first pigs they owned is in another picture. I imagine dad had Pete and Daisy, dad's team of work horses, when they lived there. I suppose dad had a truck then. I know nothing about the site because I was not in the family then. But the information I have heard about it is information mom told me, my sister, and my sister had these pictures. Dad may have hauled sugar beets in another truck he owned when he lived here. However, I do not know when dad purchased the '41 Dodge truck. Dad only told me stories about hauling sugar beets and never told me the truck he used. We know dad and mom were married in May 1939, Maybe they lived there for about 2 years, because my sister was born in 1941, and was 3 weeks old when they moved to the 39-acre property. I wasn't born until 1943, I wasn't around.

Mom's Birthday

In March 1971, Dee and I visited the Merritt Restaurant and Bakery here in Oakland by Lake Merritt. We ate in that restaurant a couple of nights each week. One of the things the bakery was known for was these enormous cakes. They were about 18 inches in diameter and at least 7 inches tall, big enough to supply many people with dessert. This bakery had lots of unusual items, cakes, and pastries, which were tasty. It was a favorite bakery for hundreds of people, and well known throughout the area.

When Dee saw these, she mentioned that my mother's 50th Birthday was coming. I had not been to Indiana for about 23 months. Dee said that I should order one of these cakes. And have the bakery decorate it with her name and add all the other birthday decorations that usually adorn birthday cakes. Dee said I should take the cake back to Indiana for mom's birthday, a surprise birthday. It was utterly my wife Dee's idea. I thought about it and decided to make my wife's idea come about. I checked my work to see if I could get the time off. That was ok. I purchased an airline ticket and chose the dates. I knew I could carry the cake and store it under the airline seat in front of me, there was plenty of space. I wanted to surprise our parents, so I could not let anyone know I was coming. I took a taxi from our house here in Oakland to the Oakland airport. When I arrived at the Dayton, Ohio airport, the closest airport to dad's house, I also took a taxi from Dayton airport to mom and dad's house. It was not very expensive. I had to tell the taxi driver how to get to mom and dad's house, about 50 miles from the airport.

Dad was doing something in the garage when I arrived at dad's house. He had on his coveralls because this was around March 13th, and not very warm. Dad saw the taxi pull into the driveway and saw me get out of the vehicle. I had my suitcase and the cake. I always try to travel light. I greeted dad and gave him a big hug. Dad started laughing when he saw me, but he did not notify mom. Mom was in the house running the sweeper when I walked in. Dad followed me into the house. I had sat the cake down out in the garage. I gave mom a big hug and told them how good it was to see them. After we talked for a little while, I went to the garage, brought in the cake, and opened the large box. I wished mom a Happy Birthday and showed her the cake. After talking more, I went out to the garage to help dad with the project he was working on. Mom must have called my sister and brother; I don't remember who else. It was clear that she could have many people come to have Birthday cake with us. I only spent 3 or 4 days there on that trip. But I did have enough time to see several of our relatives. I think my mother took me back to the airport. It was a fun and memorable trip. I always wanted to do this similar thing for dad's birthday. But dad's birthday was in June, and dad was always very busy farming around that time of year. Of course, we always sent cards and made many phone calls. There is a three-hour difference in the time change between California and Indiana. Sadly, dad passed before I could purchase a cake, fly back, and celebrate his 56th birthday this same way.

But a few years before, for dad's Birthday in 1968, we threw dad a lovely surprise Birthday celebration. Dee and I were living in Indiana at that time, in dad's house at the corner. A lot of relatives attended too. On that birthday for dad, Dee had purchased this package of candles. She put them on his cake, I think mom had baked the cake, and these candles were the kind that re-light. Dad could blow them out, but they would re-light a couple of seconds later. Dad was funny and kept blowing them out. Everyone was laughing hysterically, and dad too. Finally, dad said, I will take care of these. Then he took his pliers out of his pants pocket and pinched the candles out. But by then the memorable images were ingrained in our minds. This was dad's

51st birthday. We laughed then and have laughed so many times since that date. I would have loved to have done similar things like this again for dad. And as I mentioned, sadly, dad passed away in February 1973. The wonderful thing about dad is that he could always laugh at himself and be funny too. Dad was a great man, and I miss him.

Stanley

Stanley was an older man dad had known for a long time. I think dad knew Stanley when Stanley was relatively young. Stanley had lots of knowledge about threshing machines. Stanley operated those machines when he was a much younger man. I imagine Stanley's family were farmers from a long way back, and this is probably how he learned to operate threshing machines. Dad went to Stanley and asked him for information about dad's combine and what dad needed to do about adjusting it. I think I was about 10 years old. I remember being there as they talked; I know this was about a problem dad was having. Stanley's suggestions worked out well for dad, which fixed the problem. Stanley was a farmer, but in his older years, he had gotten away from owning any animals. I only knew Stanley as a crop farmer. But Stanley did have barns, which had housed farm animals he previously had. Stanley owned several acres around the Haysville area. And I know dad harvested some of Stanley's grains with dad's combine. Stanley also raised tomatoes for the canning factory in town. For two years, I remember dad and I helped pick tomatoes for Stanley because Stanley could not get the Latino tomato pickers to arrive for a few more days. Dad and I picked all we could, and Stanley was grateful. I know Stanley paid dad for our efforts. I do not remember how much time we spent each day. Dad really liked Stanley.

Stanley was a lovely man. He had his farm but also worked at the factory in town. I am trying to remember which company. He started working there after he gave up farming with animals. I am sure this was a much easier life. Stanley was married, and he and his wife had a daughter. The daughter was the same age as my brother. Dad and I ate at Stanley's house a couple of times. Stanley's wife was an excellent cook.

In the summer of 1960, Stanley talked to dad and asked him if I could go on vacation with him and his family. Stanley wanted me to help him do the driving. Dad never asked me if I wanted to go with Stanley and his family. Stanley's wife had never driven a vehicle. This is why Stanley wanted me to go along. Stanley had a very nice 1955 Ford automobile. Dad must have said it was ok for me to go and help Stanley drive. Stanley paid for my hotel rooms and all my food. Stanley was going to Fort Meyers, Florida, for his vacation. I helped drive his car for a couple of hours each day we traveled. I remember seeing the Gulf of Mexico and how big it was. You could not see the other side. Before this, I had seen lakes, but usually, a person could see the other shore of lakes. This surprised me. I had never traveled to any place like this before. I remember some of the activities there, especially the spider monkeys. They are wild there in about all the trees. I think we were gone for about a week. It was a delightful trip, I am happy Stanley asked me, I never would have been able to go to Florida otherwise. I believe Stanley passed some time while I was in the military. I do not remember seeing Stanley at any later date. I remember mom telling me Stanley passed while in the hospital because of a blood clot in his leg that traveled to his heart. But I do not remember the date.

Vacation

It was 1962 when our cousin Linda, from the San Diego area came to spend the summer with her grandmother Gibson. Her mother was our mother's oldest sister. She was in Indiana for the entire summer. While she was in Indiana, I spent a lot of time taking her to as many sites as possible that I knew. We went to the nearest cities for food and just looked around.

When she had to return to California, I suggested mom and dad drive her and themselves out to California as their vacation. Dad had never been out west and never had an actual holiday. I told dad that my brother and I could do the milking and chores for a couple of weeks. Dad had a very nice 1955 Dodge automobile, a very dependable automobile at the time. Finally, they agreed. They took off, and my brother and I did ok. The only problem was that the weather turned freezing, sometimes 30 degrees below zero. It doesn't get that cold in that area anymore. But it was hard then. Too cold to haul manure. Just maintain the milking, feeding, and bedding of the different animals. The little Ford tractor had a problem, so my brother and I towed it to the mechanic, who fixed it. Dad was disappointed about that, but that was the only thing I could think of doing. But it worked out.

The trip for mom and dad was not much of a vacation. Because when dad reached California, the people there had him dig a hole in the earth to put in a post to hold some kind of sign. Dad said the earth was so dry and complex it was a tough job. But dad was able to dig the hole. I hope they appreciated what dad had done for them. And then, when dad and mom were driving home it constantly rained. I know it is around 2000 miles in each direction. I just felt terrible about dad's experience. This was the only vacation dad ever took, and it did not turn out to be relaxing. But when Dee, and I were living in Indiana, I wanted dad and mom to take a vacation and go to Hawaii, or Florida, or any place they wanted. But dad always said no. He said he did not need any breaks. When I was still at home, I took care of some different neighbors who lived on their farms, when they went on their vacations. I never had any problems caring for their property while they were gone. I always felt sorry that dad never did take any time away from his responsibilities. Everyone needs rest and relaxation at different points in their lives. Dad just worked all the time. I cannot remember why our cousin was required to return to southern California at that time of year. I am sure this was around January. I only remember how cold the weather was while they were gone.

My High School Friend John

John has always been my best and longest friend from high school. John and his brothers always lived on a farm and milked cows during our high school years. I used to visit John on weekends, and many times, John, his girlfriend, and I would go to Richmond. We usually double-dated. When we went there, we would go to the movies and then to the burger restaurant drive-in afterward. We always had a good time together.

One time, John had mentioned while we were at school that he needed to haul some of his ear corn to the grain elevator. I volunteered the use of dad's big truck. On a Sunday afternoon, while John's dad was harvesting corn, I had taken dad's truck to John's farm to load it with ear corn for John and me to haul to the grain elevator the next day. I suppose John did not have space to store that amount of corn. While I was there before we loaded the truck, I let the clutch out too quickly at John's house, and the truck broke an axle in the differential. We towed the truck over onto the grass and loaded it with corn. But before we loaded the truck, we took the back plate off the differential and cleaned all the broken metal pieces out of the differential. Then the next day, dad took the broken axle to the scrap yard and found a replacement axle for that specific truck. Dad took the replacement axle down to John's place and installed the new axle with all-new differential grease. I was sorry that I messed up like that, but I was too young and not experienced enough to be handling a truck like that. This was all my mistake. But it worked out, and after school, John and I took the truckload of corn to the elevator for John. I learned a valuable lesson. Be careful with other people's property. Always show respect.

Now that I live in California, I stop to see John and Maxine each time I visit Indiana. Sadly Maxine passed about three years ago. I mentioned before how we did so many things together. Sadly, John recently passed on. He is buried next to Maxine. May they both Rest in Peace. I have lost a valued, long-time friend.

The Military and My Future

After I entered the military in 1964, I had just turned 20, I experienced many different ways of living. As I have thought back about most of these experiences, I realize how extremely different the things I have done and learned were so different from farm life. I do not know if dad realized a single drop of how different that kind of living is. This idea is why much of the following section is about me, and hopefully it will eventually explain some of the things I have done and how our father's influence was a positive part of me. I am unsure how much dad knew about me, my wife, my military service, and some of my goals. Or any of the goals my wife and I had planned together. I always wanted my father and mother to be family to my wife and me. That did not work out the way I had imagined, but those ideas are all past. Time moves on, new challenges arise, and our lives together are good. Today, I would not change any part of anything except if somehow Dad could have lived longer. And also, I wish my wife's health could improve. I have been very Blessed. We never know what life has in store for any of us.

Dad never asked me what I wanted to do after graduating high school. I wish he would have. I needed some income to survive. I needed to find work. Two weeks after graduating high school, a classmate (John) and I went to Richmond, Indiana, and started working for a highway construction company. Their home office was in Indianapolis, Indiana. We both worked for this company for the rest of the year, 1961. It was the first time I had any money in my wallet. The work closed down during winter because of the cold weather. But the company called me during the winter to take care of a couple of fencing problems that had come up. The following year, 1962, my classmate wanted to work in something other than construction. I thought about it, and before I decided, my dad offered me the opportunity to farm a neighboring farm that was up for rent. I agreed, and everything went well that year. My dad and I worked well together. But the following year, 1963, I was asked to return and work for the construction company again. I accepted their offer and worked for them the whole year. Dad never mentioned anything about my decision, but I wish he would have.

However, at the end of 1963, I received a notice from our government saying that you are 1-A and needed to take my physical exam for the Military Draft. Receiving this notice had a significant impact on me not farming in 1964. I knew the time was coming when I would have to go to the military draft. I learned a lot about how the draft worked. Some exemptions were allowed for farmers, but not if someone else could fill my space with farming if needed. I have a younger brother. Because my brother is younger than me, I would have to go someplace in the military. It was January 1964, I had gone to Indianapolis and taken my physical for the Draft. The results were 1-A. By being 1-A, I thought the military would call me to go to one of the branches. After New Year's Day, as I was coming home from work on one of the construction sites, I stopped in Muncie, Indiana, and talked to the Navy Recruiter. I was still determining what to do, but I knew I wanted to avoid going to the Army, which primarily trained in Kentucky and Tennessee.

I decided I wanted to travel and see the world. So I joined the Navy for four years of active duty and wanted to get into the submarines, even though I could not swim. I knew I could learn how to swim. I wanted West Coast duty. I wanted to see the warmer part of the world. My parents knew I was called to join the military but had no idea what I was thinking. I didn't talk to them about my decisions. They were unhappy, but I thought it would be good for my brother to learn and help with the farm. Dad and mom did need some help. I thought they would get it all worked out. Plus, I could not tell the Draft Board that I could not be Drafted. They would laugh at me.

I received more correspondence from the Navy in the first two months of 1964. I was assigned to leave for Boot Camp from Richmond, Indiana, on March 9th. I was to take the Greyhound Bus to Indianapolis. Dad and mom drove me to Richmond in my car. We said our goodbyes, and then I was off. I arrived at the military recruitment center sometime after noon. There, I had to take another physical and answer several written tests. I did pretty well. The tests I took for the Navy showed I have a reasonably high IQ. That day required many hours of talking to different people, mainly concerning where I was born and where I lived. And what type of work I had been doing, plus questions about my schooling. And any college? Did I have a criminal background? I told the people there that I wanted to be with the submarines. The submarine group was mostly complete, and they did not think I would be a good candidate for the sub's because I had a farming and construction background. Later, the Navy assigned me to be in the Seabees. I needed to learn who or what the Seabees were but I signed up for four years of active duty. I worked with the Navy for four years. I had no intention of remaining in the military after four years. I intended to be a farmer.

Because the time of day was getting late, they made me stay that night in Indianapolis at the YMCA. I signed the formal papers the following day and was on my way. I flew from Indianapolis on a DC-3 to Chicago. And on a jet from Chicago to LA and a different plane from LA to San Diego. There were 6 or 8 recruits on the plane from LA to San Diego. The Navy sent transportation to the airport and picked us up. Around midnight, I arrived at the Navy boot camp in San Diego. The men there gave us instructions, and we could sleep on benches and the floor until 4 am. Then they came, woke us up, and gave us all new uniforms, a Seabag, and all that went with it. Then I was assigned a number and a group, and then I was assigned to a barracks. Now I had to send all my civilian clothing home in the suitcase I brought with me. It was a little crazy at first but it all worked out. The one thing required was each one of us had to write a letter to our family at least once a week while at boot camp. I could tell dad and mom what I was doing, but it was hard to know how they were doing.

After graduating from boot camp after 12 weeks, I went back home for about a week. After returning from leave and back to San Diego, I was assigned to be a janitor at another part of the Navy Base. But I was ranked as a Seabee. After five months, I was transferred to The Seabee Batallion School in Oxnard, California. At the Navy base there, I attended welding and steel erection school for about three months. Then they assigned me to MCB 10 (Mobile Construction Batallion 10) at the end of my schooling. I was now a welder and sent to "D" company.

When I arrived with MCB 10, I had to acquire all new military clothing, similar to Marine and Army clothing. We called them greens. Shortly after I joined the battalion, we started Military training. A lot of this training took place at Camp Pendelton, CA. In February, the entire division flew by military jet planes to Okinawa. We did more military training there and much more physical activity. We were in Okinawa for a little over two months. While there, I received all kinds of truck driver training and other military training that I was qualified for. It was all printed on my Military driver's license. Military driver's licenses are legal and accepted here in the United States. After about 2 months, the entire battalion was loaded on ships during the last day or two of April 1965. Trucks, tanks, and everything that was to go with us.

I was assigned to drive a truck off the ship when we arrived at our destination. We set sail for Vietnam on the USS Gunston Hall LSD ship. While sailing to Vietnam, I was assigned to do the laundry detail on board the vessel. We had to wash and press all the ship's dirty clothing. I did most of the steam pressing. It was hard and hot work. On the afternoon of May 4th, they came to the laundry room and told me to get my belongings, and get on the smaller LCU boat. They required me to get in my assigned truck. It had already been loaded on the smaller LCU boat.

Some Alfa Co. drivers had loaded it on the small landing boats (LCU), used to haul the trucks and equipment to the shore. Smaller landing craft boats were used to transport us to the beach, from the large ship. We left the LSD ship we were on in the late afternoon. We headed to the shoreline shortly before dusk, but the tide had gone out before we could get to the shore, and the small landing boat could not reach the beach because of the shallowness of the ocean water and the height of the reefs there. I had a little sleep that night on the fender of the truck I was driving. Early the following morning, our small boat reached the shore, dropped the front gate, and I went off into the water and then up on the beach. Now we were in Chu Lai, North Vietnam. I was scared! I had no idea what I was going to get into. Our MCB 10 was the first Batallion to enter Vietnam on May 5th, 1965.

After arrival, I had to unload the truck I was driving because the back of it had been filled with 55-gallon barrels of fuel. After unloading the fuel I was assigned to take the truck I was driving to the quarry our people had started because it was a dump truck. It was about 2 miles away. After getting to the quarry, the truck was loaded with dirt and stone. I began driving to the area where we were building new roads. We were building roads because there was sand around this area, and most trucks would get stuck in the loose sand. The first week I was there, we worked 24 hours a day. I slept in that truck when I could. And after dark, we had to drive without headlights. I had to use the truck's blackout lights. The enemy fired at my truck and me, but we were never hit. I always had a Marine shotgun guard riding with me after dark. When being fired upon, the Marine would jump out and start running in the direction of the fire. When that happened, I just cut the engine off and jumped under the truck until the Marine returned. After the Marine returned, I would start the truck up again, and continue on.

After about three weeks of driving a dump truck, they assigned me to a different job. At about this time, the crews were starting to build an airstrip made of aluminum matting. I was assigned to this job for about six weeks of work. I made a lot of friends while working on building this airstrip. The airstrip was just barely started when I was assigned to that duty. The Airstrip was about 200 feet wide and 2000 feet long. It was to be used by the A-4 jet planes. The airstrip was finished after a lot of sweat had dripped from our bodies. The aluminum sections were heavy, with one man on each end of each piece as we were laying them down. The temperature was very warm all the time.

After we finished laying the airstrip, I was assigned to work on all different types of construction. Both as a construction worker and sometimes a truck driver, I was to haul materials to several of the work crews' job sites. There were metal buildings, wooden buildings, and bunches of other things every day. Because I was mainly driving a truck, I was assigned to pick up refugees, according to the Red Cross people, when necessary. Because the war fighting was close by. The Red Cross people did not want the locals to get injured. I was to move them from one small town and take them to the next town. What an experience it was to be hauling about 40 Vietnamese civilians in this truck. Mostly they were old people and some children, who were continually smiling at me. Luckily most of the warfighting took place after dark, and I spent most of my driving time during the daylight hours. It was an experience I will never forget.

While we were working at all the construction jobs at Chu Lai, I had a chance to go on an RNR (rest and relaxation) period. This trip was about the last few days of October. I went with one other Seabee worker to Bankok, Thailand for 7 days. This was a wonderful experience to see the beautiful city, floating markets, kick-boxing, and lots of wonderful good food. So many Budda's there. Buddhism is the Religion in Bankok. We flew there and back on an old C-123 military cargo plane. I would love to see Bankok again. I wonder what dad would have thought about this area of the world.

We landed in Chu Lai, North Vietnam, on May 5th, 1965, and departed Chu Lai, North Vietnam, on December 9th, 1965. We flew back to the United States on a C-130 Military aircraft. It took 30 hours of flying time. We departed Chu Lai and flew to Japan. Then we flew on to Guam.

At Guam, we got a bite to eat. Then we flew to Travis Air Force Base in northern California to refuel. We finally arrived at Oxnard, California, close to our home base. The one thing the military always stressed was to write letters back home to our families as often as possible. I tried to write when I could, but it was difficult because of our living conditions. But I survived and learned much about life and how precious life is. I tried to explain what I was doing to dad and mom in each of my letters. I did not tell all about the death and destruction I saw—too many broken and dead bodies. I always tried to explain the work I had been doing. Luckily, I was able to advance my rank from E-3 to E-4 while I was at Chu Lai.

After we (MCB10) arrived back in the states, most of us went on leave for about 30 days after placing our personal supplies in our barracks. I know I went home to Indiana in December of 1965. I spent almost a month at home. Then I went back to the base. After everyone had returned, we started more schooling and more military training. The date was about the end of January 1966. Early in March 1966, our battalion loaded on large Navy jet planes, and we flew to DaNang, North Vietnam. There, it was about the same as before, with lots of hard work; and building all kinds of buildings for our military's use. At this base, we also had Vietnamese people working with us. To complete a job around the new ampi-theater, I was assigned to supervise a group of about 10 Vietnamese women.

Time moved along, and everything went along as it was intended. Since I was assigned a truck, each day, I moved the crew I was assigned and their tools and all needed supplies to their work sites each morning or whatever their work time was. Start times were different because sometimes we worked at night if the weather was scorching hot. Also, I supplied another crew with all the needed supplies they required to complete their projects. We worked six and ½ days a week, with Sunday afternoons off. On Sundays afternoons, I was supposed to turn my truck back into the motor pool. I usually did not. Then after lunch, several guys would pile on the back of my truck, and we would go to the Marine's Hospital on the other side of the DaNang River. To cross the river, we had to drive over a pontoon bridge our military assembled. It sat down on the water. You would be in very deep water if you slipped off the edge. The river was about 1000 feet wide. At the hospital, everyone could drink hard liquor. At our base, we were only allowed to drink beer. Because I was driving, I rarely drank anything more substantial than Coca-Cola. I have never liked alcohol much. But the guys enjoyed doing this. Some drank more than they should have. I went along with getting to the hospital and back. We never got into trouble, but we did come close one time.

Because I was driving a truck, I had to get our supplies from our supply yard. After a while, I learned how to load my truck and how to make it easier to unload it at the job sites. Almost every time I pulled into our supply yard, there would be some Vietnamese children. They must have liked me because I always talked to them, and once in a while, I gave them a few pieces of candy. Because I was operating a truck to transfer supplies, I also needed to make lots of trips with trash to the dump site. Our military had started the dump site reasonably close to the ocean beach. The beaches there were pristine and beautiful! Usually, while driving into the dump area, some kids would run and jump on the back of my truck. The roads were deplorable, and much traveling would be about 10 MPH. After the kids were on my truck, they would throw everything they wanted to use for building materials off my truck. I did not care. They would have picked it out of the trash area anyway. None of the kids were injured, and it helped me unload the truck. The Vietnamese people's living areas along these roads were built from wood pieces and covered with cardboard boxes.

Vietnam is a lovely country. Lots of green spaces. Lots of 3-wheeled taxis and tons of people. The Monsoon rains bring lots of water in the spring of the year. But it does get sweltering in the summertime. Driving around the area, I could easily see where some of the wealthy families lived and where the poorer people lived. It looked to me that the more impoverished people had a one-room home with a dirt floor and a stove in the middle of the room. The stove usually had a lit candle sitting on it. I was told it was to keep their tea water warm. A lot of these experiences I tried to explain to dad and mom while I was home before I needed to return to the base. I do not think anyone could completely understand what my eyes saw. .

After nine months of work there, our Battalion departed from Da Nang in mid-January 1967 and flew back to California. Our Batallion, MCB 10, was to head back to Vietnam in May 1967. It meant we would have about four months to spend back in the USA. After nearly all of us had arrived back at our military base in Oxnard, Ca. from Vietnam, just about everyone went on leave to their homes for a short time. I took leave and went back home to Indiana. I had 30 days before I needed to be back on the base. While in Indiana, I spent all my time helping with all the farm chores I could. It was mid-January and early February in Indiana. On this trip, I visited many relatives and friends. I did not do anything special. But all along, I kept thinking that if I drove my car back to California, I would have a way to get back to our Base in Oxnard, Ca. I would also have transportation while there, and then I could store my car at the vehicle storage place there on the base when I had to head back to Vietnam for my 3rd trip. Also, I would have transportation back to Indiana after I was discharged in March 1968. Because I was driving back to California, a fellow Seabee had wanted me to stop in Des Moines, Iowa, to visit a young lady. I do not remember why, but I looked her up, took her to dinner, met her family, and then proceeded to California the following day. I stayed that night in a hotel. I drove on to Texas the next day. I stayed the next night in Texas and went to Flagstaff, Arizona, the following day. I spent the night in Arizona and drove to Oxnard, California, the next day. The day I drove away from Flagstaff, ice covered the road for the first two hours of driving.

After I arrived at the base towards the end of February, I needed to get all my clothing, military gear, equipment, etc., organized. Plus, much of my dress needed to be replaced because I had just plain worn it out. Vietnam was hot, dirty, and sweaty while we were there. Much of my newer clothing required alterations. The Military dress issued is usually much too large and long for me. And I had to have new rank patches sewn on because I had advanced in rank while overseas. I had advanced from E-4 to E-5. I also needed special stickers for my car to be legally on the base.

Before, while working and doing my duties in Vietnam, my friend Daryl persuaded me to study and increase my rank. That meant learning different books for advancement in rank. Growing my rank meant higher pay. It was not too hard because Daryl was of a higher rank than me. His higher rank enabled him to recommend me for advancement to the higher pay grades. As a result, when I returned from Vietnam for the first time, I was up to an E-4. When I returned from our second tour from Da Nang, I increased my rank to an E-5. One benefit of being of E-5 rank was that we could live outside the military base instead of living in the barracks while we were here in the states. And the Navy would give us an allotment of pay for doing this. The Navy did not have to pay our food expenses, but they still had to furnish our military clothing. That was about it. There were other minor benefits to getting an apartment off base, but I still had to be at our Military Base for all our daily battalion activities.

Before we departed Da Nang in January 1967, and by being E-5s, a Navy friend suggested that the two of us get an apartment off the military base. That sounded good, and we agreed to split the apartment costs. We decided on who and how we would do the food preparation. The two of us had to furnish all our personal things. The apartment provided sheets, plates, pots, pans, and silverware. We had to provide all cleaning supplies. The two of us talked, and each of us agreed as to who would furnish each of these supplies. The two of us found an apartment in Ventura, Ca., about 8 miles from the base. We looked at it, paid the first month's rent and deposit, and then we both went on leave to our homes. By living off base, for sure, I needed my transportation. That was the main factor in my decision to drive my car back to California in February 1967. My apartment sharer also drove his vehicle back for his transportation to get back and forth to the base.

I mentioned before that I would store my car in the storage lot when I needed to return to Vietnam for my 3rd tour. After we all had resumed our regular duties, I was assigned back to welding school. That meant I had to be at the base welding school by 6 am daily through the week. We did not need to stand duty while in school. The welding school was about six weeks long. It was just welding all the time, and our welds would be tested for strength and perfection. I could have been a better welder at first, since I went to this welding school before. But after a short time, I was certifying all welds and moving up the list to more stringent welding. I was a certified welder in many welding positions when I finished school. Accredited welders in the civilian world usually receive a pretty good salary.

After completing school, the entire battalion started doing more military training. That meant training with the Marines. We did rifle and pistol shooting for accuracy, plus we had lots of physical activity. We did several long hikes and runs, some during the day and some after dark. We were all getting ready for our next tour back to Vietnam. Because I was an E-5, I was assigned to be a squad leader, which meant I needed to be responsible for about ten other men. We all did very well, and each of us did as we were told while we were getting closer to the time to depart the States.

I am still determining the exact date President Johnson signed a Congressional Bill. It stated that any Military personnel, who had been in the country of Vietnam for more than 12 months, had to have two years of shore duty before the Navy could send anyone to Vietnam again. I had been in Vietnam for 16 months before this time. That meant I could not return to Vietnam for at least two years. Within a few days, the Navy gave many of us orders to leave the Batallion. Several of us had been in Vietnam for more than 12 months. I was given my orders to report to Naval Air Station Alameda. I had about four days to prepare for the move. I had to turn in all the Military equipment assigned to me. My rifle, all the Military green clothing issued to me, all the other issued survival gear, etc. At NAS Alameda, I needed my regular Navy Military issued clothing. This meant I would now wear the clothing first given to me during my boot camp training. I would be at this new base assignment for about nine months. Before I arrived at NAS Alameda, some clothing needed to be replaced and altered. I ensured I had all I needed before departing the Batallion Base.

I was given four days to travel from Oxnard, California, to Alameda, California. It was a one-day driving trip, about 375 miles each way. Luckily I had my car because it would have taken me some time to ride the bus or train to get there without it. I drove up northern California to Alameda. I looked the base over and wandered around the new area for a day or two before checking into the NAS base. I stayed with a friend for two nights in San Jose, Ca. I checked into NAS Alameda on June 1st, 1967. I had continually been writing and calling dad and mom, telling them how my life and travels were going. It was hard for them to understand everything I was doing. But everything was moving along smoothly for me.

I tried my best to explain to dad and mom what I had been doing these past two and three years. But how could they understand? What I had been doing and experiencing was so foreign to the farming industry. I wanted them to understand all my feelings while away from them. But from all my discussions with dad, no matter where we were or what we were doing, dad never asked anything about my past experiences or future life plans. I needed to think more clearly about what I wanted my future to be.

I have seen pictures of Vietnam and DaNang as it is now. Of course, it has progressed tremendously after our military left there in 1973. There are skyscrapers and tons of new modern buildings. The tallest building was about three stories in height when we were there. Several people I have talked with lived around Siagon, South Vietnam. They showed me photos, and nothing looked similar to how it was in the '60s. Time and progress move on. I guess I am just getting old. My recent experiences seem so much foreign to dad's living style. I wonder if he ever tried to understand me.

Dee, Entering My Future

Now, I need to tell all my readers that several things happened to me between late February 1967 and June 1st, 1967. I was 23 years old. I will explain. At the end of February 1967, after we all were back at the Navy base in California, a Navy friend asked me to drive him to Ventura, Ca. to see an old friend of his. He was from Texas, and his lady friend was also from Texas. One evening after we had done our duties for that day, I went to the base and picked up my friend Earl, my Navy friend, and we drove to that lady's address. Earl and the lady (Janet) talked about their friends and experiences in Texas and their plans. I was not in their conversation. I only knew what Earl mentioned later. His friend Janet had two children, and her children and I sat in their living room watching TV. We were at Janet's place for over an hour before departing. I took Earl back to the base and returned to my apartment. But just as Earl and I were leaving Janet's apartment, Janet asked me if I could come back to her apartment to meet her friend. I had no idea who her friends were. I told Janet yes, but I would not be able to stay very long, as I always needed to be at the base for welding school at 6 am the following morning. We did not set a date or time. I only said I would call her next week.

The weekend came and went. On a Monday, I was doing my laundry in the apartment building's laundry room where I lived. There was a pay phone in the laundry area, so I called Janet. Janet asked me to come over that evening to meet her friend. I told her I could after I finished doing my laundry. I went to Janet's apartment that Monday evening and arrived a little after 7 pm. Janet and her friend (Mary) were there with their four children. Janet had a daughter and a son. Mary had two daughters. They had been playing scrabble and some other kids games too. It was fun being with these young children. They were about 5 to 8 years old. We all talked, played more games, and then about 8:30 pm, I said I needed to get back to my apartment because being at school comes early in the morning, and I wanted to get some rest. Then Janet and Mary both spoke up and said, "Oh no, you cannot go yet. You have not met our other friend". I thought Mary was the friend Janet had wanted me to meet. I then asked when this other friend would arrive, and they said a little after 9 pm. So I agreed I would wait.

Janet and her kids, and I played more of one of the games while I was waiting. Sure enough, at about 9:15, Mary and this other beautiful red-haired lady walked through Janet's apartment door. As soon as I saw this red-haired lady, I said to myself, "That is the woman I want to marry." Her name was Dee. I was introduced, and then we all sat and played more scrabble games and some other board games. This lady Dee and I sat in Janet's apartment, and we talked the entire evening and into the morning too. Mary and her children had gone home, and Janet and her children had gone to bed too. Dee was tired, and I was tired, but I had met this person I really liked.

We talked and talked and talked. I found out Dee worked at a restaurant, and I asked if I could meet her at the restaurant the following evening and if I could see her again. Dee said yes, and told me the name of the restaurant. It was close to my apartment. Then, this early morning, I departed Janet's apartment at about 5 am. Dee went back to her apartment, and I went back to my apartment. After I returned to my apartment, I made a fried egg sandwich for my breakfast and then went to the welding school at the base.

I had been looking for a special lady to take home with me to our family. Someone kind, hard-working, and someone I felt comfortable around. Dee fit all my categories. Dee and I hit it off right away. I did meet her at the restaurant where she worked the following evening, and I did drive her home after her work shift was over. Ventura is a relatively small city. Each evening we were together, and after that, we talked about what we had been doing. And what each of us had hoped and planned for our future lives. I had told Dee that I was in the military and was to get discharged the following March of 1968. Dee and I were growing and spending a lot of time together. On the weekends, Dee and I took all four children, Janet's and Mary's, to some parks, the beach, and many other things. We all had fun together. After Dee and I had met, and in that short time, we had grown enormously fond of each other. I asked Dee to marry me, even though we had only known each other for about three weeks. Dee answered yes when I proposed. I told Dee that because I was in the military, I was scheduled to return to Vietnam sometime in May of that year. I also told Dee that I wanted to marry her, but I did not want to get married until I was finished with Vietnam.

My reasons for this were because of the experiences of being in a war zone; anything can happen at any time. My eyes had seen a lot of destruction. With driving a truck, it seemed to me that it could be pretty easy for the enemy to know where the driver would be sitting. While driving, I never worried about being shot or killed at all the other deployments. I just moved on and paid little attention to the gunfire overhead. And how could I know where it was coming from anyway. I did not carry my rifle in my truck. It only got dirty and scratched, and I was tired of cleaning it. If it was my time to die, so be it. This was the main reason I did not want to marry Dee until I never needed to leave the States. Plus, some Seabee buddies would get their Dear John letters while overseas. Meaning their spouses wanted to divorce them. I did not want any part of that experience. Dee agreed with my wishes and told me several times that she would wait for me. That totally made me feel good, but I would not change my mind. Marriage had to wait.

As Dee and I continued dating, things started to change for me in the military.. This change meant we could get married anytime. We talked extensively, and I decided to check into NAS Alameda myself to get up to date with my new duty station. Also to find out what my new duties would require of me. And I searched the surrounding areas for what things were good and what areas would need improvement. I learned a tremendous amount from other Navy buddies at Alameda. I made many new friends very quickly. They recommended the areas to look for an apartment. NAS Alameda is on the island of Alameda, Ca., which is close to San Francisco. It is surrounded by water and connected by three bridges and a pair of tubes/tunnels. These tubes/tunnels run under the Bay waters.

NAS (Naval Air Station) Alameda

After checking in at the base, I was assigned to the Public Works Department. It is the department that handles everything not connected to the aircraft area of the Navy. There were about 25 Navy personnel in the Public Works

Department, plus many civilians. I do not know the approximate amounts of any of us. But the base had about 5000 civilian personnel working there each day in other departments.

Several Navy ships were tied up at this NAS station, and ships were constantly coming and going. These ships had what we called Fleet Sailors. And NAS had many Navy Airborn personnel. I was a Seabee, not officially connected to any Air Division of the Navy, but I was assigned to the Airborn area. My duties at NAS included doing metal work during the weekdays and building wooden projects. We were assigned to repair several different projects too. I also had to do my duty with the Public Works Department.

My duties started as a driver when I was not working at our welding/building shop during weekday hours. In the beginning, I drove people around the base and sometimes off the military compound in a Navy taxi van. It was a little van that could haul about six people. We also had regular Ford automobiles for transporting the higher-up Brass personnel. It was only a short time before they wanted me to start driving a bus to move both Navy and civilian personnel. During the weekdays, my bus trips usually only consisted of driving people around the base. Once in a while, I would need to take a group to the city of Alameda, Oakland, and sometimes to San Francisco. On weekends, sometimes I was assigned to take Marines to Santa Rosa for military training.

At first, I was driving an older Chrysler-manufactured bus, but there was another Chevrolet bus that I liked much better. The Chevrolet bus was the one I always wanted to drive when going to San Francisco. Because many of the streets in San Francisco are narrow and have sharp turns, especially in the Chinatown area. And for sure, there was always plenty of traffic to be concerned with in San Francisco. However, I always made out ok. I was always careful, and I took my time. After awhile, the Navy purchased two new buses. They had a governor on the engine, and the mechanic had set it at 55 MPH. On trips of any distance, it seemed we were never going to get there. The speed limit was 55 MPH, but everyone on the freeway system always went 65+ MPH. My bus going at 55 MPH was too dangerous on the freeways. Plus, there were always a few Marines telling me to go faster. I could not make it go faster. How could I explain all these experiences to dad and mom? I called about once a week when I could. I never knew if they were happy to hear from me or not.

I worked hard all the time while doing my military service. I learned a tremendous amount of knowledge from books and hands-on experience. In those four years, I have many recollections of things that happened. Some were good, and some were not so good. But all were learning experiences. From a very young age, I learned about military service from a few of my Aunts and Uncles. I knew to make representing our country heartfelt, which I did. And now, as I look back, I did as good of a job as I possibly could. At least, I hope I did. When I was about 16 years old, I knew I would have to spend time in the Military. I read a little about military service and the different branches. I put in my four years of active and two years of inactive duty and used my GI bill. I hope I represented and honored our country the way I felt it needed to be defined. I Love our Country. As I have said, I wonder what dad thought about my service.

Dee and Travels

My regular duties at NAS Alameda were Monday thru Friday, 8 am to 5 pm. On weekends, when I did not need to stand duty, I wanted to see my Dee. At the same time, I lived on the base before marriage. I shared a barracks room with one of my Senior Petty Officers, Alex. If I had to stand duty on a weekend, usually one weekend a month,

I could not go to see my Dee. But when I wasn't on duty, I would drive down to Ventura, Ca., or ride the Greyhound Bus to Ventura. I usually drove my car, even though it was 370 miles each way. On the weekends, when I did not have duty, Alex would tell me to attend our meetings at 8 am, and then I should take off for Ventura. That worked out well, as I could be in Ventura by early evening. Dee usually got off work about 9 pm. Dee and her roommate, Mary, and Mary's two children allowed me to stay with them. They said I could sleep on their couch. I usually took a change of clothes and had other clothing in my car if needed. One weekend before we married, Alex drove himself and me in his car to Ventura. Alex wanted to scout out the area. Then we both drove back to Alameda that Sunday evening.

My mother had come to Alameda to visit me shortly after the Navy gave me orders to the NAS station. Mom, Uncle Bill, and Aunt Mary had come along with their son Ronnie. It was their vacation. They wanted to see the west coast and mom and Uncle Bill's sister in San Diego. That weekend, we all drove to southern California. Uncle Bill wanted to visit friends in the LA area. On the way, I stopped in Ventura and picked up Dee to go along with us. Uncle Bill's family stayed that night with their friends. Mom, Dee, and I stayed in a hotel in the LA area. Then on to San Diego to see their sister the next morning. After arriving in Chula Vista, we spent the day with them. While visiting Aunt Rita and Uncle Ralph, Uncle Ralph asked me to go to the store with him. I had no idea why until he told me I should not marry Dee. Mom and Aunt Rita had persuaded him to try to convince me not to marry Dee. Now I could see why he wanted me to go to the store with him. Of course, I paid no attention to that conversation. Then Dee and I left mom, and we drove back to northern California. I dropped Dee back in Ventura at her apartment, then went back to Alameda. This trip occurred close to the 4th of July holiday in 1967.

August, the month before we married, and while I was fulfilling my Navy duties, I looked around Alameda for an apartment for Dee and me. We could not live on the base because more senior military personnel were already occupying those living units. I finally found an apartment about 2 miles from the Navy base. It was not great, but we could manage there for seven months. Then, after we were married, not far from our apartment was another apartment building where a Navy friend lived with his wife. She was pregnant. That worked out well because that lady and Dee became good friends. Then the four of us visited often and played games, especially on the days we did not need to be at the Navy base. The husband and I commuted to the base together each day. We were in the same department.

Several other Navy friends did come by our apartment to visit too. I acquired several new good friends. One was Henry. Henry was a lifelong military career man. Dorothy (Henry's wife) was a wonderful lady from Puerto Rico. Henry and Dorothy had five children. Henry referred to them as animals. Dee sometimes tried to babysit them. Those children were a handful. We had lots of fun living in that little, cold apartment. I had told Dee that I had no intention of re-enlisting. I wanted out of the Navy and military duty. Dee knew what my plans were, and she felt good about my decisions, and so did I. I hoped dad and mom would be happy with our choices.

Marriage

Each time I visited Dee in Ventura, we talked about our future. We made our plans and picked out a wedding date. Then we went to the County Marriage License Bureau in Ventura and purchased our marriage license. After we had done that, somehow, the following week or two, Dee found the church where she wanted us to marry. Then we made an appointment to talk with the minister there and told him the date we had picked. Everything went well. Dee and I were married on Friday, September 1st, 1967, Labor Day Holiday Weekend. I drove to Ventura on Thursday. That evening I gave my car to Janet to allow Dee and all her group to get to the church for the wedding the following afternoon. I stayed in Ventura with another discharged Navy friend that Thursday night. He was married, had two children, and had a nice little sleeping area beside his garage.

Ventura is pretty warm in the Autumn My friend drove his wife and me to our wedding. Someone babysat their children. Reverend Grossitt performed the ceremony in the parsonage next to the church. There were about 15 of us. Connie L. was Dee's Maid of Honor, 7 yrs old. And Michael M. was my Best Man, 8 yrs old. The Reverend's wife was there, and she signed the marriage certificate as a witness. It was a beautiful Wedding Ceremony. Another Connie brought fresh flowers for us. The flowers were multiple kinds and different colors. I do remember Dee had some white flowers in her hands. After we said our I do's, we all returned to Dee and Mary's apartment for cake, coffee, and the opening of our wedding gifts. We both sincerely thanked everyone for attending and for all the assistance they had given us. It was such a lovely occasion. I hope everyone enjoyed themselves. Dee and I enjoyed our wedding day immensely. After everyone left the festivities, Dee and I packed all of Dee's belongings into my car and trailer.

Earlier, at the shop in Alameda, I built a trailer to haul some of our belongings back to Indiana after I was discharged. Then Dee and I left Ventura that night. Now I am with my new bride. We departed Ventura at about 11:30 pm and drove to Alameda, California. We arrived at our Alameda apartment around 7 am Saturday. We chose Labor Day weekend because it gave us an extra day to finish everything, plus get all of Dee's things to our apartment in Alameda. We unloaded everything and parked our trailer and car in their usual locations. Then Dee and I lay down and took a nice long nap. Later that evening, I took Dee to the local coffee shop (Tim's) for dinner. An excellent meal and I was so happy with Dee by my side.

Dee and I settled into our everyday lives. We were going to other Navy friends' homes every couple of days. They all became our family too. When we got together with them, we always played some kind of table board game. And sadly, most of us smoked cigarettes. A lot of beer was consumed. After Dee had been in Alameda for a couple of weeks, she wanted to get back to work as a waitress to help increase our income. Dee always worked with the Union, so it was easy for her to gain employment. I had always told Dee that I wanted to return to Indiana to be a farmer after being discharged. Dee said she was happy for us to do that. I wanted Dee to have the family life she had never had as a child.

While living in Alameda, we spent our weekends shopping at the flea markets, wandering around the whole area to see what we could see. For our Thanksgiving that year, Dee had to work that day. While Dee was at work, I baked a pumpkin pie. The pie was supposed to be our Thanksgiving dinner dessert. But there was no sugar in it; we threw it away. After Dee had returned home that day, we went to Tim's for our Thanksgiving dinner. When we arrived back at our apartment after eating, a long-haired black kitty was sitting on the doorstep. We could not ignore the kitty, so we brought it inside and fed and cared for it. We named it Dutchess. Dutchess was a wonderful kitty. The Christmas holiday came, and we had a small tree. Dutchess kept tipping it over. She wanted to play with the ornaments. I was going to the base every day, fulfilling my military duties. Dee was working each day as a waitress.

I was on duty some evenings, but we lived close to the bus stop for Dee. She could get home quickly when I could not meet her. That area of town always had lots of foot traffic, too. It was a safe area for everyone. There was a local grocery store about two blocks away. Dee liked to shop there. It was easy to walk to and carry a bag of supplies home. We did most of our shopping at the base commissary. After Dee and I married, I had been writing and calling dad and mom. I knew about the time of day to call them when they were not busy. I wondered many times; what dad would have been thinking about me and everything I tried to tell and explain to him and mom. The Life I have lived here on the west coast looks foreign compared to the farm life I experienced when I was younger. I wish dad could have been able to share some of my experiences. And life.

While Dee and I lived in Alameda, the cement floor in our apartment was very cold in the mornings, so we purchased several throw carpets to help keep our feet from getting cold. I mentioned how our kitty would jump from carpet to carpet to avoid the cold floor. We also purchased a wall lamp at the base commissary to light that kitchen better. We still have that lamp; hanging on our kitchen wall here in Oakland, California, 55 years later.

As time passed, Dee and I were saving our money and making plans for our departure from the Navy. Dad and mom knew I was planning to be a farmer. But a couple of weeks before the Navy signed me out of the military, mom had sent us a letter saying they may not need my help and to think it over about Dee and my future. Well, I paid no attention. I made up my mind years before about my future, what I imagined it would look like, while I was overseas because I had time to think. I knew then that I wanted to get married and for the two of us to return to Indiana to settle down. I had no idea I would meet Dee, but after I did and learned about her, she fit me perfectly. I loved my Dee. I wanted to be with Dee no matter what came about. I knew we could work through anything. I knew my mother did not like Dee much, but I thought mom would accept her as my wife. I never did find out exactly why my mother did not care for my wife. (Probably because they thought she was a "City Girl").

Things continued moving along, and then Friday, March 8th, (1968) came. I was supposed to get out of the Navy on March 10th. But because the 10th was a Sunday, I was separated on Friday the 8th. I went to the base that Friday morning, did my regular duties, and they told me to go to the Base Captain's office after lunch. I did, and he asked me to re-enlist, but I said no. Then he gave me my paperwork. I signed some of it and kept the rest. Also, part of the package was my departure pay slip. I went to the finance office and collected all my pay due up to March 10th.

After I was finished that afternoon, I returned to our apartment and loaded everything we were taking with us in our car and trailer, plus Dee and Dutchess. Then we left Alameda, California. The Navy had already shipped most of our things, via a moving van, to dad's farm. Dee wanted to see her friend Gayle, who lived in Hollywood, before we left California for good. We drove from Alameda to Hollywood and parked our car and trailer in front of Gayle's apartment building. I kept a wooden box full of things to take with us, as we may need an item or two along our way. I had thought about taking the box inside Gayle's apartment, but it was heavy, and Dee and I decided it would be ok out in the trailer. The second night there, someone stole the box. I really felt terrible about that, and I still do. Because it had pictures of Dee's father and all my Navy uniforms, I looked around the area for the box, but I could not find anything. Dee and I decided to go ahead and get to Indiana. We said our goodbyes to Gayle and took off. We drove during the day and stopped at motels for the nights. It took us four days to drive to dad and mom's farm in Indiana.

Dee and I have had a wonderful life together. For sure, Dee and I were made to be with each other. I wish dad could have been more of a part of our lives. I always thought dad would like Dee and appreciate all we were trying to do. I always thought dad would have made similar decisions and goals, which Dee and I have been attempting to do. Dee and I always had love in our hearts and hoped to express it as much as possible. I know dad really liked Dee. Yes, Dee had different ways and ideas, but we always agreed and enjoyed our lives together.

Arriving at Dad's Farm

We arrived at dad and mom's farm about 5 pm. I do not remember the exact date in 1968. I parked our car and trailer down at the barn area of the farm. I knew dad and mom would be milking because of the time. I did not think that would be a problem. Dee and I went into the milkhouse, and I walked into the milking parlor. Mom was there, I gave her a big hug, and dad was in the middle of the milking parlor. I walked down and gave dad a big hug. Sadly, dad was not happy to see Dee or me. Then dad said to get Dee and me out of the milking parlor, because we were making the cows nervous. I did not know what to do or what to say to Dee, dad, or mom. Dee and I went back into the milkhouse. I think Dee and I went outside for a short time. This was the first time I wondered if I had made a big mistake by returning to Indiana. But it was my goal to be a farmer.

After dad and mom finished the milking, the 4 of us talked briefly, and I helped clean the barn and complete the farm chores. Then we went to dad and mom's house for the evening meal. I have no idea what mom prepared. Dad and mom owned the property up the road, the 160-acre property. Dee and I were going to occupy that house on that property, but it wasn't ready for occupancy for another couple of weeks. We stayed with dad and mom for about two weeks before we had the house prepared for us to move in. Then we took the things the Navy had shipped because they had arrived. We put them on my wagon temporarily. Then we moved everything in. When Dee and I came to Indiana, we had saved $500, plus our traveling expenses. We used that money to purchase furniture, stoves, tables, a refrigerator, etc., for that house. There were no furnishings inside the house. Before we moved in, Dee and I agreed with dad and mom that we would help on the farm, and they would pay us $50 per week, plus we could have all the milk and eggs we wanted. Each day, Dee and I would go to the farm early, help with the milking, feeding, bedding, etc., and do the same things again each evening. We attended farm sales to get furniture and other items needed to complete our home. I used our car and trailer to haul these items. As fieldwork started, I was helping with everything, knowing what needed to be done. Later, I purchased an old Chevrolet pickup truck from a friend. I had been using my car and trailer, but the farm really needed a pickup truck.

After Dee and I had been back in Indiana for about six weeks, mom arranged a wedding reception at dad and mom's house for Dee and me. This was a big surprise for both of us. It was such a nice thing, and we received many beautiful gifts. Some of those gifts we are still using today, 55 years later.

After some time, Dee felt she wanted to return to waitress work mainly because we needed more money. The $50 needed to be more to cover gasoline, food, insurance, etc. The $500 was all used up. Dad and mom had put limits on what Dee could do at the farm. Dee did not feel needed around the farm at all. She wanted to help us out by going to work. Dee was an outstanding waitress. Dee found a waitress job in Greenville, Ohio. Her working hours were 8 pm to 2 am. I would take her to work, come home, rest, and then return to pick her up. There were a couple of times I was late picking Dee up, because I was so tired

I could not wake up when the alarm went off. I started setting two alarm clocks. Dee worked there for about three months. Dee did not like working there because most patrons were drunk, spoiled young men. I suggested Dee find something better and closer to our house. Dee never did drive a vehicle. I always had to find the time and ways to get Dee to work and home from work.

In September 1968, I had my tonsil taken out. Tremendous pain. There was not much fieldwork at the farm at that time of year. Shortly after, I found a job at the Union City Body Company. A stock person at first, and then an opening for a welder came up. I took that welding position. I needed to do something to get more income. It required me to work the second shift. Luckily, Dee found a waitress job in Winchester, Indiana. And its hours were almost the same as mine. But that job was challenging because Dee was required to mop the entire restaurant floor after the restaurant was closed. The mops were very heavy, even for me. But it worked out. So after I finished my shift, I went to the restaurant and mopped the restaurant floors while Dee could do much of the lighter work. Dee did not like working there very much either. I knew why. Luckily, the Westinghouse factory in Union City, Indiana, was hiring, and Dee applied and started working there doing something to electric motors. Dee was never mechanically inclined, but a friend (Jeannettia) helped Dee learn the job. It was also working the 2nd shift. The only thing was, Dee's hours started an hour before mine. Jeannettia agreed to drop Dee off at my car when Dee's shift was over, and Dee would wait for me in our car. It was good, except it was pretty cold in the wintertime. With both of us working 2nd shift, I was able to help dad with the farming before I had to go to work. And when I came home from work, I fed and cared for the beef cattle; dad raised in the barn where we lived. This schedule was not the best, but it was working. Dee and I usually drove our old truck to work, and golly, it was cold when the winter temperature was around zero. Dad never did tell me anything about my decision to work in a factory. I know dad did not think factory workers earned their pay. Dad thought the workers were over paid, and did little work to earn it.

I am still determining the exact date, but it was around October 1968. It was one of the times when mom and I were walking from the milk barn back to their house for all of us to get ready for the evening meal. Often, Dee and I would eat with mom and dad, and the next time they would come to our house to eat with us. Both Dee and mom were good cooks, and the food tasted great. But this time, as mom and I were walking back to the house, mom suggested I "divorce Dee and send her back to California." I knew from the start that mom never really liked Dee very much. Probably because Dee was not a country girl, and Dee was a beautiful woman. As we got closer to the house, I told Mom, "I don't know." That was all that was said then, and I just let it pass. But I loved my Dee, and I could never send her away. However, one frigid winter evening, after we had gotten home from work, Dee told me that she did not like that cold weather. But she loved me, and could we find a warmer climate for both of us to work and live? I made my decision right then. The next day, Dee and I talked again, and I told Dee that I wanted her and me to move back to California. When I left the military, a man told me about a welding job in northern California. I knew Dee was unhappy in Indiana, and our mother did not care for Dee. It seemed to me that it was best for the two of us and our future to make a change. Dee and I talked about it and decided when to make a move, so we saved as much money as we could. We did not owe anything, and we could be free. But at that time, I made up my mind that we would never ask my parents for anything, ever. And to this day, we have never asked for anything of my parents, only to respect our Love.

About four weeks before we left Indiana, dad was down at

the barn when I was feeding his cattle. That is when I told dad that Dee and I would move back to California. Dad started crying. The only time I had ever seen my father cry was at his mother's funeral. I felt terrible, but it had to be. All the furnishings we had purchased to occupy the house we were living in, we left for my brother and his wife, plus the truck. I do not think dad ever knew exactly how much my mother did not like Dee. I am sure dad never knew what mom had asked me to do. I never told him. I wish I could have, but I did not want to create any more stress for my dad. Dad had enough pressure from his business. Dad knew that I loved him tremendously. And I do know; dad really liked Dee. Sometimes, when dad was at our house, dad and Dee would laugh uncontrollably about something one of them had said. It was wonderful!

I do not know if dad and mom ever knew how much I wanted to be a farmer. That was my whole plan after I graduated from high school. That was my intention all the time I was in the military. And after I met Dee, she knew I wanted to go to Indiana to be a farmer. And that was ok with Dee. Dee loves animals of all kinds. Yes, she was scared at first, but that was because it was all so strange to her. And Dee knew about cows and milking them because her grandfather cared for them at a Pennsylvania farm. I know Dee, she would have made a good farmer's wife. I only know dad did not want Dee and me to move back to California.

But before Dee and I discussed moving to California, this was around September 1968; as dad and I drove home from the Shaw farm in his pickup truck, dad suggested I purchase a farm. I would have loved to do that and knew precisely the farm I wanted. Dad did too, and I am sure I could have purchased it at a reasonable price. The owner liked me because I had helped them extensively before I had to go into the military. Dad wanted me to get into farming, which would have been a great opportunity. But I told dad I couldn't do that because Dee and I didn't even have $50 in the bank, and how could I afford an expense like that? How could I pay for a farm? Dad did not know how much mom did not want Dee around. That is all dad ever said about me purchasing a property. Not having any money in the bank was why I found a job at the Union City Body Company. Dee and I were not big spenders; however, we needed cash to pay our bills and living expenses. We had insurance, fuel bills, food to buy, Dee liked to send greeting cards, etc. We had to pay for these somehow. We did not have to pay rent for our house because that was the agreement between dad and me. I would care for the cattle in the barn in exchange for the rent of his house.

I felt terrible then and feel bad now, but I knew those decisions were the only way for Dee and me. I decided no more farming, and I have never looked back. Dee and I were determined to make it, no matter what may get in our way. And Dee and I are successful today. Health is an issue, but we never know what tomorrow can bring for any of us. I wonder if dad ever knew why Dee and I moved back to California. I am sure mom never told dad anything about her and my conversation. I do not think mom really wanted me to return to Indiana or to think about becoming a farmer, especially if Dee was with me. I never knew what dad thought.

Dad purchasing more

Dad and mom had purchased the 167 acre farm property on the corner. It is at the intersection of Greenville Pike, and St Rd 227, one-half mile from their current farm. It was July 1964. It was the property with a lovely house where Dee and I lived for 14 months. The time was after I had gotten out of the military. However, the 167 acre property needed lots of clearing and work to get it looking the way dad wanted it to look. Dad never liked grownup fencerows, and this property had lots of them. They take away from productive and valuable producing land. Dad had a contractor work on it, along with my brother and another neighbor. But after dad died, it lost his loving care. Of course, mom inherited all the properties after dad passed. Mom did her best to care for all the properties, but dad's TLC was not there anymore.

Sometime after dad died, mom sold off 7 acres of the 167 acre property. She sold the house, barn, and a couple of outbuildings, to the people who lived there. They are continuing to occupy that seven-acre property today in 2023

The 160 Acre Property

After our mother died, I acquired this property. I inherited enough money to pay for part of it, and I had to pay from my savings that portion over my inheritance to obtain it. It was during the year 2013. I plan to keep it going for several more years. I wanted to stay with farming as an occupation, but that idea never worked out for me. However, this is the closest I have come to agriculture. One of our neighbors rents it and does this property's actual farming and tilling. It works out well. Thankfully my sister and brother-in-law have a tractor and can mow around the edges of the fields to help keep the grass and weeds under control. My brother-in-law and I needed to do quite an extensive cleanup of this property after I took ownership. I still need to keep up maintenance to keep it looking the way my dad would want it to look. I wish I could spend much more time out in the fields of this property, but my wife needs my caregiving every day in Oakland because she is disabled. Therefore, I am limited in how much time I can spend on this land. I check on it twice a year.

I was thinking about this 160-acre property, just north of

dad's original 80-acre home on St Rd 227. I helped Maurice Gray care for this property before joining the military. Maurice rented it from its then-owner. Maurice started farming after moving back to his home in Indiana from Texas. Maurice had a stroke just about the year I graduated high school. He was unable to do anything physical after that. I do not know who was farming this property between then and when dad purchased it. Then while I was away in the military, my parents bought this land. Dad cleaned it up, built a barn, and upgraded everything. Dad installed many fences to contain the cattle and used temporary electric fences to split the fields. This property is rolling, with some hills and valleys. Dad put in some drainage ditches to help with the soil's drainage. The layout of the land is unusual but pretty. For many years, when I was in high school and when dad and I did a lot of raccoon hunting, we used to hunt in and through this wooded area several times during the hunting season. This wooded area was relatively clean compared to many other wooded regions we hunted in. Did we catch any raccoons there? I am very thankful to have ownership of this property.

Dee and My Move Back to California

While in the military at NAS (Naval Air Station) Alameda, I worked as a welder, mainly repairing garbage dumpsters for the Navy Base. The civilian gentleman supervisor, which I was working for, and who assigned the work to me told me that after I was discharged, he could put me to work for his department, repairing these dumpsters and any other projects that came into his shop. The shop where he was the supervisor was just across the fence from our Seabee's shop. The dumpsters, which needed repair, would be dropped off at his yard, and then I would bring them over to our space and use my tools there. Of course, after I was released from the Navy in 1968, I had no intentions of ever returning to northern California. But we never know what the future may bring.

However, several months later, when Dee and I decided to move back to California, applying for that repairing job was the position I had hoped to acquire. This was the main reason why we moved back to this area. When Dee and I moved back to this area, the Navy cut back on civilian personnel at the NAS base. I talked to the same supervisor, who told me about the cutbacks. He told me that he could not fill that position with me. Well, I was very disappointed. But after we settled into an apartment, Dee returned to waitress work the next day. I was looking through the newspapers for employment—very little work. But a lady at the California Unemployment Office told me that the Salvation Army was looking for truck drivers. I went to the Salvation Army store and applied for the position. I went to work the next day. The wages were small, but now I had some income. I drove a truck to pick up donated articles for about two months. The foreman I worked for then liked my work and gave me the heaviest route. I drove out of the store parking area around 7:30 am. It was always around 5 pm when I returned to the truck parking area. That was after I had unloaded the donations I had picked up that day. Most days, I drove about 100 miles and made about 25 pickups. All trucks had to be unloaded before parking because homeless people tended to get in the rear of the trucks during the night and scatter everything around. And they would help themselves to whatever they could find. I was determined to work enough to acquire some money to ensure our move back to California was successful.

After working for the Salvation Army for two months, one of our neighbors who lived next to the apartment where Dee and I were living told me that Del Monte Corporation down the street was hiring. I called the Salvation Army foreman the following day and told him I could not drive that day. Then I went to the Del Monte Office and applied for a job. Del Monte hired me, and I went to work for Del Monte the next day. I called the Salvation Army foreman again and told him what I had done that morning. He thoroughly understood and said I could always come back to drive for him. So I started at Del Monte and worked for Del Monte Corporation in Alameda, Ca. for 22 years. I would have stayed employed with Del Monte longer than 22 years, except they decided to move the plant where I had been working from Alameda to Stockton, Ca. I did not want to move to Stockton, which is about 65 miles each way from our home. That was the end of Del Monte for me. After leaving Del Monte's employment, I went to work for a beer distributor for 51 weeks. While there, a co-worker told me of a position working for the City of Alameda in their electrical warehouse. I applied and was hired. I left the beer distributor. In Alameda, I learned much about electricity and what it takes to get electrical power into our homes. This was the employer I was working for when I retired in 2005.

When Dee and I returned to California in May of 1969, we found a small one-bedroom apartment in Alameda, Ca. It was ok but very small. Then in July of 1970, Dee found a house for us to rent in Oakland, Ca. We lived in that house for about a year when we decided to look at buying a place of our own. It would be much better to invest in something tangible instead of giving our monthly rent money to someone else. We looked around, but we needed more money saved. But after looking at a few houses, we found our current home. We applied to purchase it and have lived here for 51+ years.

None of this was anything like what I had planned during the early years of my life. As Dee and our lives together were growing and moving along, we were steadily progressing in all areas of our lives. We reached some goals which we planned for our future. Dee and I are very flexible and would take things as they come. We are very thankful and appreciative. I always wondered what the future would bring for Dee and me. I also thought about my parents and how they were doing. Dee had no living parents. I felt that dad and mom would slow up, stop milking cows, and semi-retire at some point. That did not happen. But it would be good if dad could visit Dee and me here in California during some winter months. I realize this house is small, but we could survive for a few weeks. If my parents had visited often, we would have invested in a larger home or built onto this house. But after dad passed on, this house worked out very well for Dee and me. I still miss our father. This book has really brought up so very many memories. Memories I buried for 50+ years. This is why I decided to write about our father and so many of the beautiful things he did. Plus, so many of the things he and I did together. Wonderful memories. I have really missed him.

The End of My Father's Life

I will write this section as best and accurately as my recollection tells me.

Our father passed away in February 1973. Dad had been seriously ill since the first part of May 1972. Dad had had a significant heart attack but did not realize it. His health grew much worse as time moved along. Dad should have had more specialized medical care.

In May 1972, my sister and her husband visited Dee and me here in Oakland. I was 29 years old. We had called dad and mom to let them know my sister was heading home. We asked how they were doing. Mom said that dad had been sick. I wondered what the illness was. Mom explained that dad thought he had gotten ill from using and inhaling some kind of crop spray a few days before. Mom said dad had gone to see the doctor. Dad's doctor (who was not very good and also lost his medical license a few years later) told dad that he thought dad had something like the flu and sinus infection from the spray. But the doctor did tell dad he wanted to put dad in the hospital to run some tests. At least the doctor was smart enough to want to investigate further. But mom said that if it were just the flu, dad would get over it in a couple of days. Dad decided not to go into the hospital for any tests. But with that phone call, I felt that dad was pretty sick. I also felt dad's symptoms did not sound like the flu. I told mom I would jump on a plane as soon as possible. I wanted to return to Indiana to help dad and hopefully help dad get to feeling better and recuperate. I could get him to doctor's appointments, plus help with the milking and farming. But mom insisted, "No, you stay there in California," and that "she would take care of dad" and do the milking.

Dee and I lived in our current house in May 1972, and Dee was always very supportive of me. Especially for trying to do whatever I could when it came to my family or any problems that may arise. Dee suggested I go to Indiana to help and to see what I could do in November 1972. I talked to the people at my job, and they told me to take time off to do what I needed to do. I went to the farm, helped with the milking and chores, and harvested as much of the crops as possible. The date was around the first of December. Dad was in and out of the hospital. Mom and I visited dad each evening while he was in the hospital. The winter had set in, and it was cold. I tried to run the harvester at night after the earth became frozen because the earth was very soft with moisture during the day. It worked well at first. A neighbor man also helped by driving dad's truck to the elevator after I had filled it with the grain. After about three weeks, I had accomplished some, but one day it started snowing hard. I decided to return to California and Dee, with plans to return to Indiana in a couple more weeks. But after I had returned to

California, some of dad's neighbors finished the harvesting for dad. I think my brother was there and helped some, but mom said the neighbors did the harvesting.

I was calling mom about every night to see how dad was doing. I never saw Dad alive after the middle of December, after I had returned to California. Each time I called and talked to mom, she made it sound like dad was doing pretty well. But mom was covering over everything about dad's illness and not telling me anything about any hospitalizations or other doctor's visits. Dad had been in and out of the hospital a lot, but she never told me of it. Yes, Dee and I were distraught when we learned that dad had passed on.

Another of the last times I saw my father alive was in the Ball hospital in Muncie, Indiana. I sat beside him on his hospital bed. We talked, and he told me he wanted to leave us, his children, with something, meaning some monetary value. I knew what he was referring to, but I told him, "Dad, I do not want anything without you. Nothing is worth anything, if you are not here with it". I meant it then, and I mean it today. I wish he could have lived many years longer. But I never realized how very sick he was at that time. I thought at the time, dad would recuperate some and be able to have some more years of life. I have always felt that his smoking and diet shortened his lifespan. After dad became seriously ill from heart failure, he could not work. I went to Indiana to try to help harvest some of his crops later that year. Dad was well enough to get his crops planted that spring but too ill to harvest them. I did not get much accomplished, but I wanted to get anything done that I could. Dad had just purchased a new combine that needed several adjustments, which took precious time. I only hope all the things I have done in my lifetime would please my father.

It was a mistake on my part not to go back sooner. I always wished I returned and ensured dad received the best treatment possible. But dad became increasingly ill later in the year 1972.

I did go back in the latter part of October to see how dad was doing, but by then, dad had been admitted into the hospital in Muncie, Indiana. When I visited dad in the hospital, he was somewhat strong and in a room in the upper part of the hospital. The one vital thing that I remember from that visit, as dad and I were sitting on the side of the hospital bed, dad told me that he had lost consciousness while lying on the kitchen floor. Plus, he could not remember how long he lay on the kitchen floor before his conscience returned. Dad never told me which day of May that was. Also, dad said to me that he was suffering a lot. I did not know how he felt physically, but I knew he did not feel very good.

Of course, the hospital had plenty of tests done by then, and it was determined dad was suffering from "Heart Failure," which started in May. Later I discovered that half of his heart had died because of little or no blood circulation. If dad had gone to the hospital for tests in May, he possibly could have lived a little longer and maybe had heart surgery to help him. Of course, he would have needed to change his eating, work, exercise drastically, and stop smoking. But because of the severe damage to his heart in May, and not receiving any care then, dad's time here on earth was very limited. While I was visiting Dad, dad was discharged from the hospital. But he just had to go home and rest. That is what dad did, but his heart was already severely damaged. It also became necessary for dad to regularly see the Cardiologist doctor treating him, who was an excellent doctor. Dad was admitted in and out of the hospital on a couple of occasions. As a result of dad's illness and failure to get immediate care back in May, dad passed away the following February.

After dad had become so ill in November, I did go to Indiana to visit dad and tried to help with the daily chores. We usually took turns staying at the hospital with dad each time I was there. The doctors wanted some family members to be there at all times. They probably were afraid dad could have another heart attack at any moment. I tried to do the night shift, and mom and my sister did the day shift for a while. The last time I saw dad alive, he was sitting in his recliner chair in his living room. But then it snowed quite a large amount, and then I decided to get back to California to help my wife. My sister and brother-in-law picked me up at dad's house, and took me to the airport. I remember crying and crying because I felt I would never see my father alive again. The picture in my mind today is dad sitting in his recliner chair that morning. I never saw dad alive again. But I had intended to travel back to Indiana after a couple more weeks to help again. But before I could return to Indiana, Dad's neighbors had come to dad's aid, harvested all the grains that needed to be harvested, and hauled them to the grain elevator for him. Mom explained this to me, so I never returned until after dad passed away.

At dad's viewing at the funeral home, many people came to express their condolences to the family. I truly appreciated that, plus seeing so many of them. I tried to thank every one of them for coming. Most viewings at the funeral home are very unhappy. I could not feel that way on that specific day. I spent most of my time speaking to the visitors with a smile and sometimes chuckling with some visitors too. However, I was celebrating dad in my mind. Because in my mind, there were so many times and things that dad missed out on commemorating his life here on earth. I wanted to celebrate dad's life and my love for him. This day would be the last day dad was still above the ground. I wanted to show him respect, celebrate, and express my love for him. May dad be Resting in Peace.

After dad died, my wife and I returned to Indiana the next day. We stayed with mom, helped some with what I could, and of course attended the viewing, funeral service, and burial. Mom, my sister, my brother, and I talked a little about the future of the farms. Also, what mom wanted to do for her future, and the properties' futures. That is when mom said she and my brother would continue the schedule dad had always used and continue caring for the farms. That was ok with me because I knew it was not my place to move back to Indiana and try to take things over. I did not want to do this; besides, my wife and I had settled in California. My mother, brother, and I would have worked better together, but this was not anything I could do.

A little history of dad's milk cows and milking every morning and evening. After dad became sick, mom did it by herself daily. That was a large amount of work for her, only one person. But mom told me she sold the entire herd of cattle the day before dad passed away. Mom never told dad what she had done. Mom did the right thing. Because the cardiologist told mom that dad would never be able to work his farm again, that dad would never be able to milk cows again. Under these circumstances, there was no future for dad working the farms again. The cardiologist knew how bad dad's health was. He was telling us the truth without revealing how long dad was going to be able to live. That doctor was excellent and knew how dad's life would end. However, he was a very kind doctor and always told me, dad was suffering from "more heart failure."

After our father died, mom inherited all the properties, and our mother tried her best to keep the farms together and productive. Our brother took over doing most of the heavy work. Also, after some time, mom cash rented out some of the properties, and sometime later, she rented out all the farm properties. That meant some other farmer would be tilling and planting the soils and harvesting too. Plus, they would be responsible for maintaining the crops and soil until harvest time. I would like to know when most landowners started renting their land on a cash rental basis. As far as I know, dad always rented land from other landowners on a split costs basis. But mom rented the lands on a cash-rent basis. These contracts stipulate that the renter will maintain the fencerows and ditches and work to help keep down soil erosion. But nature will do what it wants, and farmers cannot control everything. All of dad's properties miss him.

Dad has been gone for 50 years now. I try to visit his gravesite each time I am in Indiana. Our mother is buried beside him, along with several other relatives nearby. Hopefully, they all are playing Euchre in Heaven. I miss them all and think of many of them often. But dad is and always was the most important to me. I still miss dad, but I know his time here on earth was over some time ago. But I Truly Loved my Father.

After mom passed on from this world in 2012, we three children inherited dad and mom's estate. The estate was divided the way mom had it written in her will. The three properties were in mom's will. The sad thing was that we could not keep the 80-acre property. We sold it. I wish we could have kept it, but that just did not work out. I hope the new owners appreciate having it.

Mementos and Memories

I have many beautiful mementos that my dad used in my younger years, such as overalls, pipes, lighters, watches, and a few other mementos. It is good to have them, but sometimes they make me remember and miss him repeatedly. To this day, I have always felt so very close to my father. When he was sick, I would have given him my heart if I could have. He deserved a much longer life here on earth. This is why I am writing this book, to explain a little about the kind of remarkable person Elvin Leon Burk was.

Over the years, I have also been lucky enough to acquire several mementos from many other relatives—some from the Burk side and some from the Gibson side. My sister and I have remarked to each other that for reasons unknown to us, dad and mom never visited very often with other relatives of their families—only a very few. I remember seeing dad's brothers and their families in my earlier years. And when my mother's family members were around, we sometimes called on them. But we rarely spent Sunday afternoons visiting relatives. Sometimes relatives would come to our house to see dad and mom on Sunday evenings. After the milking was finished we all could sit, talk, and visit.

Dad stopped at about 5 pm every evening to do the milking and required me to help. Dad may have made people feel uncomfortable. But that is the way it was. At 5 pm, whatever we were doing would stop, and the milking would get started, and usually, I would do much of the other farm duties after we got the milking organized. We were finished after about 90 minutes. We may have yet to complete everything perfectly that evening, but tomorrow we could catch up and finish the jobs we may have shorted that evening. We could play longer if people were still playing ball or doing other things together. But many times, especially if Aunt Mary was visiting, she would want me to get a fire going in the little firepit I had made. I could get it started and let it burn. Then I could do some more chores and then return to the fire. But farmwork was never work. Farmwork was something we wanted to do. And it was always enjoyable to have visitors too. It was easy to get the hot dog roasting fire going and share everything dad and mom had. Everyone enjoyed the hot dog roasts, plenty of good food, music, and juicy gossip.

I cannot express this thought too much! I sincerely thank you, dad, for everything you taught me and all the knowledge you tried to pass on to me. I am only sorry my head was so hard, but I realize now and thank you for all your efforts and knowledge. God Bless you, Dad.

Extra's

I recently found this saying, I don't know where it came from, but it is true.

"Our futures are what we make of them. "Our past is our history to learn from

I am now approaching my 80th birthday, and I wanted to express my thoughts about dad and what he meant to me. I have tried to follow my thoughts in writing about the time of each event as my age remembered.

To my readers; I hope I have been clear with my thoughts, about my father, and his and my relationship. Plus how much I respected his work, and teachings. I have tried to explain the kind, even though my thoughts are a little scattered, the hard working, wonderful father we three children had. And I hope you enjoy reading about Elvin Burk, through my eyes. Thank you.

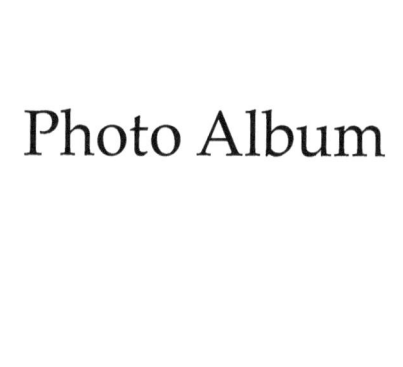

Dad

Dad's 3rd grade class
Wayne School

Dad 1941

Dad 1941

Dad

Dad and Mom
before marriage

Dad and Mom
after marriage

Dad and Mom
1936

Dad holding me
with my sister standing

Bessie
Dad's first cow

Wiggles

Dad's first pigs

Dad holding me

Dad with my sister

Dad, my sister and I

We 3 kids,

Dad at Grandma Gibson's house

Dad's immediate fami Anise, Roy, dad, Ira an Ollie

Dad, Steve and I with Boston Blackie and Nelliebelle

Dad, Steve and I with Old Sport and Andy

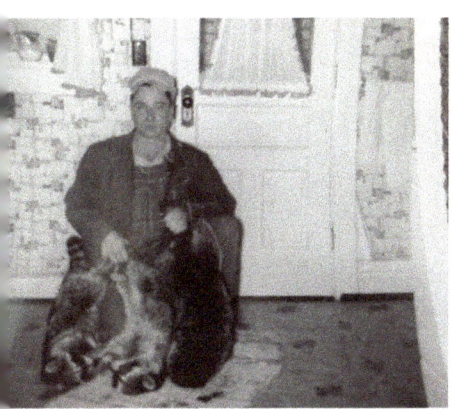

Dad with 3 raccoons

Me holding 2 raccoons
8 years old

My sister, our mother
and me

My sister,
the '41 Dodge Truck
and me

Dad and Granddad and the '41 Dodge

Dad and me

Dad loading Sugar Beets

Dad, my sister and me

og (Andy), Uncle Ray
holding me and dad

Dad and my nephew

Dad giving my
nephew a ride

Dad reading to my nephew

Dad with his Christmas present

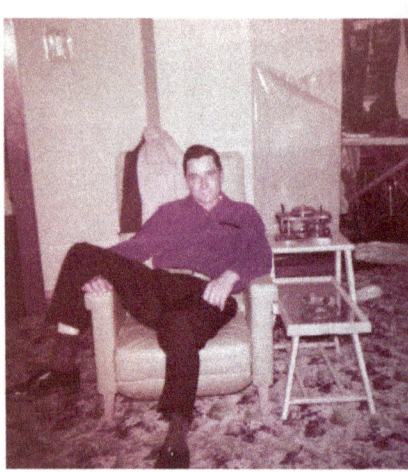

Dad relaxing in his favorite recliner

Dad's birthday with a cake and ice cream

Dad relaxing with Fanny

Dad and Fanny
She wants to hitch a ride

Dad combining soy beans

Dad havesting wheat

Dad's favorite tractor

Getting ready to unload firewood

Dad posing with his favorite tractor

Dad with Uncle Bob

My friend John and Uncle Bill

Aunt Grace and Dad singing

Aunt Grace and Dad posing

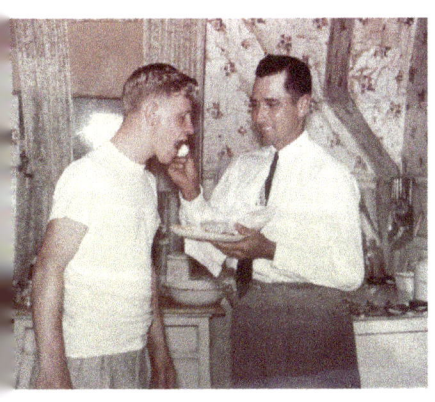

Elvin Devenport was named after dad Two Elvins

Aeriel view of the 80 Acre farm

The Pleasent Hill Race Track

ABOOKS

ALIVE Book Publishing and ALIVE Publishing Group
are imprints of Advanced Publishing LLC,
3200 A Danville Blvd., Suite 204, Alamo, California 94507

Telephone: 925.837.7303
alivebookpublishing.com

www.ingramcontent.com/pod-product-compliance
Lightning Source LLC
Chambersburg PA
CBHW040309170426
43195CB00020B/2900